# Absolute DISCARDED
# Beginner's Guide
# to C Programming

## With 2000+ C Codes And
## 23+ Complete Chapter's.

## -Harry H. Chaudhary.
### (IT Manager @ Anonymous International)

Author Note:

Every possible effort has been made to ensure that the information contained in this book is accurate, and the publisher or the Author can't accept responsibility for any errors or omissions, however caused.

All liability for loss, disappointment, negligence or other damage caused by the reliance of the Technical Programming or other information contained in this book, of in the event of bankruptcy or liquidation or cessation of trade of any company, individual; or firm mentioned, is hereby excluded.

All other marks are property of their respective owners. The examples of companies, organizations, products, domain names, email addresses, logos, people, places, and events depicted herein are fictitious. No association with any real company, organization, product, domain name, email address, logo, person, place, or event is intended or should be inferred.

The author and publisher have taken care in the preparation of this book, but make no expressed or implied warranty of any kind and assume no responsibility for errors or omissions. No liability is assumed for incidental or consequential damages in connection with or arising out of the use of the information or programs contained herein.

This book expresses the author views and opinions. The information contained in this book is provided without any express, statutory, or implied warranties. Neither the authors, and Publisher, nor its resellers, or distributors will be held liable for any damages caused or alleged to be caused either directly or indirectly by this book.

ISBN 13: **978-1500533236.**
ISBN-10: **1500533238.**

**Marketing & Distribution By Amazon Inc. & Other 1500 worldwide Bookstores.** Print Paperback Edition **Available on Amazon.com and** Digital PDF Edition **Available on** Google Books **and** Google Play **and Lulu.com with Discount.**

*For Publish this book in other language or request permission or license of this book work contact Author's Assistance- Author.Harry@Gmail.com*

# Dedication

"This book is most dedicated to all those who make the daily sacrifices,

Especially those who have made the ultimate sacrifice, to ensure our freedom & security."

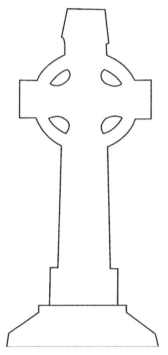

You told me that everything will be okay in the end,
You also told me that, if it's not okay, it's not the end.
"I'll search for you through 1000 worlds & 10000 lifetimes until I find you"

## About Author:

**Harry,** H. Chaudhary is an Indian computer Programming and Bestselling Java Author and **scientifically Hacking professional** has a unique experience in the field of computers Programming, **Hacking and Cyber Security.**

He has helped many Countries Governments and many multinational Software companies of around the globe to secure their networks and securities. He has authored several books on Various Computers Programming Languages and computer security & Hacking. **He is basically known for his international bestselling Programming book "Core Java Professional."**

He is technically graduate software engineer and Master. He is the leading authority on C Programming and C++ Programming as well as on Core Java and Data Structure and Algorithms. His acclaimed C and C++, C# & Java books. He has over 5 years of experience as a software methodologist. His teaching and research interests are in the areas of artificial intelligence, programming languages.

He is living two lives. One life, He is a Computer program writer for a respectable software company. The other life is lived in computers, where he go by the hacker alias 'Harry" and are guilty of virtually every computer crime. Currently he is working as offline IT manager @ world famous community **Anonymous international Community.**

## Author side:

You may have noticed something missing here: no impressive of credentials. I haven't been a professor at a Prestigious University for a quarter-century; neither am I a top executive at a Silicon Valley giant. In some ways, I'm a student of Technology, just like you are.

And my experience over the years has shown me that many of the people who know the most about how technology works also have rather limited success in explaining what they know in a way that will allow me to understand it. My interests, and I believe my skills, lie not in being an expert, but an educator, in presenting complex information in a form that is sensible, digestible and fun to read my books.

"What is real? How do you define *real*? If you're talking about what you can feel, what you can smell, what you can taste and see, then real is simply, electrical signals interpreted by your brain."

"... I am just now beginning to discover the difficulty of expressing one's ideas on paper. As long as it consists solely of description it is pretty easy; but where reasoning comes into play, to make a proper connection, a clearness & a moderate fluency, is to me, as I have said, a difficulty of which I had no idea ..." – Harry

# ∞ Inside Topics at a Glance ∞

# Preface:

## ∞ Essential C Programming Skills--Made Easy! ∞

Learn the all basics and advanced features of **C programming** in no time from Bestselling Programming Author Harry. H. Chaudhary. This Book, starts with the basics; I promise this book **will make you 100% expert level champion of C Programming**.

Anyone can learn C Programming through this book at expert level. Engineering Students and fresh developers can also use this book. In software development section I explained live software project. As we all knows Author Harry is basically known for his *"Easy Techniques-Explanations in Programming World - Learn with Fun Style !"* **To use this book does not require any previous programming experience.**

This book covers common core syllabus for **BCA, MCA, B.TECH, M.TECH, BS (CS), MS (CS), BSC-IT (CS), MSC-IT (CS),** and Computer Science Professionals as well as for Hackers. This book contains 1000+ Live C Program's code examples, and 500+ Lab Exercise & 200+ Brain Wash Topic-wise Code book and 20+ Live software Development Project's. All what you need ! Isn't it ?

This Book is very serious C Programming stuff: A complete introduction to C Language. You'll learn everything from the fundamentals to advanced topics. If you've read this book, you know what to expect a **visually rich format designed for the way your brain works**. If you haven't, you're in for a treat. You'll see why people say it's unlike any other **C book you've ever read.**

Learning a new language is no easy. You might think the problem is your brain. It seems to have a mind of its own, a mind that doesn't always want to take in the dry, **technical stuff you're forced to study**.

The fact is your brain craves novelty. It's constantly searching, scanning, waiting for something unusual to happen. After all, that's the way it was built to help you stay alive. It takes all the routine, ordinary, dull stuff and filters it to the background so it won't interfere with your brain's real work--recording things that matter. How does your brain know what matters?

# CHAPTER
## ∞ **1** ∞
## (Introduction To C)

Introduction-

### Stuff you need to know about language levels –

Programming languages have different levels, depending on how much they resemble human Languages. Programming languages that use common words and are relatively easy for most folks to read and study are called high level languages. The opposite of those are low-level languages, which are not easy to read or study.

High-level languages include the popular BASIC programming language as well as other languages that just aren't that popular any more BASIC reads almost like English, and all its commands and instructions are English words — or at least English words missing a few vowels or severely disobeying the laws of spelling.

The lowest of the low-level programming languages is machine language. That language is the actual primitive grunts and groans of the microprocessor itself. Machine language consists of numbers and codes that the microprocessor understands and executes.

Therefore, no one really writes programs in machine language; rather, they use assembly language, which is one step above the low-level machine language because the grunts and groans are spelled out rather than entered as raw numbers.

Why would anyone use a low-level language when high-level languages exist? Speed! Programs written in low-level languages run as fast as the computer can run them, often many times faster than their high-level counterparts. Plus, the size of the program is smaller.

A program written in Visual Basic may be **34K** in size, but the same program written in assembly language may be **896 bytes** long. On the other hand, the time it takes to develop an assembly language program is much longer than it would take to write the same program in a higher-level language. It's a trade-off.

The C programming language is considered a mid-level language. It has parts that are low-level grunting and squawking, and also many high-level parts that read like any sentence in a Michael Crichton novel, but with more character development.

In C, you get the best of the high-level programming languages and the speed of development they offer and you also get the compact program size and speed of a low-level language. That's why C is so bitchen.

**Note:** No, I'm not being flip. C was developed at AT&T Bell Labs in the early 1970-72s. At the time, Bell Labs had a programming language named B --B for Bell. The next language they created was C - one up on B.

- C is the offspring of both the B programming language and a language named BCPL, which stood for Basic Combined Programming Language. But you have to admit that the B story is cute enough by itself.

- You would think that the next, better version of C would be called the D language. But, no; it's named C++.

- C is considered a mid-level language. See the nearby sidebar, "Stuff you don't need to know about language levels," for the boring details.

- The guy who created the C programming language at Bell Labs is Dennis Ritchie. I mention him in case you're ever walking on the street and you happen to bump into Mr. Ritchie. In that case, you can say "Hey, aren't you Dennis Ritchie, the guy who invented C?" And he'll say "Why — why, yes I am." And you can say "Cool."

10

# History of C -

C programming language is perhaps the most popular programming language. C was created in 1972 by Dennis Ritchie at the Bell Labs in USA as a part of UNIX operating system. C was also used to develop some parts of this operating system. In 1960's "Basic Combined Programming Language (BCPL) called B language was developed at Cambridge university.

It was not fully satisfied language. 'B' language was modified by denies Ritchie was implemented at bell laboratory in 1972. C is generally supported by most compilers. C was developed by a system programmer Dennis Ritchie in 1972, at American Telegraph & Telecommunication (AT & T) Bell Laboratories in New Jersey USA.

From that time C programming language has been the de facto programming language when fast programs are needed or the software needs to interact with the hardware in some way.

Most of the operating systems like Linux, Windows™, and Mac™ are either developed in C language or use of this language for most parts of the operating system and the tools coming with it.

This course is a quick course on C Programming language. In our first lesson we will first write our first C program. We will then learn about printing to screen, variables and functions. We assume that you are familiar with at least one of the popular operating systems.

For this course you can use the following compilers or Programming Environments. --

- **Gcc** and **cc** in UNIX and Linux operating systems.

- **Borland C or Turbo C** in DOS operating system or in Command line environment of windows operating system.

- "Bloodshed **Dev-Cpp**" integrated development environment (IDE) gives you a complete and compact programming environment.

- It comes with "MinGW" and "GCC" C Compilers and you should not need anything else for this course.

## The C Development Cycle -

Here is how you create a C program in seven steps in what's known as the development cycle:

**1.** Come up with an idea for a program.
**2.** Use an editor to write the source code.
**3.** Compile the source code and link the program by using the C compiler.
**4.** Weep bitterly over errors (optional).
**5.** Run the program and test it.
**6.** Pull out hair over bugs (optional).
**7.** Start over (required).

No need to memorize this list. It's like the instructions on a shampoo bottle, though you don't have to be naked and wet to program a computer. Eventually, just like shampooing, you start following these steps without thinking about it. No need to memorize anything. The C development cycle is not an exercise device. In fact, programming does more to make your butt fit more snugly into your chair than anything.

**Step 1** is the hardest. The rest fall naturally into place.

**Step 3** consists of two steps: compiling and linking. For most of this book, however, they are done together, in one step. Only later if you're still interested do I go into the specific differences of a compiler and a linker.

## From Text File to Program:

When you create a program, you become a programmer. Your friends or relatives may refer to you as a "computer wizard" or "**guru**," but trust me when I say that programmer is a far better title.

As a programmer, you job is not "programming." No, the act of writing a program is coding. So what you do when you sit down to write that program is code the program. Get used to that term! It's very trendy.

The job of the programmer is to write some code! Code to do what? And what type of code do you use? Secret code? Morse Code? Zip code?

*The purpose of a computer program is to make the computer do something.*

The object of programming is to "make it happen." The C language is only a tool for communicating with the PC.

As the programmer, it's your job to translate the intentions of the computer user into something the computer understands and then give users what they want. And if you can't give them what they want, at least make it close enough so that they don't constantly complain or — worse — want their money back.

The tool you have chosen to make it happen is the C programming language. That's the code you use to communicate with the PC. The following sections describe how the process works. After all, you can just pick up the mouse and say "Hello, computer!"

- Programming is what TV network executives do. Computer programmers Code.

- You use a programming language to communicate with the computer, telling it exactly what to do.

## The source code - (Text file)

Because the computer can't understand speech and, well, whacking the computer — no matter how emotionally validating that is for you does little to the PC, your best line of communications is to write the computer a note a file on disk.

To create a PC epistle, you use a program called a text editor. This program is a primitive version of a word processor minus all the fancy formatting and printing controls. The text editor lets you type text — that's about all.

Using your text editor, you create what's called a source code file. The only special thing about this file is that it contains instructions that tell the computer what to do.

And although it would be nice to write instructions like "Make a funny noise," the truth is that you must write instructions in a tongue the computer understands. In this case, the instructions are written in the C language.

- The source code file is a text file on disk. The file contains instructions for the computer that are written in the C programming language.

- You use a text editor to create the source code file. See Appendix A for more information on text editors.

## Creating the Goodbye Harry.C source code file:

Use your text editor to create the following source code. Carefully type each line exactly as written; everything you see below is important and necessary. Don't leave anything out--

```
#include <stdio.h>
int main()
{
printf("Goodbye Harry, cruel world!\n");
return(0);
}
```

As you review what you have typed, note how much of it is familiar to you. You recognize some words (include, main, "GoodbyeHarry, cruel world!", and return), and some words look strange to you (stdio.h, printf, and that \n thing).

When you have finished writing the instructions, save them in a file on disk. Name the file GOODBYEHARRY.C. Use the commands in your text editor to save this file, and then return to the command prompt to compile your instructions into a program.

## Stuff you need to remember -

+ In Windows Notepad, you must ensure that the file ends in .C and not in .TXT. Find a book about Windows for instructions on showing the file name extensions, which makes saving a text file to disk with a .C extension easier.

+ Note that the text is mostly in lowercase. It must be; programming languages are more than case sensitive — they're case-fussy. Don't worry when English grammar or punctuation rules go wacky; C is a computer language, not English.

+ Also note how the program makes use of various parentheses: the angle brackets, < and >; the curly braces, { and }; and the regular parentheses, ( and ).

## Save It! Compile and Link It! Run It!

Four steps are required in order to build any program in C. They are **save**, **compile**, link, and **run**. Most C programming language packages automatically perform the linking step,

14

Though whether or not it's done manually, it's still in there. Save! Saving means to save your source code. You create that source code in a text editor and save it as a text file with the C (single letter C) extension.

Compile and link! Compiling is the process of transforming the instructions in the text file into instructions the computer's microprocessor can understand. The linking step is where the instructions are finally transformed into a program file. (Again, your compiler may do this step automatically.)

Run! Finally, you run the program you have created. Yes, it's a legitimate program, like any other on your hard drive. You have completed all these steps in this chapter, culminating in the creation of the GOODBYEHARRY program. That's how C programs are built.

At this stage, the hardest part is to knowing what to put in the source file, which gets easier as you progress through this book. (But by then, getting your program to run correctly and without errors is the hardest part!)

You find the instructions to save, compile, and run often in this book. That's because these steps are more or less mechanical. What's more important understands how the language works. That's what you start to find out about in the next chapter.

## History of C Language -

As I mentioned earlier that C was developed by a system programmer Dennis Ritchie in 1970-72, at American Telegraph & Telecommunication (AT & T) Bell Laboratories in New Jersey USA. It was written originally for programming under UNIX operating system.

C was developed from BCPL (Basic Combined Programming Language-B) which was improved and renamed as B. B was developed in 1960's at Cambridge University.

C is actually a symbolic instruction code, a set of commands that perform actions on a computer. The C language is often referred as middle level language because we can write high as well as low level programs through C.

Languages prior to C are FORTRAN (Formula Translation), COBOL (Common Business Oriented Language), BASIC (Beginners All Purpose Symbolic Instruction Code) and Pascal. Languages after C are C++, Java, C# etc. C permits very close interaction with the inner working of the computer.

# What is C?

C is a programming language used to write a program. Programs are the set of instructions given by a programmer to the computer in high level language. C uses a compiler to translate the high level program into machine code before executing any instructions. Compiler is itself a computer program. Other translators are Interpreter and Assembler.

The original high level program is called the source program(.C) and the resulting machine language program is called the object program(.obj). 'It was named "**C**" because its features were derived from an earlier **language called** "B", which according to Ken Thompson was a stripped-down version of the BCPL programming **language'**

## Assembler vs. Compiler -

In general, compiler is a computer program that reads a program written in one language, which is called the source language, and translates it in to another language, which is called the target language. Traditionally, source language was a high level language such as C++ and target language was a low level language such as Assembly language.

However, there are compilers that can convert a source program written in Assembly language and convert it to machine code or object code. Assemblers are such tools. So, both assemblers and compilers ultimately produce code that can be directly executed on a machine.

## What is a Compiler?

Compiler is a computer program that reads a program written in one language, which is called the source language, and translates it in to another language, which is called the target language. Most often, the source language is a high level language and the target language is a low level language. So, in general compilers can be seen as translators that translate from one language to another. In addition, compilers perform some optimizations to the code.

A typical compiler is made up of several main components. The first component is the scanner (also known as the lexical analyzer). Scanner reads the program and converts it to a string of tokens.

The second component is the parser. It converts the string of tokens in to a parse tree (or an abstract syntax tree), which captures the syntactic structure of the program. Next component is the semantic routines that interpret the semantics of the syntactic structure. The code optimizations and final code generation follow this.

16

# What is an Assembler?

Assembler is a software or a tool that translates Assembly language to machine code. So, an assembler is a type of a compiler and the source code is written in Assembly language.

Assembly is a human readable language but it typically has a one to one relationship with the corresponding machine code. Therefore an assembler is said to perform isomorphic (one to one mapping) translation. Advanced assemblers provide additional features that support program development and debugging processes. For example, the type of assemblers called macro assemblers provides a macro facility.

## What is the difference between an Assembler and a Compiler?

Compiler is a computer program that reads a program written in one language and translates it in to another language, while an assembler can be considered a special type of compiler which translates only Assembly language to machine code. Compilers usually produce the machine executable code directly from a high level language,

But assemblers produce an object code which might have to be linked using linker programs in order to run on a machine. Because Assembly language has a one to one mapping with machine code, an assembler may be used for producing code that runs very efficiently for occasions in which performance is very important (for e.g. graphics engines, embedded systems with limited hardware resources compared to a personal computer like microwaves, washing machines, etc.).

## Difference between:

| | Assembler | Compiler |
|---|---|---|
| 1. | It translates the mnemonic codes such as PRN, ADD, and SUB etc. to machine language code. | It translates the high level language to assembly language. |
| 2. | The program, which executes using assembler, executes faster, because it directly converts the source code in machine language. | It takes time to execute a program, because it first translates the source code into another compiler's language and then using assembler converts it into machine language. |

**Difference between: Compiler and Interpreter -**

A interpreter is similar to sentence-by-sentence translation, whereas a compiler is similar to translation to the whole passage.

|    | Compiler | Interpreter |
|----|----------|-------------|
| 1. | Compiler translates the entire high level language program into the machine language program at once before executing it. This optimizes the use of machine language instructions in the translated program. Therefore normally compiled programs run faster than Interpreted programs. The original high level language program is called as *source program*. The compiled program i.e. machine language program generated by the compiler after translation is called object program. | The Interpreter translates the program written in high level language into machine language at the time of executing that program, instructions by instructions. That is, it reads the first instruction written in the program and converts that into equivalent machine language instructions. Then the CPU watches those machine language instructions. After that, the Interpreter reads and translates the next instruction and so on. |
| 2. | Compiler Takes **Entire** program as input | Interpreter Takes **Single** instruction as input. |
| 3. | Object code is permanently saved for future use. | No object code is saved for future use. |
| 4. | Non time consuming translation method. | Time consuming translation method |
| 5. | It requires large space in the computer. | Interpreter are easy to write and do not require large memory space. |
| 6. | Speed of a compiler is very fast. | Speed is very slow. |
| 7. | Any change in source program after the compilation requires recompiling of entire code. | Any change in source program during the translation does not require's retranslation of entire code. |
| 8. | Intermediate Object Code is **Generated.** | **No** Intermediate Object Code is **Generated.** |

| 9. | Conditional Control Statements are Executes **faster.** | Conditional Control Statements are Executes **slower.** |
|---|---|---|
| 10. | **Memory Requirement** : **More** (Since Object Code is Generated) | **Memory Requirement** is **Less.** |
| 11. | Program need not be **compiled** every time. | Every time higher level program is converted into lower level program. |
| 12. | **Errors** are displayed after **entire program** is checked. | **Errors** are displayed for **every instruction** interpreted (if any) |
| 13. | **Example** : C Compiler. | **Example** : BASIC. |

**Explanation: Compiler Vs Interpreter**

Just understand the concept of the compiler and interpreter -

1. We give complete program as input to the compiler. Our program is in the human readable format.

2. Human readable format undergoes many passes and phases of compiler and finally it is converted into the machine readable format.

3. However interpreter takes single line of code as input at a time and executes that line. It will terminate the execution of the code as soon as it finds the error.

4. Memory requirement is less in Case of interpreter because no object code is created in case of interpreter.

**Drill Note** – *Most of students really don't know the difference between Compiler & Interpreter. Learning a new language is no easy. You might think the problem is your brain. That's why I am trying to explain differences in many forms.*

A Compiler and Interpreter both carry out the same purpose – convert a high level language (like C, Java) instructions into the binary form which is understandable by computer hardware.

They are the software used to execute the high level programs and codes to perform various tasks. Specific compilers/interpreters are designed for different high level languages.

However both compiler and interpreter have the same objective but they differ in the way they accomplish their task i.e. convert high level language into machine language. Look seriously below-

**Compiler –**

A compiler is a piece of code that translates the high level language into machine language. When a user writes a code in a high level language such as Java and wants it to execute, a specific compiler which is designed for Java is used before it will be executed. The compiler scans the entire program first and then translates it into machine code which will be executed by the computer processor and the corresponding tasks will be performed.

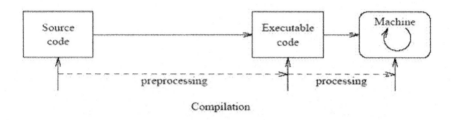

Compilation

Shown in the figure is basic outline of the compilation process, here program written in higher level language is known as source program and the converted one is called object program.

**Interpreter -**

Interpreters are not much different than compilers. They also convert the high level language into machine readable binary equivalents. Each time when an interpreter gets a high level language code to be executed, it converts the code into an intermediate code before converting it into the machine code. Each part of the code is interpreted and then execute separately in a sequence and an error is found in a part of the code it will stop the interpretation of the code without translating the next set of the codes.

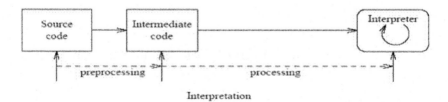

Interpretation

20

## Merits of C Programming -

**1. C is a general purpose** programming language. You can generate games, business software, utilities, mathematical models, word processors, spreadsheets and other kinds of software.

**2. C is a structured** programming language. It uses structured statements such as while, for loops in place of goto statements which cause bugs (error) in the program.

**3. System independence-** C does not require any services from the operating system, it runs independently. C can run on any operating system.

**4. High efficiency-** C compilers are generally able to translate source code into efficient machine instructions. C language data and control mechanisms are well matched to most small computers and microcomputers.

**5. System programming-** C is used for system programming i.e. writing operating systems. The UNIX operating system is also rewritten from C.

## Difference between Syntax and Semantics -

| Semantics | Syntax |
|---|---|
| It is the logic or planning of the program. Semantics can be written in any of the following ways:<br><br>1.    Flowcharts.<br>2.    Algorithms.<br>3.    Pseudo codes. | It is the way of writing the program in a particular programming language. Syntax changes from language to language. |

## FLOWCHART -

It is a symbolic representation of the program logic. There are some predefined symbols used for the logic. A flowchart shows the actual flow of the logic of a program.

A flowchart is nothing but diagrammatic representation of various steps involved in solution of a problem. The flowchart indicates the direction of flow of a process, relevant operations and computations, point of decisions and other information which are a part of the solution. Once developed and properly checked, the flowchart provides an excellent guide for writing the program.

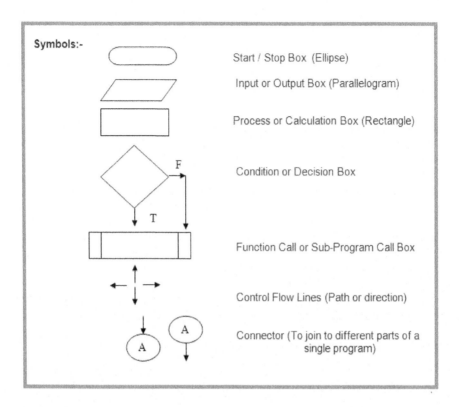

Symbols:-

Start / Stop Box (Ellipse)

Input or Output Box (Parallelogram)

Process or Calculation Box (Rectangle)

Condition or Decision Box

Function Call or Sub-Program Call Box

Control Flow Lines (Path or direction)

Connector (To join to different parts of a single program)

## ALGORITHMS -

Once a problem is been properly defined, a detailed, finite, step-by-step procedure for solving it must be developed. This procedure is known as algorithm. Algorithm can be written in ordinary language, or using formal procedures that lie somewhere between ordinary and programming languages.

Algorithm to add two numbers –

1. Read A,B.
2. Set SUM := A+B.
3. Write SUM.
4. Exit.

## PSEUDOCODE -

Sometimes, it is desirable to translate an algorithm to an intermediate form, between that of a flowchart and the source code. Pseudocode is an English approximation of source code that follows the rules, style, and format of a language but ignores most punctuation's.

22

```
main()
{
        integer a,b,sum;
        read in a and b;
        add a & b and set it to sum;
        write sum;
}
```

**Structure of C program (Source Code) -**

Let us discuss the structure of a C program using an example:
/*sum of two numbers*/

```
#include<stdio.h>            /* For printf() & scanf() */
#include<conio.h>            /* For clrscr() & getch() */
main()                       /* Starting point of the program execution*/
{
        int a,b,sum;                /* Variable Declarations */
        clrscr();                   /* Clear Screen */
        printf("enter two numbers"); /* Request for Input */
        scanf("%d %d",&a,&b);       /* Input from user */
sum=a+b;                            /* Adding two numbers */
printf("sum=%d",sum);               /* Output Sum */
getch();                            /* To hold output screen */
        }                           /* End of main */
```

**Explanation of C Program -**

**STORY OF HEADER FILES -**

Header files contain definitions of functions and variables which can be incorporated into any C program by using the pre-processor *#include* statement. Standard header files are provided with each compiler, and cover a range of areas, string handling, mathematical, data conversion, printing and reading of variables.

To use any of the standard functions, the appropriate header file should be included. This is done at the beginning of the C source file. For example, to use the function *printf()* in a program, the line --

### *#include  <stdio.h>*

Should be at the beginning of the source file, because the definition for *printf()* is found in the file *stdio.h* All header files have the extension .h and generally reside in the /include subdirectory.

> *#include <stdio.h>*
> *#include "mydecls.h"*

The use of angle brackets <> informs the compiler to search the compilers include directory for the specified file. The use of the double quotes "" around the filename inform the compiler to search in the current directory for the specified file.

**KEYBOARD INPUT -**

There is a function in C which allows the programmer to accept input from a keyboard. The following program illustrates the use of this function,

```
#include <stdio.h>
main()                        /* program which introduces keyboard input */
{
int  number;
printf("Type in a number \n");
scanf("%d", &number);
printf("The number you typed was %d\n", number);
}
```

An integer called *number* is defined. A prompt to enter in a number is then printed using the statement

> *printf("Type in a number \n:");*

The *scanf* routine, which accepts the response, has two arguments. The first ("%d") specifies what type of data type is expected (ie char, int, or float).

The second argument (&number) specifies the variable into which the typed response will be placed. In this case the response will be placed into the memory location associated with the variable *number*. This explains the special significance of the & character (which means the address of).

**#include –**

The #include directive instructs the C Preprocessor to find the text file **"stdio.h"**. The name itself means **"standard input and output"** and the ".h" means it is a header file rather than a C source file (which have the ".c" suffix). It is a text file and may be viewed with any text editor.

**Comments –**

Comments are placed within /* and */ character sequences and may span any number of lines.

**Main -**

The main function is most important. This defines the point at which your program starts to execute. If you do not write a main function your program will not run (it will have no starting point). In fact, it won't even compile.

**Braces –**

C uses the brace character "{" to mean "begin" and "}" to mean "end". They are much easier to type and, after a while, a lot easier to read.

**Printf () –**

The printf function is the standard way of producing output. The function is defined within the Standard Library, thus it will always be there and always work in the same way. This example shows that printf and scanf share the same format specifiers.

When presented with "%i" they both handle integers. scanf, because it is a reading function, reads integers from the keyboard. printf, because it is a writing function, writes integers to the screen. Expressions Note that C is quite happy to calculate "a-b" and print it out as an integer value. It would have been possible, but unnecessary, to create another variable "c", assign

The printf function writes output to the screen. When it meets the format specifier %i, an integer is output.

**Scanf() -**

The scanf function is the "opposite" of printf. Whereas printf produces output on the screen, scanf reads from the keyboard. The sequence "%i" instructs scanf to read an integer from the keyboard. Because "%i %i" is used two integers will be read. The first value typed placed into the variable "a", the second into the variable "b". The scanf function reads input from the keyboard. When it meets the format specifier %i the program waits for the user to type an integer.

The space between the two "%i"s in "%i %i" is important: it instructs scanf that the two numbers typed at the keyboard may be separated by spaces. If "%i,%i" had been used instead the user would have been forced to type a comma between the two numbers.

**\n –**

The sequence of two characters "\" followed by "n" is how C handles new lines. When printed it causes the cursor to move to the start of the next line.

**Return –**

Return causes the value, here 0, to be passed back to the operating system. How the operating system handles this information is up to it. MS-DOS, for instance, stores it in the ERRORLEVEL variable. The UNIX Bourne and Korn shells store it in a temporary variable, $?, which may be used within shell scripts. "Tradition" says that 0 means success.

A value of 1, 2, 3 etc. indicates failure. All operating systems support values up to 255. Some support values up to 65535, although if portability is important to you, only values of 0 through 255 should be used.

**& -**

The "&" is very important with scanf. It allows it to change the variable in question this is also known as **Ampersand** . Thus in--

```
scanf("%i", &j)
```

The "&" allows the variable "j" to be changed. Without this rather mysterious character, C prevents scanf from altering "j" and it would retain the random value it had previously (unless you'd remembered to initialize it).Since printf does not need to change the value of any variable it prints, it doesn't need any "&" signs. Thus if "j" contains 15, after executing the statement:

```
printf("%i", j);
```

we would confidently expect 15 in the variable because printf would have been incapable of alerting it.

**The Format of C -**

- Statements are terminated with semicolons.
- Indentation is ignored by the compiler.
- C is case sensitive - all keywords and Standard.
- Library functions are lowercase.
- Strings are placed in double quotes.
- Newlines are handled via **\n**
- Programs are capable of flagging success or error, those forgetting to do so have one or other chosen randomly!

26

## The Format of C -

### Semicolons –

Semicolons are very important in C. They form a statement terminator they tell the compiler where one statement ends and the next one begins. If you fail to place one after each statement, you will get compilation errors.

### Free Format -

C is a free format language. This is the up-side of having to use semicolons everywhere. There is no problem breaking a statement over two lines - all you need do is not place a semicolon in the middle of it (where you wouldn't have anyway).

The spaces and tabs that were so carefully placed in the example program are ignored by the compiler. Indentation is entirely optional, but should be used to make the program more readable.

### Case Sensitivity -

C is a case sensitive language. Although int compiles, "Int", "INT" or any other variation will not. All of the 40 or so C keywords are lowercase. All of the several hundred functions in the Standard Library are lowercase.

### Random Behavior –

Having stated that main is to return an integer to the operating system, forgetting to do so (either by saying return only or by omitting the return entirely) would cause a random integer to be returned to the operating system.

This random value could be zero (success) in which case your program may randomly succeed. More likely is a non-zero value which would randomly indicate failure.

**Drill Note-  WAP means "Write a Program", For Topic wise Programming example pleae see Last section of this book.**

**Important features of the above C program:**

1. The instructions of a C program are typed in lowercase but the variables and user defined things can be written in uppercase.

2. The first line of this program is the comment. Every comment starts with slash and asterisk (/*) and ends with asterisk and slash (*/). A comment helps the programmer in explaining the logic of the program. It improves the readability of the program.

   These comments can be placed anywhere in the program. The compiler does not read these comments. Nesting of comments is not allowed. Comments are the explanation of a statement in the program to improve the readability of the program.

3. Comments are not necessary; it is a good practice to begin a program with a comment indicating the purpose of the program, its author and the date on which the program was written.

   Any number of comments can be written at any place in the program example a comment can be written before the ---statement, after the statement or within the statement. A comment can be split over more than one line such a comment is called a multi-line comment.

4. The second and third lines of the program are called as header files **(stdio.h and conio.h)** which contains information that must be included in the program before compiling. # is a pre-processor directive or compiler directive. This statement directs the compiler to include header files in the program before compiling the program. We can **also write** <stdio.h> as "stdio.h".

5. Every C program consists of one or more modules called *functions*. One of this functions is called main( ). The execution of every program begins with main function, which may call other functions. Whole program is written in this main function enclosed in curly brackets. Use of more than one main() is illegal.

6. Declaration of the variables is done immediately after the opening braces of the program. We cannot declare variables in the middle of a program.

7. Note that every statement in the main function ends with a semicolon(;).

8. Next is the printf( ) statement:- printf("Enter two numbers");
   printf is an output command which requests the user to enter a number. This message is known as "prompt message" and is printed on the output screen as  Enter two numbers

9. The values entered in the computer via the next statement scanf( ).
   scanf("%d %d",&a,&b); scanf is an input command which takes some value from the user according to the given format specifier and stores it at the desired variable. The & is called as address of operator.

10. The next is the assignment statement:- sum= a+b;
    which adds the values in variable a and b and the assign it to variable sum;

11. The last printf( ) is used to show the calculated value  for sum on the screen.

12. Finally the getch( ) function is used to show the output screen.

13. All the statements inside the main() are slightly ahead than main(). This is called as indentation. This shows that all the statements are inside the main() function.

Core Java Professional.

By Harry H. Chaudhary.

Available On Amazon.com
Google Play || Google Books
Ultimate Java Book for Beginner's.

People. Innovation. Excellence.

## Multiple Choice Questions:

**1. C is a :**
- a. high level language.
- b. low level language.
- c. middle level language.
- d. assembly level language.

**2. Logic of a program is called:**
- a. syntax.
- b. semantics.
- c. flowchart.
- d. debugging.

**3. C language has been developed by**
- a. Ken Thompson.
- b. Dennis Ritchie.
- c. Patrick Naughton.
- d. Ed Frank.

**4. Flowcharts are used to decide-**
- a. sequence of steps involved in Finding solution.
- b. An aid to making algorithm.
- c. To prepare decision table.
- d. To debug a program.

**5. C programs are converted into machine language with the help of -**
- a. An Editor.
- b. A compiler.
- c. An operating system.
- d. None of the above.

**6. C can be used on-**
- a. Only MS-DOS operating system.
- b. Only Linux operating system.
- c. Only Windows operating system.
- d. All the above.

Answers:
1(c)   2(b)   3(b)   4(a)   5(b)   6(d)

# Theory Questions.

1. Explain the historical development of c

    a. When c was developed?
    b. Who develop the c?
    c. Where c was developed?
    d. C is a high, middle or low level?
    e. On which operating system it can work?

2. What are the major components of a C program? What significance is attached to the name main.
3. What are comments. Where can comments can be placed.
4. Are C program required to be typed in lowercase? Can uppercase be used for anything in a C program. Explain.
5. Which symbol is used to end a C statement. Do all statements end this way?
6. Why are statements indented in a C program.
7. What is a flow chart? Draw the various symbols used in flow chart.

# Lab Exercise.

1. WAP to input two numbers from the keyboard and print their sum.
2. WAP to input two numbers from the keyboard and print their average.
3. WAP to calculate the area of a circle.
4. WAP to print the total seconds in a given time (hrs, min, sec's).
5. WAP to convert temp.  From Fahrenheit to centigrade. C=(F-32) * 5/9
6. WAP to SWAP (interchange) two numbers.
7. WAP to SWAP (interchange) 2 numbers without using third variable.
8. WAP to SWAP (interchange) three numbers.
9. WAP to SWAP three numbers without using fourth variable.
10. WAP to calculate the remainder of 2 numbers without using % operator.

# Fill in the blanks.

1. ___is the creator of C language. It was developed at ___in _____year.
2. _____ operating system is developed in C.
3. _____ can be stated the ancestor of C.
4. C language is translated into machine code using a _____.
5. C can be used with _____, _____ and _____ operating systems.

C - Programmer
Harry.

# CHAPTER
## ∞ 2 ∞
## (Elements of C Language)

**C Tokens –**

Tokens are the smallest individual unit known as tokens. C recognizes six types of tokens. C programs are written using these tokens and the syntax of the language. Following are the C Tokens:

- Keywords.
- Identifiers.
- Literals.
- Operators.
- Seperators.

**1. Keywords -**

Keywords are the reserved words whose meaning has already been explained to the C compiler. These words are defined in the language itself. There are 32 keywords in C.

| auto | double | int | struct | break |
|---|---|---|---|---|
| else | long | switch | case | enum |
| register | typedef | char | extern | return |
| union | const | float | short | unsigned |
| continue | for | signed | void | default |
| goto | static | sizeof | volatile | do |
| while | if | -- | -- | -- |

## 2. Identifiers –

Identifiers are the names given to variables. Using this identifier we can access that variable. All other names in a C program such as array name or a function name are also known as Identifiers.

## Variables -

An entity that may vary during program execution is called a variable. Or you can say Variable is the place inside the main memory that is basically used to store some particular type of data that vary during the program execution. Variable names are names given to locations in memory. These locations can contain integer, real or character constants. All the variables that are used in the program should be declared i.e. typed at the top with their respective data types. The variable declaration tells two things:

1.    It tells the compiler the name of the variable.
2.    It also tells the type of value the variable will hold.
**E.g.:    int a;
            float b;
            char c;**

Variable name may be consist of letter, digits and under line(-) with following the below rules -

1) They must begin with a letter.
2) Upper case & lower case are significant mean total is differ.
3) Variable name should not be a keyword.

*The basic format* for declaring variable is

[Data type name]   var1, var2, -------;

The variable declaration tells *two things -*

34

- It tells the compiler the name of the variable.
- It also tells the type of value the variable will hold.

**Eg:**    Int a;
        Float b;
        Char c;

Here **a** is an integer variable, **b** is a float variable and **c** is a character variable. **;** is called as termination symbol or end of statement.

## Primary type declaration:

A variable can be used to store a value of any data type. That is the variable name does not have anything to do with the variable name.

**e.g.  int a,b,c;**

Where **a,b,c** are the names given to the variables. All the variables of the same data type are separated by a comma. The declaration statement must end with a semicolon.

Suppose we want to declare three variables, then...... We write as-

        int a, b, c;

At the same time of declaring these three integer variables, three memory locations are created in the main memory of the computer for storing each type of integer variables operational data. These of each allocation field are known as a location.

## Naming a variable

It is better that you use meaningful names for your variables even if this causes them to become long Names. Also take this in mind that C is case sensitive.

A variable named "COUNTER" is different from a variable named "counter". Functions and commands are all case sensitive in C Programming language.

You can use letters, digits and underscore _ character to make your variable names. Variable names can be up to 31 characters in ANSI C language.

**Valid Names -**

Only letters, digits and the underscore character may be validly used in variable names. The first character of a variable may be a letter or an underscore, although The Standard says to avoid the use of underscores as the first letter.

Thus the variable names "temp_in_celsius", "index32" and "sine_value" are allvalid, while "32index", "temp-in-celsius" and "sine$value" are not. Using variable name like "_sine" would be frowned upon, although not syntactically invalid.

Variable names may be quite long, with the compiler sorting through the first 31 Characters. Names may be longer than this, but there must be a difference within the first 31 characters.

## 3.    Literals/Constants:

Constants in C refer to fixed values that do not change during the execution of a program. In C there are 2 types of constants:

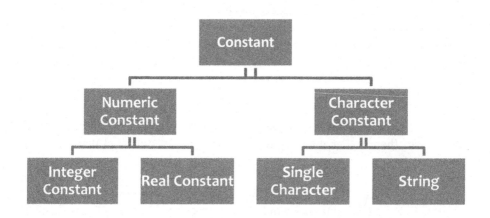

**Numeric constants:-**

**A) Integer constants –**

They are a sequence of digits. There are three types of integers: decimal, octal, hexadecimal.

**Decimal numbers** contain set of digits 0 to 9 which can be positive (+) or negative (-).

E.g.: 6, 46, 398, 658736, -89, +598 are all integers
Spaces, comma or special symbols are not allowed.
E.g.: 12 897, 364,897, $56, 78@56 are all invalid or wrong numbers.

**Octal numbers** consist of any combination of digits fro 0 to 7, with a leading 0.
E.g.:037, 0435, 0551.

**Hexadecimal numbers** has 16 digits 0 to 9 and alphabets A to F (10-15), the sequence of digits is preceded by 0x or 0X.
E.g.:0X2, 0x9f, 0xbcd.

**B) Floating or Real constants -**

Integer constants are not sufficient to represent all the quantities such as price, distance, temperature, etc. These numbers have a decimal point(.) i.e. fractional parts like 65.987, 0.000569, 89.36.

A floating number can also be represented as exponential or scientific notation for e.g. 0.0000123 can be written as $1.23*10^{-5}$ or 1.23e-05.Thus the general form is:

> Mantissa e exponent
> So, 1.23 is called mantissa and -05 is called as exponent

**C) Character constant –**

**i) Single character constants:**

> A single character alphabets in uppercase('A' to 'Z') or lowercase ('a' to 'z') or digits(0 to 9) or a special symbol(@, #, $, %, *, &, +, -, ., :, / etc.) which are enclosed in single quotes (' ').

E.g.: 'a' or 'A' or '7'or'+' are all character constants.

**Note:** All escape sequences are also considered characters.

## ii) String constants:

A string constant is a single character or a group of characters enclosed in double quotes (" ").

Like: "hello", "4598", "hello235", "5+3".

**Note -** The character constant '7' is not the same as digit 7. Every character constants has an equivalent integer number.

'A' to 'Z' has ASCII 65 to 90. i.e. 'A' has ASCII 65 'B' has ASCII 66 and so on.

'a' to 'z' has ASCII 97 to 122
'0' to '9' has ASCII 48 to 57
' ' (space) has ASCII 32.
☺ (smiling space) has ASCII 1.

## Data Types –

C language is rich in data types. ***There are 4 classes of data types:***

1.   Primary data types (int, float, char)
2.   User defined data types (enumerator, typedef)
3.   Derived data types (array, function, pointers, structure, union)
4.   Empty data sets. (void)

## Primary Data Types -

| Integer | Real | Character |
|---------|------|-----------|
| int or short or short int *occupies 2 bytes-* <br><br> *range: -32768 to +32767* <br><br> long int or long *occupies 4 bytes range: -* <br><br> *-2,147,483,648 to+2,147,483,647* | float *occupies 4 bytes-range:3.4e-38 to 3.4e38* <br><br> double *occupies 8 bytes-range:1.7e-308 to 1.7e+308* <br><br> long double *occupies 10 bytes—* <br><br> *range: 3.4e-4932 to* 1.1e+4932 | char *occupies 1 byte Range—* <br><br> *-128 to +127* |

38

**Formula to calculate range -**

$$2^{n-1}$$

Where n is the number of bits occupied by the data type.

*Range of int:*
int occupies 2 byte i.e. 16 bits ( since 1 byte is equal to 8 bits)

So, $216^{-1} = 2^{15} = 32768$.
Thus range becomes:    -32768 to +32767

**Note-**    This formula cannot be used to calculate the range of real data types
(float, double, long double)

**Modifiers used with primitive data types -**

Signed, unsigned, and short may be applied to character and integer
primitive data types. The modifier long can also be applied to double.

**Signed and Unsigned -**

The range of int or signed int is -32768 to +32767 and it uses 2 bytes,
but sometimes the program requires only the positive values and these values
may exceed the range of int.

In such cases the data type can be made unsigned by adding the
negative range to the positive one. Thus the range of unsigned int becomes:
                    0 to 65535

The unsigned int uses only 2 bytes. Thus we can say that the unsigned
data type uses the same number of bytes as the signed data.

**Note:** The real data types cannot be made unsigned.

**Format specifiers:**

There are quite a number of format specifiers for printf and scanf.
Here are the basic ones:

| | |
|---|---|
| **%d** | print an int argument in decimal. |
| **%i** | print an int argument in decimal, hexadecimal or octal. |
| **%h** | print an short int argument in decimal. |
| **%ld** | print a long int argument in decimal. |
| **%u** | print a unsigned int argument. |

| | |
|---|---|
| **%lu** | print a unsigned long int argument. |
| **%f** | print a float argument. |
| **%lf** | print a double argument. |
| **%Lf** | print a long double argument. |
| **%e** | exponential notation. |
| **%g** | float or exponential notation. |
| **%o** | print an int argument in octal (base 8) |
| **%x** | print an int argument in hexadecimal (base 16) |
| **%X** | print an int argument in hexadecimal (base 16)in uppercase |
| **%c** | print a character. |
| **%s** | print a string. |

**Escape sequences -**

Certain non printable characters, which are used in the printf( ) function are called as escape sequences. Escape sequences always begin with backslash ( \ ). Commonly used escape sequences are:

**Escape sequences--**

| | |
|---|---|
| **\a** | Bell beep. |
| **\b** | back space(brings cursor one position left) |
| **\f** | form feed(ejects current paper from printer and loads a new one) |
| **\n** | New line character. |
| **\r** | carriage return(brings cursor to the beginning of the line) |
| **\t** | Horizontal tab. |
| **\v** | Vertical tab. |
| **\\** | To print backslash. |
| **\"** | To print double quotations. |
| **\'** | To print single quotations. |
| **\?** | To print question mark. |
| **\0** | Null (End of string) |

## Operators –

Operators can be used to perform the required computations on the values.

**Types of operators:** There are three types of operators:

1. Unary Operator: Operators which work on one operand only.
2. Binary Operator: Operators which work on two operands.
3. Ternary Operator: Operators which work on three operands.

## The Rule of Precedence -

Each operator in C has precedence associated with it. This precedence is used to determine how an expression involving more than one operator are evaluated.

There are distinct levels of precedence and an operator may belong to one of the levels. The operators at the higher level of precedence are evaluated first.

## The Rule of Associativity -

The operators of the same precedence are evaluated either from left to right or from right to left, depending on the level. This is known as the Associativity property of an operator. There are 45 operators in C:

## Classes of operators:

Operators are divided into mainly **9** classes:

1. Arithmetic operator.
2. Unary operators.
3. Relational operators.
4. Assignment operators.
5. Equality operators.
6. Logical operators.
7. Conditional operators.
8. Bitwise operators.
9. Comma operators.

| Rank | Operators | Descriptions | Associativity |
|------|-----------|--------------|---------------|
| 1 | ( ) | Function call. | Left to right. |
| | [ ] | Array element reference | |
| | -> | Structure operator (used between pointer and member) | |
| | . | Structure operator (used between object and member) | |
| 2 | - | Unary minus | Right to left. |
| | + | Unary plus | |
| | ++ | Increment | |
| | -- | Decrement | |
| | ! | Logical not | |
| | ~ | One's complement | |
| | * | Value of address (used with pointers) | |
| | & | Address of | |
| | sizeof | Sizeof | |
| | (type) | Typecasting | |
| 3 | * | Multiplication | |
| | / | Division | Left to right. |
| | % | Modulus | |
| 4 | + | Addition | Left to right. |
| | - | Subtraction | |
| 5 | << | Left Shift | Left to right. |
| | >> | Right Shift | |
| 6 | < | Less than | |
| | <= | Less than equal | Left to right. |
| | > | Greater than | |
| | >= | Greater than equal | |
| 7 | == | Equality (conditions) | Left to right. |
| | != | Not Equal | |
| 8 | & | Bitwise AND | Left to right. |
| 9 | ^ | Bitwise XOR | Left to right. |
| 10 | \| | Bitwise OR | Left to right. |
| 11 | && | Logical AND | Left to right. |
| 12 | \|\| | Logical OR | Left to right. |
| 13 | ? : | Condition Operators | Right to left. |
| 14 | =, *=, /=, %= +=, -= &=, ^= \|=, <<=, >>= | Assignment operators | Right to left. |
| 15. | , | Comma operator | Left to right. |

# 1. Arithmetic operator -

These operators include **+, -, \* , /, %** the + and - operators here are used to add and subtract two operands respectively. * is used to multiply while / is used to divide.

```
int i=2,j=3,k,l;
float a,b;
k=i/j*j;
l=j/i*i;
a=i/j*j;
b=j/i*i;
printf("%d, %d, %f, %f",k,l,a,b);
Output:- 0, 2, 0.000000, 2.00000
```

% is called modulus operator, this operator is used to calculate remainder.

```
int a=5,b=3,c;
c= a%b;
printf("%d", c);
Output:- 2
```

**Note:** The modulus operator does not work on floating numbers.

# 2. Unary operators -

+,-, ++,- -, sizeof, (typecasting) The + and – in the unary operators are used to show the sign of the numbers. The ++ operator is used to add 1 to the variable.

```
int a=5,b=4;
a++;
b--;
printf("%d,%d",a,b);
```

**Output:- 6, 3**
if we use a++ or ++a both will increase the value of a by 1. a++ is called **postfix** while ++a is called **prefix.**

| Postfix | Prefix |
|---|---|
| int a=5,b;<br>b=a++;<br>printf("%d, %d",a,b);<br>**Output:- 6,5** | int a=5,b;<br>b=++a;<br>printf("%d, %d",a,b);<br>**Output:- 6,6** |
| int i=3;<br>i=i++;<br>printf("%d",i);<br>**Output:- 4** | int i=2;<br>printf("%d %d",++i, ++i);<br>a.      3 4<br>b.      4 3<br>c.      4 4<br>d.      Output may vary from<br>         compiler to compiler.<br>**Output:- b** |

## 3. Relational operators -

<, >,<=,>= These operators are boolean operators( those operators which give answer in 1 or 0. here 1 is considered true and 0 is false).

| | |
|---|---|
| int x=10,a,b;<br>a= x>2;<br>b=x<2;<br>printf("%d, %d",a,b);<br><br>**Output:- 1,0** | int x=10,y=20,z=5,i;<br>i=x<y<z;<br>printf("%d",i);<br>a.   1<br>b.   0<br>c.   Error<br>d.   None of the above<br>**Output:- a** |

## 4. Assignment operator -

=, +=, -=, *=, /=, %= These operators are used to assign value to a variable.

```
a=5;          /* assignining  5 to variable a*/
a=5+2;        /*valid*/
a=b;          /*valid*/
5=a;          /*invalid*/
a+b=5;        /*invalid*/
```

The other operators of assignment are used for doing an arithmetic operation on a variable and then assigning the value to the same variable:

```
a+=5; is equivalent  to a=a+5
a-=5; is equivalent to     a=a-5
a*=5; is equivalent  to a=a*5
a/=5; is equivalent  to    a=a/5
a%=5; is equivalent  to a=a%5
```

5. **Equality operator - = =, !=**

These two operators are used to check whether the given expression has the right and left sides equal or not. This operator is also a Boolean operator it also gives answer in 0 or 1.

```
int a,b,c=5;
a= =5;
b!=2;
printf("%d, %d",a,b);
```

**Output:- 1,0**

6. **Logical Operator - &&, ||, !**

These operators are also Boolean operators. **&&** and **||** operator are used with two expressions. These expressions generally have either relational operators or equality operators in them.

| Expression 1 | Expression 2 | && | ¦¦ |
|---|---|---|---|
| 0 | 0 | 0 | 0 |
| 1 | 0 | 0 | 1 |
| 0 | 1 | 0 | 1 |
| 1 | 1 | 1 | 1 |

The **NOT** operator is used to reverse the expression:

| Expression | ! |
|---|---|
| 0 | 1 |
| 1 | 0 |

```
int a=10,b=5,c,d;
c= a>3 && b!=3;
d= (a= =10 ¦¦ b>20);
printf("%d, %d",c,d)
```
**Output:- 1, 1**

**Using the short circuit operator:**

```
int a=5,b=4,c;
c= (b = =3 && a++);
printf("%d, %d, %d", a,b,c);
```

**Output:- 5, 4, 0**

46

Now let us try to understand this output, in the expression there are four types of operators, b= =3 has equality operator. a++ is a unary operator. These two expressions are connected to each other with a logical AND. And at last value is assigned to variable c.

In this expression b = = 3 in a false expression thus would give 0. The next operator is a logical AND, this operator works on two different expressions (AND gives answer as 1 only if both the expressions are true) the first one being b = = 3 and the second one a++. The first expression for AND is false so it will not evaluate the next expression to speed up the execution of the program.

```
int i=3,j=2,k=0,m;
m = ++i && ++j || ++k;
printf("%d %d %d %d", i , j, k,m);
Output:-2 3 0 1
```

```
int i=3,j=2,k=0,m;
m = ++j && ++i || ++k;
printf("%d %d %d %d", i , j, k,m);
Output:-2 3 0 1
```

```
int i=3,j=2,k=0,m;
m = ++i || ++j && ++k;
printf("%d %d %d %d", i , j, k,m);
Output:- 2 2 0 1
```

```
int i=3,j=2,k=0,m;
m = ++i && ++j && ++k;
printf("%d %d %d %d", i , j, k,m);
Output:-2 3 1 1
```

## 7. Conditional Operator -

This is the only ternary type of operator in C. It works on three operands. This class of operators is a set of two operators(? and :) which work together. Let us understand the syntax of this operator first:

### Condition ? true statement : false statement;

The above expression says if condition is true i.e. if it returns a non zero value, then the value returned will be true statement, otherwise the value returned will be false statement.

**Consider the following e.g.**

| | |
|---|---|
| 1. int x=2,y;<br> y = x > 5 ? 3 : 5;<br><br> **Output: 5**<br><br>since the value of x is less than 5 so the condition is false hence the part of statement after semicolon( : ) will be executed.<br><br>2. int a=5,b=4,c;<br> a>b? g = a: g = b;<br><br>**Output:-** This will give an error 'Lvalue required'. The error can be overcome by enclosing the statement in the : part within a pair of parenthesis. a>b? g = a: (g = b); In absence of parentheses the compiler believes that b is being assigned to the result of the expression to the left of second =. Hence it reports an error.<br><br>The limitation of the conditional operators is that only one statement is allowed after ? or : .<br><br>**Note:** it is not necessary to use the conditional operators only with arithmetic statements,<br><br>3. Are the two statements same:<br> a<=20?b=30:c=30;<br> a<=20?b:c=30;<br>**Output:-** No | 4. int a=10,b;<br> a>=5?b=100:b=200;<br> printf("%d",b);<br> **Output-** lvalue error occurs.<br><br>The second assignment should be written in parentheses as follows:<br> a>=5?b=100: (b=200);<br><br>5. Rewrite the following set of statements using conditional operators:<br> int a=1,b;<br> if(a>10)<br>    b=20;<br><br>**Output:-** int a=1,b,dummy;<br>      a>10?b=20:(dummy=1);<br><br>Note that the following will not work:<br> a>10?b=20:;;<br><br>6. Can you suggest some other way to write the following expression such that 30 is used only once?<br> a<=20?b=30:c=30;<br><br>**Output:-** ((a<=20)?&b:&c)=30); |

## 8. Bitwise operators –

Some programs require working on the bits(0 and 1) such as programs interacting with the hardware parts of the computer. Thus C contains several special operators which allow working on the bits.

*The bitwise operators are generally categorized into three types:*

1. The one's complement operator(~)
2. The logical bitwise operator.(&, |, ^)
3. The shift operators.(<<, >>)
   In all there are 6 bitwise operators.

**One's complement operator:**

Also referred as the complementation operator. It is a unary operator that inverts the bits of the operand, i.e. all 0s become 1 and all 1s become 0s. The operand for the operator must always be an integer value(int, short int, long int, unsigned, char).

unsigned int  a= 5, b;
b = ~a;
printf("%u",b);

**Output:-** will be 65530.

Let us evaluate the output now: the binary equivalent of the number 5 will be
0000 0000 0000 0101.

As already said one's complement convers all the 1s to 0s and all 0s to 1s.so the complement will be   1111 1111 1111 1010 and converting the number to a decimal number will give—

$1*2^{15}+1*2^{14}+1*2^{13}+1*2^{12}+1*2^{11}+1*2^{10}+1*2^9+1*2^8+1*2^7+1*2^6+1*2^5+1*2^4+1*2^3+0*2^2+1*2^1+0*2^0$

32768+16384+8192+4096+2048+1024+512+256+128+64+32+16+8 +0+2+0 and the final answer will be 65530.

**9. The logical bitwise operators:**

There are three logical bitwise operators bitwise AND(&),bitwise OR( | ),bitwise OR( ^). Each of these operators requires two integer values to work.

Each of the operands are individually converted into their respective binary numbers.The left most bit of the binary number is called the most significant bit or MSB. While the right most bit is called the least significant bit.

| Operand 1 | Operand 2 | & | \| | ^ |
|-----------|-----------|---|----|---|
| 0 | 0 | 0 | 0 | 0 |
| 0 | 1 | 0 | 1 | 1 |
| 1 | 0 | 0 | 1 | 1 |
| 1 | 1 | 1 | 1 | 0 |

The above table explains the working of all the logical bitwise operators.

**The shift operators:**

The two bitwise shift operators are left shift (<<) and the right shift (>>). Each of these operators also requires two operands. The first integer operand that represents the bit pattern to be shifted. The second operand indicates the number of bits to be shifted.

```
int a,b;
a=20<<2;
b=20>>2;
printf("%d %d",a,b);
Output:- 80, 5
```

The program will convert 20 to its binary equivalent i.e. 0000 0000 0001 0100 shifting 2 bits to the left would result the bits to be 0000 0000 0101 0000 and the integer number will be 80. if the bits of the integer number 20 are shifted 2 bits to the right side the binary number will be 0000 0000 0000 0101.

Thus shifting the number to right by 1 reduces the number to half, while shifting the number to left by 1 bit doubles the number.

**10. Comma operator -**

, operator works from left to right but returns the right most value. This operator is generally used in the for loop. The expressions separated by comma operator are solved from left to right. On using the comma operator the value and the type of right most operand is returned. For e.g. in the assignment statement below:

i = (j = 1, k = 2, 3, 4);
The expressions j = 1, k = 2, 3, 4 are evaluated first. Then the value of the expression is returned as 4 and assigned to i.

| 1. | int a; | 2. | int a; |
|----|--------|----|--------|
| | a = 5,6; | | a = (5,6); |
| | printf("%d",a); | | printf("%d",a); |
| | Output:- 5 | | Output:- 6 |

# Some Solved Programs:

1. If a four digit number is input through the keyboard, write a program to obtain the sum of the first and last digit of the number.

```
int n,a,b,sum;
printf("Enter a four digit number: ");
scanf("%d",&n);
a=n%10;
b=n/1000;
sum = a + b;
printf("Sum of the first and last digit is %d", sum);
getch();
```

2. Print the range of a number. E.g. number 78 is between 70 and 79, 102 is between 100 and 109.

```
int n,lower_r,upper_r;
printf("Enter a number: ");
scanf("%d",&n);
lower_r = n %10 * 10;    /*the arithmetic operators work from left to right*/
upper_r = lower_r + 10;
printf("Range is %d - %d", lower_r,upper_r);
getch();
```

3. Print the various denominations of a given rupee. E.g. if a person has 1779 in his pocket the program should print the following.

500 x 3 = 1500, 100 x 2 = 200, 50 x 1 = 50, 20 x 1 = 20, 10 x 0 = 0, 5 x 1 = 5, 2 x 2 = 4, 1 x 0 = 0

```
int Rs,a,b,c,d,e,f,g,h;
clrscr();
printf("Enter the amount: ");
scanf("%d",&Rs);
a= Rs/500;
Rs = Rs%500;
b = Rs/100;
Rs=Rs%100;
c=Rs/50;
```

52

```c
Rs=Rs%50;
d=Rs/20;
Rs=Rs%20;
e=Rs/10;
Rs=Rs%10;
f=Rs/5;
Rs=Rs%5;
g=Rs/2;
Rs=Rs%2;
h=Rs/1;
printf("The various denominations of the given rupees are\n\500 X %2d\n100 X %2d\n 50 X %2d\n 20 X %2d\n 10 X %2d\n  5 X %2d\n\ 2 X %2d\n  1 X %2d",a,b,c,d,e,f,g,h);
getch();
```

Ohhh Yes! Demm Man ....
We don't know that
We are new Fuc*in Programmers! LoL

## Multiple choice questions:

1. A whole number with a decimal point is known as:
   - a. floating point number.
   - b. character.
   - c. integer.
   - d. none.

2. The declaration unsigned u indicates:
   - a. u is a character
   - b. u is an unsigned integer
   - c. u is unsigned character
   - d. u is unsigned long integer

3. Which statement must not end with semicolon:
   - a. #define
   - b. variable declaration
   - c. assignment
   - d. none

4. Point out the valid variable names:
   - a. gross salary
   - b. gross-salary
   - c. AVG
   - d. AVG.

5. If a is an integer variable, a =5/2 will return a value.
   - a. 2.5
   - b. 3
   - c. 2
   - d. 0

6. The expression, a=7/22*(3.14+2)*3/5 is evaluated to
   - a. 8.28
   - b. 6.28
   - c. 3.14
   - d. 0

7. The expression a=30*1000+2768 evaluates to
   - a. 32768
   - b. -32768
   - c. 113040
   - d. 0

8. The expression a=4+2%-8 evaluates to
   - a. -6
   - b. 6
   - c. 4
   - d. none of the above

9. Hierarchy decides which operator
   - a. is most important
   - b. is used first
   - c. is fastest
   - d. operates on largest numbers

10. In C a variable can not contain
    - a. blank spaces
    - b. hyphen ( - )
    - c. decimal point
    - d. all the above

11. Arithmetic instructions can not Contain--
    - a. variables.
    - b. constant.
    - c. variable names on right of equal.
    - d. variable names on left of equal.

12. Which of the following is odd one out
    - a. +
    - b. -
    - c. /
    - d. **

13. What will be the value of d assuming it to be float after the operation d=2/7.0
    - a. 0
    - b. 0.2857
    - c. can not be determined.
    - d. none of the above.

Answers-

1(a)   2(b)   3(a)   4(c)   5(c)   6(d)   7(b)   8(b)   9(b)
10(d)   11(c)   12(d)   13(b)

## Theory Questions –

1. Explain what are data types? Name all the data types in c language with their size in bytes (in dos operating system). List all the format specifiers. Also write the formula by which we can calculate the range of a given data type.
2. Calculate the range of int by this.
3. How many keywords are present in C. Give the name of all the keywords?
4. Explain all the naming rules of a variable in c.
5. Characteristics of a program.
6. Name all the escape sequences.
7. What do you mean by precedence of operators? List all the available
8. operators in c in the order of their precedence. (higher to lower)
9. What do you mean by typecasting? Explain implicit and explicit typecasting

## Give the output of the following -

| | |
|---|---|
| **1**. int i =4, z =12;<br>  if( i = 5\|\| z>50)<br>printf("\nwelcome in matrix");<br>  else<br>printf("\n you may go now");<br><br>**Output: welcome in matrix**<br>First in if i is assigned with 5 that is non zero value and assume as true now this value involve with (\|\|) OR op. and in the case of OR operator if first condition is true it is not go for the next one and jumps out with true value this is known as "short circuit ". | **13**. What should we do to treat the constant 3.14 as a long double?<br><br>**Output: Use 3.14l**<br><br>**14**. What will be the output of the following statement:<br>  printf("% %d %d",sizeof(3.14f),<br>  sizeof(3.14), sizeof(3.14l));<br><br>  a.    4 4 4<br>  b.    4 garbage value garbage value<br>  c.    4 8 10<br>  d.    Error<br>**Output:** c |
| **2**. int i=4,z=12;<br>  if(i = 5&& z>5)<br>       printf("hello");<br>  else<br>       printf("bye");<br><br>**Output: hello**<br>First i is assigned with 5 that is non zero and assume true now second | **15**. How floats are stored in binary form?<br>**Output:** Floating point numbers are represented in IEEE format. The Ieee format for floating point storage uses a sign bit, a mantissa and an exponent for representing the power of 2. the sign bit denotes the sign of the number: a 0 represents a positive value and a 1 |

condition (z>5) is checked and it is true so both condition are true and finally generate the true so the statement under if is executed and message "hello" is printed.

3. int i =4,j = -1,k =0,w,x,y,z;
   w = i||j||k;
   x = i&&j&&k;
   y = i|| j&&k;
   z = i&&j||k
   printf("\nw=%d x=%d y=%d z=%d",w,x,y,z);

**Output: w =1 x =0 y =1 z =1**
i =4 that is a non zero value means true condition.
j =-1 that is also a non zero value means true condition.
k =0 that means false condition.

4. int i =4,j =-1,k =0,y,z;
   y =j+5&&j+1||k+2;
   z = i+5 || j+1 && k+2;
   printf("\n y =%d z =%d",y,z);

**Output: 1 1**
In the first statement j+5 =4(T) and j+1 =0(F) and k+2 =2(T)
Now first (j+5 && j+1) →(4 && 0) gives 0 (F) and second comparison will be (0 || k+2)→(0||2)→1(T) so y =1.
In the second statement i+5 =9 and in the exp. (i+5 || j+1 && k+2)→(9|| j+1&& k+2) and we know in the case of || op. if first condition is true then control don't go for the next condition it jumps out with true result means 1 so z =1.

5. int i = -3, j = 3;
   if (!i+!j*1)
          printf("Hello");
   else
          printf("Bye");

denotes a negative value. The mantissa is represented in binary after converting it to its normalized form. The normalized form results in a mantissa whose most significant digit is always 1. the IEEE format takes advantage by not storing this bit at all. The exponent is the integer stored in unsigned binary format after adding a positive integer bias. This ensures that the stored exponent is always positive. The value of the bias is 127 for floats and 1023 for doubles

16. int p = 8, q = 20;
    if(p = = 5 && q<5)
            printf("Hello Matrix");
    else
            printf("Bye Matrix");

**Output: Bye Matrix**
At first compiler execute the exp in if and there the first compare p = = 5 that gives false(0) and here && is involve in exp. so control jumps out without checking for the next condition and gives false in if. Now because there is false condition in if control jumps to the else block and printed "Bye Matrix".

17. int i = -1, j = 1,k,l;
    k = i&&j;
    l = i||j;
    printf("%d %d",i,j);

**Output: -1 1**
Here simple print the value of i and j that don't effect the value of i and j so the value of i and j remains same and gets printed through printf( ).

18. int j = 4,k;
    k = !5 && j;
    printf("k =%d",k);

**Output: 0**

**Output: Bye**
Here first we know the priority of all used op. Here !(not) gets higher priority then *(multiplication) and then +(addition)
i = -3( T ) then !i→( ! T )→F(0)
similarly !j gives  F (0) and 0*1 gives 0 and now exp. will convert (0+0)→ 0 so condition is false and control jumps out to the else block and execute it resultant "Bye" is printed.


**6**. int a= 40;
  if(a>40 && a<45)
       printf("a is between 40 and 45");
  else
       printf("%d",a);

**Output: 40**
Here a>40 is the first compare that gives false and exp. contains && op. In the case of the && if first condition is false then control jumps out with false condition and in if condition is false so finally control jumps to the else block and print the value of a that is 40.

**7**. int a = 65;
   printf("\n a>=65 ? %d: %c",a);

**Output 65**

**8**. float a= 0.7;
  if(a<0.7)
       printf("Hello");
  else
       printf("Bye");

**Output:** Hello

**9**. We want to round off x, a float, to an int
  value. The correct way to do so would be:

Here ! gets the first priority and when solved(!5)→(!T)→(F). And in the case of && op. first condition  is false then control don't go for the next statement and jumps out with false condition means 0 so k =0.

**19**. int i = -1, j = 1,k,l;
   k = !i&&j;
   l = !i||j;
   printf("%d %d",i,j);

**Output: -1 1**
Here i and j gets printed that doesn't effect in the above steps and remains same.

**20**. int x = 20, y = 40, z = 45;
   if(x>y && x>z)
       printf("x is max");
   else if(y>x && y>z)
       printf("y is max");
   else
       printf("z is max");

**Output: z is max**
Here first condition in if is checked (x>y && x>z) and (x>y) gives false and && op. is involved and here first condition is false control gives false result and jumps out to the next else if block and check for the condition here also first condition y>x is true and then second condition is y>z that is false and finally exp. gives false and control jumps to the else block and printed out "z is max".

**21**. int i = 4,j,num;
   j = (num<0?0:num*num);
   printf("%d",j);

**Output: Garbage**
Because num is not initialize and when condition is checked it becomes false and compiler execute the num*num and assign in j. so j is also contains garbage value.

a.    y=(int) (x+0.5);
b.    y=int (x+0.5);
c.    y=(int) x+0.5;
d.    y=(int) ((int) x+0.5);
**Output:** a

**10**. Which are the three different types of real data types available in C and what are the format specifiers used for them.
   **Output:** float  4 bytes
         %f
            double       8 byte
         %lf
            long double 10 byte
         %Lf **11**. By default any real number is treated as
   **Output:** double

**12**. What should we do to treat the constant
   3.14 as a float?
   **Output:** Use 3.14f

**22**. int a,n=30;
      a =( n>5 ? ( n<=10 ? 100 :200):500);
      printf("%d",n);

**Output: 30**
Here we see that n is used to check the condition but a can change by condition but n is not change in the above program and we print out the value of n that is 30.

**23**. int k = 4;
      ( !k != 1?
printf("\nHello"):printf("Bye"));

**Output: Hello**
Here ! op. encounter in the same statement two times so we solve the exp using associativity that is left to right. now clearly ( !k) is solved that gives[( !4)→0] and exp. convert as 0!=1 that is true so the first printf after ? gets executed and print out "Hello".

# Point out the error if any.

| | |
|---|---|
| **1.** int x =2,y =3;<br>  ( x = = y ? printf("%d",a));<br><br>**Output:** Error<br>Ternary op.( ? :) must be use in pair here in the above program : is missing.<br><br>**2.** int a = 3;<br>  ( a = =3 ? printf("Hello Matrix");:<br>  printf("Bye Matrix"););<br><br>**Output:** Error<br>Here the ";" after the first printf( ) will terminate the statement whether it must be terminate after the ":"(colon) statement i.e. after the second printf() statement.<br><br>**3.** int a = 5 ,b = 10;<br>  a = =10 && b!=10 ?<br> print("come in"):<br>printf("you can go"); | **Output:** No Error<br><br>Here first condition is executed that becomes false so control jumps to the printf() after the colon and gets printed "you can go".<br><br>**4.** int a = 65 ,b;<br>  b = ( a = =65 : printf("you are correct"):printf("you are wrong"));<br><br>**Output:** Error<br>Here "?" is missing from the ternary op.<br><br>**5.** int a = 10,b;<br>  a >=5?( b =10): ( b =15);<br>  printf("%d %d",a,b);<br><br>**Output:** No Error.<br><br>In the above program first condition is checked that comes false and execute the statement after the colon sign that assign 15 in b. and then print out the value of a and b that is 10 and 15 respectively . [This statement can be written as b= (a>=5 ? 10 :15);  Floating Point |

## Lab Exercise –

1. WAP to calculate the sum of digits of a three digit number e.g. 125 is 8
2. WAP to merge three number. E.g. a= 1, b= 2, c = 8 is 128.
3. WAP to print the reverse of a 3 digit number.
4. Compute the gross salary of Mr. HARISH. Input his basic salary. His DA is 40% of basic salary, and HRA is 20% of basic salary.

C - Programmer
Harry.

# CHAPTER

# ∞ **3** ∞

## (Control Statements-Conditions)

## Introduction-

Programs are much more useful if they can make decisions about what tasks need to be performed. Making a decision in a C program usually involves testing the value of one or more variables,

*for example, 'if X is greater than Y then carry out task 1,*

*else carry out task 2'.*

C programs can use a range of tests to satisfy many different circumstances. The example given above uses the *if-else* construct and is just about the most simple test that a C program can perform.

However, it is not too difficult to imagine that, having made this decision, task 1 or task 2 may also be an *ifelse* type of test, leading to the execution of other, more specialized, tasks (perhaps including more tests). This can be achieved in C by using as many **nested** *if-else* constructs as required.

The *switch* construct is similar to the nested *if-else* but is more appropriate when different tasks must be selected (switch to) depending on the value of a variable.

1.  Condition or Selection or Decision Control Statement
2.  Switch case Control Statement.

## 1. Selection Statements (Decision Control Structure) :-

Selection statement allows the program to choose any one path from different set of paths of execution based upon the outcome of an expression or the state of a variable.

a. **if**
b. **if else**
c. **nested if else**
d. **if-else-if**

| (a) Syntax of if | (b) Syntax of if else |
|---|---|
| if(condition)<br>{<br>    statements;<br>} | if(condition)<br>{<br>}<br>else<br>{<br>} |

| (c) Syntax of Nested if else | (d) Syntax of if-else-if Ladder |
|---|---|
| if(condition)<br>{<br>    if (condition)<br>    {<br>    }<br>    else<br>    {<br>    }<br>}<br>else<br>{<br>    if (condition)<br>    {<br>    }<br>    else<br>    {<br>    }<br>} | if(condition1)<br>{<br>}<br>else if(condition2)<br>{<br>}<br>else if(condition3)<br>{<br>}<br>else<br>{<br>} |

## 2. Switch Case –

```
switch(expression)
{
        case 1:
                statement 1 sequence;
                break;
        case 2:
                statement 2 sequence;
                braek;
        case 3:
                statement 3 sequence;
                break;
        --
        --
        --
        case n:
                break;
        default :
                default statement sequence;
}
```

Decision and Switch Case control statements allow the computer to take a decision as to which statement is to be executed next.

## Common programming errors -

1.      The if statement does not include the word then. For this reason it is an error to write:

```
if(condition) then
        Statement;
```

2.      In the if statement, the condition must be enclosed in parenthesis. Thus it is an error to write:

```
if condition
        statement;
```

3.      In the if statement, no semicolon follows the word else. For this reason, it is a logical error to write. Now false statement will always execute.

```
if(condition)
        true statement;
else;
        false statement;
```

4. Using a single equal sign = (for comparing) instead of a double equal sign = = will be considered as logical error.

5. In a switch, the integer expression that follows switch must be enclosed in parenthesis. Thus it is an error to write

```
switch i
{
    .........
    .........
}
```

## Some Solved Problems -

1. **To calculate the real roots** of the quadratic equation

```
#include<math.h>                          /*to use function sqrt*/

float a,b,c,d,r1,r2;
printf("enter three numbers: ");
scanf("%f %f %f",&a,&b,&c);
d=b*b-(4*a*c);
if(d<0)
        printf("roots are imaginary");
else
{
        r1=(-b+sqrt(d))/(2*a);            /*to calculate square root */
        r2=(-b-sqrt(d))/(2*a);
        printf("The roots are %f %f",r1,r2);
}
```

2. If cost price and selling price of an item is input through the keyboard, WAP to determine whether the seller has made profit or incurred loss. Also determine how much profit he made or loss be incurred.

```
float cp,sp;
printf("Enter the cost price and the seling price of the item: ");
scanf("%f %f",&cp,&sp);
if(sp>cp)
        printf("profit is Rs. %.2f",sp-cp);     /*%.2f is used to
                                                 print number up to
                                                 2 decimal places
                                                 only*/
else if(cp > sp)
        printf("loss is Rs %.2f",cp-sp);
else
        printf("No Profit No Loss");
```

64

3. **WAP to create a calculator** which can do addition, subtraction, multiplication, division, & modulus (remainder).

```
int a,b,ch;
printf("Enter two nos. ");
scanf("%d%d",&a,&b);
printf("1:\tAdd\n2:\tSubtract\n3:\tMultiply\n4:\tDivide\n5:\tModulus\nEnter your choice: ");
scanf("%d",&ch);
switch(ch)
{
        case 1:
                printf("%d\n",a+b);
                break;
        case 2:
                printf("%d\n",a-b);
                break;
        case 3:
                printf("%d\n",a*b);
                break;
        case 4:
                printf("%f\n",(float)a/b);
                break;
        case 5:
                printf("%d\n",a%b);
                break;
        default:
                printf("Invalid Input");
}
getch();
```

## Drill Note:

I want to use the opportunity and give you a caution at the end of this lesson. As there are many commands and programming techniques in any programming language, you will not be able to remember all of them.

The only way to remember things is to practice them. You need to start developing your own small programs. Start with lesson exercises and continue with more sophisticated ones. If you do not do this, all your efforts will become useless in a while. I always quote this in my programming classes:

# Fill in the blanks –

1. If an expression c=e1&&e2&&e3, then if e1 is false, e2 and e3 _____ be evaluated.

2. The logical operator == checks for the _____ of the two values.

3. All characters are internally represented as _____.

4. The statement
   " if (ch>= 'a' && ch<= 'z') returns ('A' + ch- 'a')"
   will return _____ for a given character between 'a' and 'z'.

5. In the printf statement between the % and the conversion character there may be an h if the integer to be printed as _____.

6. The data type double is actually double precision _____.

7. Operators *, /,% have _____ precedence.

8. Operators &, ^, = = have _____ precedence.

9. A _____ converts thew assembly language programs to machine code.

10. Braces { and } are used to group the declarations and statements together into a _____ statement.

11. The operator size of returns size of a data type in a _____.

12. Given that a is unsigned integer variablewhose value is 0 X 6db7, the expression.
    b=a<<6;
    will assign b the value_____

13. The expression 11%3 will evaluate to _____.

14. ? : is a _____ operator.

15. In a C expression with mixed data type containing variables of the float and double the result is of the type _____.

16. The unary operator ~ is used for performing the _____ on the variable.

17. The following C expression
    1+2*3-5
    evaluates the expression to _____.

# What will be the output of the following program -

**1.** int i =4;
switch (i)
{
       default:
           printf("Matrix");
       case 1:
           printf("Computer");
           break;
       case 2:
           printf("Education");
           break;
       case 3:
           printf("Hello");
}
**Output:-** MatrixComputer

**2.** int i =4, j=2;
switch (i)
{
       case 1:
           printf("Hello");
           break;
       case j:
           printf("Bye");
           break;
}
**Output:-** Error constant expressions are required in *switch*, we cannot use j.

**3.** int i =1;
switch (i)
{
       case 1:
           printf("Hello");
           break;
       case 1 * 2 + 4:
           printf("Bye");
           break;
}
Output:- No error. Constant expressions like 1*2+4 are acceptable

**4.** int i =4;
switch (i)

**13.** int a=300,b,c;
if(a>=400)
         b=300;
         c=200;
         printf("\n%d %d",b,c);
**Output:-b** contains garbage and c=200. Because a is initialize with 300 and when condition is checked then it becomes false and b can't assign with 300 so still b contain garbage value and if doesn't contain any braces so the scope of if is only on next statement so c is out of the if scope and it will be assign with 200.

**14.** int a=500,b,c;
if(a>=400)
         b=300;
         c=200;
         printf("\n%d %d",b,c);
**Output:** -300 200. Because a is initialize with 500 and when condition is checked then it becomes true and b is assign with 300 if doesn't contain any braces so the scope of if is only on next statement so c is out of the if scope and it will be assign with 200.

**15.** int x =10,y =20;
if(x = = y);
         printf("\n%d %d",x,y);
**Output:-10 20.**
Because if contains ; so it is understand as
if(x = =y)
  {
  ;
  }
printf("\n%d %d",x,y);
now it is clear that if contains null statement and after executing if control reach on printf( ) that print

```c
{
}
printf("Hello World");
```
Output:- A switch can occur that does not have any statement.

**5.** 
```c
int i =1;
switch (i)
{
        printf("Matrix");/*common for both
                cases*/
        case 1:
            printf("Hello");
            break;
        case 2:
            printf("Bye");
            break;
}
```
**Output:-** Hello
Though there is no error but the first printf can never get executed. In other words all the statements in a switch must belong to some case or the other.

**6.** Can we use switch statement to switch on string?
**Output:-** No *switch* can work only on integer constants or constant expressions.

**7.** We want to test whether a value lies in the range 2 to 4 or 5 to 7. Can we do this using switch?
**Output:-** yes but it is not practical if the ranges are bigger.

**8.** 
```c
switch(a)
{
        case 2:
        case 3:
        case 4:
        /*some statements*/
        break;
        case 5:
        case 6:
        case 7:
```
out the value of x and y that is 10 and 20 respectively.

**16.** 
```c
int a = 3;
float b = 3.0;
if(a = = b)
        printf("\n a and b are equal");
else
        printf("\n a and b are not equal");
```
**Output:-**a and b are not equal because a and b both are assigned with 3 and when condition is checked it becomes true so the next statement to if is executed and print out "a and b are not equal".

**17.** 
```c
int x=3,y=5;
if (x = =3)
        printf("\n %d",x);
else;
        printf("\n%d",y);
```
**Output:-**
3
5
Because x is initializing with 3 and when condition is checked it becomes true and will print out 3. Now control jumps out of the if structure and gets execute the next print statement that print out the value of y that is 5. Now the question is why next printf( ) is executed? This is so happens because the next statement after else is ; not printf( ). That means else contain Null statement and next printf( ) is out of the if structure.
18. 
```c
int x = 3,y,z;
y = x =10;
z = x<10;
printf("\n x =%d y =%d z = %d");
```
**Output:-**
x = 10 y =10 z =0

```
        /*some other statements*/
        break;
}
```
The way *break* is used to take the control of switch can *continue* be used to take the control to the beginning of the switch?

**Output:-** No, *continue* can work only with loops and not *switch.*

**9.** char card = 3;
```
switch(card)
{
        case 1:
            printf("\n King");
        case 2:
            printf("Queen");
        default:
            printf("Jokar");
}
printf("\nYou have losing the game:");
```
**Output:-**     Joker
                You have lost the game:
In the above program the case variable is card that value is 3. and there is no case constant that is 3 so no perfect match here and compiler execute the printf( ) statement after the default that print out "Jokar" and then control comes out to the switch block when comes out met with a printf( ) statement that print "You have lost the game".

**10.** int prize = 3;
```
switch(prize)
{
        case '3':
                printf("\nSilver:");
                break;
        case 3:
                printf("\nGold")
                break;
        default:
                printf("\n Bronze");
}
```
**Output:-** It will always print "Gold"
Here compiler match the value of the

here in first x is initialize with 3 and in the next statement x again assign with 10 and the value of x is again assign in y so the value of y is also 10. now in the next statement conditional operator(<) gets higher priority that's why first condition is checked and if becomes false and gives the value 0. so z is assign with 0.

Note: when a condition is true it gives 1(non-zero) and when it becomes false it gives 0(zero) and vice versa.

**19.** int k=35;
printf("%d %d %d",k = =35,k = 50,k>40);
**Output:-**0 50 0
When printf( ) statement is executed the first the expression and comparison take place and the expression is solved from right to left order so first condition (k>40) is checked because k = 35 so it becomes false and gives 0. now continuing in order right to left next k = 50 is executed and it assigns 50 in k  and now k is compared with 35 that gives false because k is 50 not equal 35 and gives 0. and printing will take place from left to right.

**20.** int a=97;
char b ='a';
if(a = = b)
                printf("hello matrix");
else
                printf("bye matrix");
**Output:-**hello matrix
here a and b are compared against equality but b contains 'a' that ASCII value is 97. so both a and b are equal and condition becomes true and gets execute the statement next to the if statement.

case variable with the case constant, the comparison will be between 3 and '3' that is unsuccessful match because one is integer and another is character and when character is converted with the ASCII value it will be 68 that is not equal to 3. and then control jumps to the next case that will be the perfect match so it will print "Gold" and jumps out to the switch block due to break statement.

**11.** int c =3;
switch(c)
{
      case 0:
          printf("Windows and Dos:");
      case 1+0:
          printf("Networking and security:");
      case 4/2:
          printf("Programming:");
      case 8%5:
          printf("Unix and Linux:");
}
**Output:-** Unix and Linux:
In this program first compiler solve the exp. of case constant and then match the case variable with the case constant. Here 8%5 gives 3 that will match with the case variable and that will print "Unix and Linux:"

**12.** int k;
float j = 2.0;
switch(k = j+1)
{
      case 3:
          printf("you have passed:");
          break;
      default:
          printf("Leave It");
}
**Output:-** you have passed:
Here first compiler solve the exp k = j+1 and gives k = 3. and now k becomes case variable that value is matched with the

**21.** int x = 15;
printf("%d %d %d ",x!=15,x =20,x<30);

**Output:-1 20 1**

Here in the printf( ) statement first expression or comparison take place in the order R to L and firs x<30 is checked because x is 15 so this is true and gives 1 now x is assigned with 20 and then x!=15 take place and gives 1 because of true condition because x is assigned with 20 first. and now the result gets printed in the order L to R.

**22.** int ch = 'a'+ 'b' ;
switch(ch)
{
      case 'a':
      case 'b':
          printf("you have secured a");
      case 'A':
          printf("you are confused:");
      case 'b' + 'a':
          printf("you have secured both a and b:");
}

**Output:-** you have secured both a and b.

**23.** In the above program fist exp. ch = 'a' + 'b' is solved. Because character constant will convert with their ascii value and ch = 65 + 66→ch = 131 and then switch variable will match with the case constant and because there same constant is exist as in the above exp.('b'+'a'→131) so condition

| | |
|---|---|
| case constant and print out "you have passed" and then jumps out to the switch block because of "break" statement. | becomes true and the statement "you have secured both a and b:" will print. |

## Point out the errors, if any, in the following programs:

| | |
|---|---|
| **1.** float a =12.25, b=5.2;<br>if(a = b)<br>printf("\n a and b becomes equal");<br><br>**Output:-** No Error.<br><br>Here in the if statement a is not compared with b, a is assigned with b that is non zero(5.2) and now in if non zero value gets executed as true and gets execute printf statement under the if.<br><br>**2.** if('A'<'a')<br>        printf("\n A is smaller than a");<br><br>**Output:-** No Error.<br><br>Here in if statement A(capital) is compared with a(small) and we know the character is first replaced by it's ASCII value and than any comparison make places and because ASCII of A is 65 and ASCII of a is 97.<br><br>so the condition gets execute with true result.<br><br>**3.** int x =10;<br>if(x>=2) then<br>        printf("Good");<br><br>**Output:-**<br><br>Error→ "then" can't be used in c.<br><br>**4.** int j =10, k =12; | **7.** int a=10,b=15;<br>if(a = =b)<br>        printf("equal");<br>elseif<br>        printf("a is max");<br>else<br>        printf("b is max");<br>**Output:-**<br>Error→elseif is not a single keyword in c. both are must be separate so space is required between else and if.<br><br>**8.** int ch=1;<br>switch(ch)<br>{<br>        case 0;<br>           printf("\nClub");<br>        case 1;<br>           printf("\nDiamond");<br>}<br>**Output:-** Error.<br>Because there will be the semicolon instead of colon after the case.<br><br>**9.** int temp;<br>scanf("%d",temp);<br>switch(temp);<br>{<br>        case (temp<=20)<br>          printf("Oh! Damn Cool");<br>        case (temp>20 &&<br>temp<=30)<br>          printf("Rainy season:");<br>        case (temp>30 &&<br>temp<=40)<br>printf("\nwish me I am on<br>                 Everest:");<br>        default : |

```
if(k>=j)
{
    {
        k=j;
        j=k;
    }
}
```
**Output:-** No Error

Any no. of braces can be used.

**5.** int a =10, b = 15;
```
if(a%2 = b%5)
    printf("wonderful");
```

**Output:-**
Error→ Lvalue required.
first the expression in if is solved and % op. gets higher priority than = so first b%5 gives 5 and a%2 gives also 5. (Order R to L) and exp. becomes 5=5. And now assignment take place but we know we can't assign a value in constant.

**6.** int a,b;
```
printf("Enter two num:");
scanf("%d %d",a,b);
if(a>b)
        printf("a is max");
else
        printf("b is max");
```

**Output:-**

Error→ &(ampersand) is required in scanf().
Here no error will be reported by the compiler but we can't get desired result because when we input any two num on run time it will not store in a and b because it don't know the address of a and b automatically we must give it

```
printf("\n Let's Go for a Picnic:");
}
```

**Output:-**

Error. Relational op. can't be used in cases.

**10.** float a = 3.5;
```
switch( a)
{
        case 0.5:
            printf("Hello C:");
        case1.5:
            printf("Working in C:");
        case 2.5:
        printf("Test your C Skill:");
        case 3.5:
            printf("Simply C:");
}
```

**Output:-**

Error. Floating point constants is not allowed in cases.

**11.** int a = 3,b= 4,c;
```
c = b-a;
switch(c)
{
        case 1||2:
            printf("Hello Matrix:");
            break;
        case a||b:
            printf(\nBye Matrix");
            break;
}
```

**Output:-**

Error. A case need constant value or constant exp. Logical op. is not allowed in cases.

72

# Lab Exercise (WAP- Write a Program)-

1. WAP to check whether a number input through the keyboard is even or odd.

2. WAP to print the maximum out of two numbers.

3. WAP to print the maximum out of three numbers.

4. WAP to print the maximum out of four numbers.

5. WAP to print the maximum out of four numbers. (Short logic)

6. WAP to print the second maximum out of three numbers.

7. WAP to check whether a year is leap year or not.

8. WAP to calculate the grade of a student after the input of marks of that student.
   Percentage >= 90          grade is 'A'
   Percentage >= 70          grade is 'B'
   Percentage >= 50          grade is 'C'
   Percentage < 50 grade is 'F'

9. WAP to compute the tel. bill of a customer. Montly Rental Rs.100.Rates are as follows.

   No of calls 1to     100          rate = 0
   No of calls 101 to 200          rate = 0.80
   No of calls 201to 500          rate = 1.00
   No of calls 501to --          rate = 1.20

10. WAP to compute the pension of an employee.

    If the person is male.

    Age  >= 90          pension is 4000
    Age  >= 60          pension is 6000
    Age  < 60          pension is 0

    if the person is female.

    Age  >= 90          pension is 3000
    Age  >= 60          pension is 5000
    Age  < 60          pension is 0

11.  WAP to check whether a 3 digit number is a magic number or not. (Palindrome) A number is a magic number if its reverse is same as the original number.

12.  Any year is entered through the keyboard, WAP to determine the year is leap or not. Use the logical operators && and ||.

13.  Any character is entered through the keyboard, WAP to determine whether the character entered is a capital letter, a small case letter, a digit or a special symbol.

14.  WAP using conditional operators to determine whether a year entered through the keyboard is a leap year or not.

# CHAPTER

## ∞ **4** ∞

## (Control Statements (Looping))

## Introduction-

Sometimes we want some part of our code to be executed more than once. We can either repeat the code in our program or use loops instead. It is obvious that if for example we need to execute some part of code for a hundred or more times it is not practical to repeat the code. Alternatively we can use our repeating code inside a loop.

while(not a hundred times)

{

code

}

The loop repeat the some portion of the program until a specified number of time or until a particular condition is being satisfied. **Or** In other words you can say, The Looping is a process of repeating a single statement or a group of statements until some condition for termination of the loop is satisfied.

There are a few kinds of loop commands in C programming language. We will see these commands in next sections.

**There are four Parts of a loop -**

1.  Initialization.
2.  Conditions
3.  Statements
4.  Incrementation or Decrementation.

***Don't forget***, Looping is a process of repeating a single statement or a group of statements until some condition for termination of the loop is satisfied.

**Type of loops -**

*Entry control loops:* Those loops in which condition is checked before the execution of the statement. Thus if the condition is false in the beginning the loop will not run even once.

**e.g.** for loop, while loop.

*Exit control loops:* Those loops in which the condition is checked after the execution of the statement. Thus if the condition is false in the beginning the loop will run at least once.

***e.g.*** do while loop

**while loop –**

C has three loops, while is the simplest of them all. It is given a condition (in parentheses, just like with the if statement) which it evaluates. If the condition evaluates to true (non zero, as seen before) the body of the loop is executed. The condition is evaluated again, if still true, the body of the loop is executed again. This continues until the condition finally evaluates to false. Then execution jumps to the first statement that follows on after the loop

while loop is constructed of a condition and a single command or a block of commands that must run in a loop. As we have told earlier a block of commands is a series of commands enclosed in two opening and closing braces.

In the while loop, the condition is evaluated and if it is true the statement of the loop is executed. After the execution of statement and increment or decrement, the loop condition is tested again. This process of repeated execution of statement, increment or decrement and testing of condition continuous till the condition finally becomes false and the control of the loop is transferred to the next statement.

Once again if more than one statement is required in the body of the loop, begin and end braces must be used.

It is the simplest of all the loops. This loop is used as follows:

```
initialize;
while(condition)
{
        statement;
        increment or decrement;
}
```

        while loop is an entry control loop. The condition is evaluated and if it is true the statement of the loop is executed. After the execution of statement and increment or decrement, the loop condition is tested again. This process of repeated execution of statement, increment or decrement and testing of condition continuous till the condition finally becomes false and the control of the loop is transferred to the next statement.

**Syntax:**

```
initialization;

while(condition)

{

        statement;

        incrementation or decrementation;

}
```

**Free syntax:**

```
while( condition )

        command;

while( condition )

    {

    block of commands

    }
```

        Loop condition is a boolean expression. A boolean expression is a logical statement which is either correct or incorrect. It has a value of 1 if the logical statement is valid and its value is 0 if it is not. For example the Boolean statement (3>4) is invalid and therefore has a value of 0. While the statement

(10==10) is a valid logical statement and therefore its value is 1.

## Semicolon Warning! -

Avoid Semicolons After while . We have already seen that problems can arise if a semicolon is placed after an if statement. A similar problem exists with loops, although it is more serious. With if the no op statement is potentially executed only once. With a loop it may be executed an infinite number of times.

## Example -

```
#include<stdio.h>

main()

{

int i=0;

while( i<100 )

{

printf("\ni=%d",i);

i=i+1;

}

system("pause");

}
```

In above example i=i+1 means: add 1 to i and then assign it to i or simply increase its value. As we saw earlier, there is a special operator in C programming language that does the same thing. We can use the

expression i++ instead of i=i+1.

## Type Conversion -

From time to time you will need to convert type of a value or variable to assign it to a variable from another type. This type of conversions may be useful in different situations, for example when you want to convert type of a variable to become compatible with a function with different type of arguments.

Some rules are implemented in C programming language for this purpose.Automatic type conversion takes place in some cases. Char is automatically converted to int. Unsigned int will be automatically converted to int.

If there are two different types in an expression then both will convert to better type.In an assignment statement, final result of calculation will be converted to the type of the variable which will hold the result of the calculation (ex. the variable "count" in the assignment count=i+1; )

For example if you add two values from int and float type and assign it to a double type variable, result will be double.

**Using loops in an example -**

**Write a program** – To accept scores of a person and calculate sum of them and their average and print them.

```c
#include<stdio.h>
#include<conio.h>
main()
{
int count=0;
float num=0,sum=0,avg=0;
printf("Enter score (-1 to stop): ");
scanf("%f",&num);
while(num>=0)
{
sum=sum+num;
count++;
printf("Enter score (-1 to stop): ");
scanf("%f",&num);
}
avg=sum/count;
printf("\nAverage=%f",avg);
printf("\nSum=%f\n",sum);
system("pause");
}
```

This example we get first number and then enter the loop. We will stay inside loop until user enters a value smaller than 0. If user enters a value lower than 0 we will interpret it as STOP receiving scores.

**Here are the output results of a sample run:**

Enter score (-1 to stop): 12

Enter score (-1 to stop): 14

Enter score (-1 to stop): -1

Average=13.000000

Sum=26.000000

**Drill Note-**

Once again I am telling you, for more programming examples according to chapter topics please read last chapter of this book where I mentioned more than **200 C Programs for your practice.**

When user enters -1 as the value of num, logical expression inside loop condition becomes false (invalid) as num>=0 is not a valid statement. Just remember that "while loop" will continue running until the logical condition inside its parentheses becomes false (and in that case it terminates).

Print the sequence 1, 2, 3, 4, 5,..............N

int i,n;

```
printf("Enter the value of N ");

scanf("%d",&n);

i=1;

while(i<=n)

{
        printf("%d,",i);

        i++;

}
printf("\b ");        /*to remove the comma (,) printed at the last */
```

**do while loop -**

The do while loop in C is an "upside down" version of the while loop. Whereas while has the condition followed by the body, do while has the body followed by the condition.

This means the body must be executed before the condition is reached. Thus the body is guaranteed to be executed at least once.if the condition is false the loop body is never executed again.

It is an exit control loop. The loop is used as follows:

```
initialize;
do
{
        statement;
        increment or decrement;
}
while(condition);
```

Here the condition is tested after the execution of the statement and increment or decrement. Thus in this type of loop the program proceeds to evaluate the body of the loop first and the condition is tested after that. Thus even if the condition is false in the beginning then also the statement will be executed at least once. It is an exit control loop.

```
int j = 5;

printf("start\n");

do

printf("j = %i\n", j--);

while(j > 0);

printf("stop\n");
```

**output –**

```
start
j = 5
j = 4
j = 3
j = 2
j = 1
stop
```

**e.g**

**WAP** to Print the sequence 1, 2, 3, 4, 5,..............N

```
int i,n;

        printf("Enter the value of N ");

        scanf("%d",&n);
```

```
i=1;

do

{

printf("%d,",i);

i++;

} while(i<=n);

printf("\b ");      /*to remove the comma (,) printed at the last */
```

**Drill Note-** Most Important thing , do while guarantees execution at least once.

**for loop -**

As I told earlier, there are many kinds of loops in C programming language. We will learn about for loop in this section.

"For loop" is something similar to while loop but it is more complex. "For loop" is constructed from a control statement that determines how many times the loop will run and a command section. Command section is either a single command or a block of commands.

**Drill Note-** Remember that *for* loop encapsulates the essential elements of a loop into one statement. For more examples please see last chapter of this book

*for loop* is also an entry control loop which provides a more concise loop control structure. The loop is used as:

```
for (initialize; condition; increment or decrement)
{
        statement;
}
```

Initialization part is performed only once at "for loop" start. We can initialize a loop variable here.

Test condition is the most important part of the loop. Loop will continue to run if this condition is valid (True). If the condition becomes invalid (false) then the loop will terminate.

Run every time command' section will be performed in every loop cycle. We use this part to reach the final condition for terminating the loop.

For example we can increase or decrease loop variable's value in a way that after specified number of cycles the loop condition becomes invalid and "for loop" can terminate.

At this step we rewrite example 3-1 with for loop. Just pay attention that we no more need I=I+1 for increasing loop variable. It is now included inside "for loop" condition phrase (i++).

**Example –**

```
#include<stdio.h>
#include<conio.h>
            main()
            {
            int i=0;
            for(i=0;i<100;i++ )
            printf("\ni=%d",i);
            system("pause");
      }
```

**Drill Note- Stdio.h – Standard Input Output.**

**Drill Note- Conio.h – Console Input Output.**

**Drill Note-** Essentially all you need to remember the two semicolon characters that must separate the three parts of the construct.

**Example –**
      Write a program that gets temperatures of week days and calculate average temperature for that week.

```
#include<stdio.h>
#include<conio.h>

            main()
            {
            int count=0;
            float num=0,sum=0,avg=0;
```

```
for(count=0;count<7;count ++)
{
printf("Enter temperature : ");
scanf("%f",&num);
sum=sum+num;
}
avg=sum/7;
printf("\nAverage=%f\n",avg);
system("pause");
}
```

**Example -**

Below example will print a multiplication chart (from 1*1 to 9*9). Run the program and see the results.

```
#include<stdio.h>

main()

{

int i,j;

for(i=1;i<10;i++)

{

for(j=1;j<10;j++)

printf("%3d",i*j);

printf("\n");

}

system("pause");
```

*for And while Compared -*

The construct:

For (initial-part; while-condition; update-part)

Body

**Is equivalent to:**

Initial-part;

While (while-condition)

{

Body;

Update-part;

}

Here, the initialization works first then the condition is evaluated if the condition is true the execution of the statement takes first and then the increment or decrement of the variable takes place the condition is again tested and the process goes on till the loop condition becomes false.

The initialization takes place using some assignment operator. If more then one variable is to be initialized then assignments are separated by commas.

After all the assignments are written a semicolon is used to separate them from conditions. If there are more than one condition then they are separated by either logical AND (&&) or logical OR ( || ).

After all the conditions are given a semicolon is used before giving the increments or decrements.

If there are more than one statement in the body of the loop then using the parenthesis is compulsory.

A unique aspect of for loop is that one or more parts of for loop can be omitted if they are not required. However the semicolons separating the different parts of the loop are necessary.

A delay loop can also be set up using the null statement: for(i=100;i>0;i--);

In this loop there is no statement thus first the variable i is initialized by 100, the condition is tested ,then the decrement takes place, again the condition is tested, i is decreased again and it is repeated till the condition becomes false.

Another unique feature of the for loop is nesting that is placing one loop as a statement for another loop. In ANSI C the nesting is allowed up to 15 levels, however some compilers allow even more.

## Jump statements  (New Topic)-

Loop performs a set of statements, till the condition becomes false. The number of times a loop is to be repeated is decided in advance and a condition is set. But sometimes it becomes necessary to skip certain part of the loop or terminate the loop if a particular condition is true then jump statements come to action:

### C supports four jump statements:

i.    break.
ii.   continue.
iii.  goto.
iv    return.

## break -

The break statement is used inside a loop, to directly come out of the loop. We have already used *break* in switch statement. It is used to skip the execution of the loop any further and transfer the control of the program to the statement following the loop.

## continue-

Sometimes it is necessary to skip the execution of the statement when certain condition is true. continue does not terminate the loop but jumps directly to the next iteration. In for loop continue brings the control to the next increment or decrement but in while or do while loop continue causes the control of the loop to jump directly to the condition.

## goto-

It is also used to jump from one part of the program to the other or exit from the deeply nested loop. But using goto is not a good practice because it makes the logic complicated and long programs unreadable.

## return -

Used in a function to return some value and to jump from called function definition to calling function definition.

## exit() -

It is not a jump statement. It is used to terminate the program or directly exit from the program without following the intermediate statements. It is a library function included in *stdlib.h and process.h*. exit is used as: exit( )

*Drill Note* - break, goto, continue, return are all keywords.

## Let's Discuss these all in detail-

### Break Statement-

It must seem strange that C has a construct to deliberately create an infinite loop. Such a loop would seem something to avoid at all costs!

Nonetheless it is possible to put infinite loops to work in C by jumping out of them. Any loop, no matter what the condition, can be jumped out of using the C keyword break. We saw the loop below earlier :

```
printf("enter an integer: ");
while(scanf("%i", &j) != 1) {
while((ch = getchar()) != '\n')
;
printf("enter an integer: ");
```

### *break is Really Goto!*

It doesn't necessarily address the problem very well because it now uses the equivalent of a goto statement! The goto is the scourge of modern programming, because of its close relationship some companies ban the use of break. If it is to be used at all, it should be used in moderation, overuse is liable to create spaghetti

### *break, switch and Loops-*

This is exactly the same break keyword as used in the switch statement. If a break is placed within a switch within a loop, the break forces an exit from the switch and NOT the loop. There is no way to change this

### *continue*
"continue" statement

**Drill Note** – Continue statement can be used in loops. Like break command **"continue"** changes flow of a program. It does not terminate the loop however. It just skips the rest of current iteration of the loop and returns to starting point of the loop.

### Example -
```
#include<stdio.h>
main()
{
```

```
while((ch=getchar())!='\n')
{
if(ch=='.')
continue;
putchar(ch);
}
system("pause");
}
```

In above example, program accepts all input but omits the '.' character from it. The text will be echoed as you enter it but the main output will be printed after you press the enter key (which is equal to inserting a "\n" character) is pressed. As we told earlier this is because **getchar()** function is a buffered input function.

Whereas break forces an immediate exit from the nearest enclosing loop the continue keyword causes the next iteration of the loop.

In the case of while and do while loops, it jumps straight to the condition and re-evaluates it. In the case of the for loop, it jumps onto the update part of the loop, executes that, then re-evaluates the condition.

### continue is Really Goto-

Statements applying to the use of break similarly apply to continue. It is just another form of goto and should be used with care.

Excessive use of continue can lead to spaghetti instead of code. In fact the loop above could just as easily be written as:

```
for(j = 1; j <= 10; j++)

if(j % 3 != 0)

printf("j = %i\n", j);
```

### continue, switch and Loops -

Whereas break has an effect on the switch statement, continue has no sucheffect. Thus a continue placed within a switch within a loop would affect the loop.

### Drill Note –

if (then) else - watch the semicolons

switch can test integer values

while, do while, for - watch the semicolons again

# Answer the Following Questions -

**1.** The three parts of the for loop are:

    a. The i _____ expression
    b. The c_____ expression
    c. The i_____ expression

**2.** The break statement is used to exit from:
    a. An if statement.
    b. A for loop
    c. A program
    d. The main() function

**3.** A do-while loop is useful when we want that the statements within the loop must be executed:
    a. Only once
    b. Atleast once
    c. More than once
    d. None of the above.

**4.** In what sequence the initialization, condition, execution is done in the do-while loop-

a. Initialization, testing, execution.
b. Initialization, execution, testing
c. Testing, execution, Initialization

**5.** Which of the following statements is used to take the control to the beginning of the loop—

a. exit
b. break
c. continue
d. none of the above.

**6.** int i=1;
   for( ; i++ ;)
        printf("%d", i);

**7.** int a=5;
   do
   {
        printf("%d\n",a);
        a = -1;
   }while(a >0);

**8.** What will be the value of sum after the execution of the following program:
int sum, index;
sum=1;
index=9;
do
{
       index=index-1;
       sum=sum*2;
}while(index>9);

## Answers –

1.  initialization,condition,increment      2. b     3. b     4. b     5. C
6.  1,2,3..32767, -32768,...infinite loop      7. 5     8. 2

# SOME SOLVED PROGRAMS -

1. **Print the numbers in reverse order from N to 1**
   **N.............5, 4, 3, 2, 1**

   ```
   int i,n;
   printf("Enter the value of N ");
   scanf("%d",&n);
   for(i=n;i>=1;i--)
   printf("%d,",i);
   printf("\b ");      /*To remove the comma (,) printed at the last */
   ```

2. **Print the Fibonnicci series1, 1, 2, 3, 5, 8, 13,....................N**

   ```
   int prev,next,cnt,sum,n;
   printf("Enter the value of N ");
   scanf("%d",&n);
   prev=0;
   next=cnt=1;
   while(cnt<=n)
        {
        printf("%d,",next);
        sum = prev + next;
        prev = next;
        next = sum;
        cnt++;
        }
   printf("\b ");
   ```

3. **To print the Factorial of number N**

   ```
   int n,i;
   long int fact;
   clrscr();
   printf("Enter the number to get Factorial: ");
   scanf("%d",&n);
   for(i=n,fact=1;i>=1;i--)
   fact = fact * i;
   printf("Fact is %ld", fact);
   ```

4. **/\*WAP to print the following**
   ```
   1
   12
   123
   1234
   12345              up to N rows*/
   ```

```
int n,i,j;
clrscr();
printf("Enter the number of Rows: ");
scanf("%d",&n);
for(i=1;i<=n;i++)
        {
                for(j=1;j<=i;j++)
                printf("%d",j);
                printf("\n");
        }
```

5. **WAP** to check if the given sequence of numbers is in ascending order or not. The sentinel value for the sequence is -1.

```
enum {false,true};
int prev,n,flag=true,i;
printf("Enter number 1 ");
scanf("%d",&n);
prev = n;
i=2;
while(n != -1)
{
        printf("Enter number %d ",i++);
        scanf("%d",&n);
        if(n < prev && n != -1)
                flag=false;
        prev=n;
}
if(flag = = false)
        printf("Not in ascending order");
else
        printf("In ascending order");
```

6. **To print the sum of 9+99+999+............ n terms.**

```
long int term,sum=0;
int n,cnt;
clrscr();
printf("Enter the value of n");
scanf("%d",&n);
for(cnt=1,term=9;cnt<=n;cnt++)
{
printf("%ld\n",term);
sum+=term;                    /*adding the term to sum using
                              assignment operator*/
term=(term*10) + 9;
}
printf("%ld",sum);
```

7.                  /*pascal triangle
                        1
                        11
                        121
                        1331
                        14641 */
```c
main()
{
int i,j,n,b;  /*b=preceding no*/
printf("enter the number of rows: ");
scanf("%d",&n);
for(i=0;i<n;i++)
{
b=1;
        for(j=0;j<=i;j++)
{
        if(i==0||j==0)
printf("%3d",b);            /*3d is used for providing each
                            number a space of 3 characters*/
else
{
        b=b*(i-j+1)/j;
        printf("%3d",b);
        }
}
        printf("\n");
        }
```

## 8. Convert decimal no. to its binary equivalent

```c
main()
{
        int n,i,a,r;
        printf("enter the no.: ");
        scanf("%d",&n);
        for(i=15;i>=0;i--)
        {
                a=1<<i;
                r=n&a;
                if(r= =0)
                        printf("0");
                else
                        printf("1");
        }
}
```

9. **WAP** to compute the natural logarithm of a given number

```
#include<math.h>
main()
{
        int x, i;
        float result=0;
        printf("\nEnter the value of x:");
        scanf("%d",&x);
        for(i=1;i<=7;i++)
        {
                if(i==1)
                        result=result+pow((x-1.0)/x,i);
                else
                        result=result+(1.0/2)*pow((x-1.0)/x,i);
        }
        printf("Log(%d) = %f",x,result);
}
```

## SOME SOLVED PROGRAMS –

1. **check a number to be prime or not*/**

```
enum bool{false,true};
        int i,n;
        enum bool FLAG=true;
        clrscr();
        printf("Enter a number: ");
        scanf("%d",&n);
        for(i=2;i<=n/2;i++)
        {
                        if(n%i= =0)
                        {
                                FLAG=false;
                                break;
                        }
        }
        if(FLAG= =true)
                printf("Prime number");
        else
                printf("Not Prime Number");
```

## 2. WAP to generate n random numbers.

```
#include<stdlib.h>
    int a,i,n;
    randomize();    /*initializes the random number generator
    with a random number*/
    printf("enter the no. to be printed: ");
    scanf("%d",&n);
    i=1;
    while(i<=n)
    {
    a=random(100)+1; /*generates a number between 0 and 99*/
    printf("%d\n",a);
    i++;
    }
```

## 3. WAP to produce the following output:

```
a b c d e f g f e d c b a
a b c d e f   f e d c b a
a b c d e       e d c b a
a b c d           d c b a
a b c               c b a
a b                   b a
a                       a
```

```
int n,i,j,k,l;
printf("Enter the number of Rows: ");
scanf("%d",&n);
for(i=n;i>=1;i--)
{
for(j=1;j<=i;j++)
        printf("%c",j+97-1);
for(k=1;k<=2*(n-i)-1;k++)
        printf(" ");
for(l=i;l>=1;l--)
{
        if(l==n)
        continue;        /*passes the control of the loop directly to
                          the decrement statement*/
        printf("%c",l+97-1);
}
        printf("\n");
}
```

94

**Drill Note-**

*In comments you can write whatever you want no matter its in upper case or lower case or special character, you are free to write.*

**4. WAP** to print the total no. of characters typed by the user. Input will be terminated by enter key.

```
char ch;
int i=0;
printf("Enter a sentence: ");
while((ch=getche())!='\r')          /*getche( ) is an input function */
{
        i++;
}
printf("\n%d",i);
```

**5. WAP to reverse a number and find its octal equivalent.**

```
#include<math.h>
main()
{
int n, rev, a, oct, cnt;
printf("\nEnter a number");
scanf("%d",&n);                    /*reverse the number*/
rev=0;
        while(n>0)
        {
                a=n%10;
                rev=rev*10+a;
                n=n/10;
        }
        n=rev;
        cnt=oct=0;
        /*converting to octal*/
        while(n>0)
{
        a=n%8;
        n=n/8;
        oct=oct+a*pow(10,cnt);
        cnt++;
}
        printf("The octal equivalent of %d is %d",rev,oct);
}
```

**Drill Note-**

Once again I am telling you, for more programming examples according to chapter topics please read last chapter of this book where I mentioned more than **200 C Programs for your practice.**

## Odd loops –

**1.** for(i=1;i<=5;i--)
      printf ("%d",i);
**Output:-** 1,0,-1,-2……

**2.** for(i=1;i<=5;++i)
      printf ("%d",i);
**Output:-** 1,2,3,4,5

**3.** for(i=1;++i<=5;)
      printf ("%d",i);
**Output:-** 2,3,4,5

**4.** for(i=1;i++<=5;)
      printf("%d",i);
**Output:-** 2,3,4,5,6
**5.** for(i=1;i<=5;printf("%d",i++));
**Output:-** 1,2,3,4,5

**6.** for(i=1;i<=5;printf("%d",++i));
**Output:-** 2,3,4,5,6

**7.** for(i=1;i=5;i++)
      printf ("%d",i);
**Output:-** 5,5,5,5……

**8.** for(i=1;i=0;i++)
      printf("%d",i);
**Output:-** the condition will be considered false because at the place of condition there is an assignment of 0.

**9.** for( ; ;)
**Output:-** a blank screen will be generated.

**10.** for(i=1;i++<=5;i++)
      printf("%d",--i);
**Output:-** 1,2,3,4,5

**11.** for(i=1;i= =5;i++)
      printf("%d",i);
Output:- No output will be generated because the condition is checking if the value of i is 5 which is false in the beginning.

**12.** for(i=1;i<=5;)
      printf("%d",i++);
**Output:-** 1,2,3,4,5

13. for(i=1;5;i++)
      printf("%d",i);
**Output:-** 1,2,3,4,5…………

**14.** for(i=1;i<=5;i++);
      printf("%d",i);
**Output:-** 6
      The loop does not have any statement because of the presence of the semicolon after increment. Such loops are called as *null loops.*

**15.** int i=1;
   for(;i<=5;i++)
      printf("%d",i);
**Output:-** 1,2,3,4,5

**16.** int i=1;
   while( )
   {
      printf("%d",i);
      i++;
   }
**Output:-** Error as condition is missing and this is not allowed in while loop.

**17.** int i=1;
   while(i<=5)
      printf("%d",i++);
**Output:-** 1,2,3,4,5

**18.** for(i=1;i<4;i++)
      printf("%d",(i%2)?i:2*i);
**Output:-** 1,4,3,8,5

# Common programming Errors -

1.  While statement does not include the word do. Thus it is not logical to write –

        while(condition) do
        {
        statement;
        }

2.  The break and continue statements affect only the innermost loops.**e.g.**

        for(………….)      /*loop 1*/
        {
        for(……………..)   /*loop2*/
        {

                  …………..
                  …………..
                  break;
                  …………..
                  …………..
        }
                  …………..
        }

The break statement would cause the exit from loop 2 but not from loop 1.

# What would be the output of the following programs.

**1.** int i =1;
while( i<= 10);
{
        printf(" \n%d",i);
        i++;
}

**Output:-** No output because a infinite loop.

In the above program a ";" is encounter after the while so it is understand as following by the compiler
while(i<=10)
{
        ;
}
clearly in the body of loop there is no increment and only null statement so condition still remains true that cause an indefinite loop and because of null statement no output is generated.

**2.** char ch;
while(ch =0; ch<=255;ch++)
        printf("\n %d-%c",ch,ch);

**Output:-** Error.

In the above program "while" loop is used in the place of "for" that cause generate an error because of different syntax.

**3.** int a =4;
while( a = =1)
{
        a = a-1;
        printf("%d",a);
        --a;
}

**Output:-** No output

**10.** int a =4, b =0, c;
while(a>=0)
{
        a--;
        b++;
        if( a = =b)
            continue;
        else
            printf( "\n %d  %d",a,b);
}
**Output:-** 3  1
           1  3
           0  4
          -1  5
In the above program first a = 4,b = 0 and when condition checked it becomes true and control execute the body of loop and a is decrease by 1 and b i increase by 1. so a = 3 and b = 1 now again condition is checked a = = b that is false and control jumps to the else block and print the value of a and b that is 3 and 1 respectively now when control reach to the end of the loop again jumps to the condition now again condition remains true and again body of loop executed resultant a = 2 and b = 2 and when condition a = = b is checked it becomes true that continue the loop using "continue" statement and control jumps to the loop condition that is true because a = 2 that is greater then 0.again body of loop executed and a =1,b = 3 and gets printed because the condition in if is false and from the end of the loop control jump to the condition that is true and a =0 and b =4 that is not equal so printed out and repeatedly when condition is checked it is true and execute a = -1 and b = 5 that is not equal and gets printed through else block and this time when

98

Because condition is false for the first time and control immediately comes out from the body of loop without execute anything.

**4.** int a =4,b,c;
b = --a;
c = a--;
printf("\n%d %d %d",a,b,c);

**Output:-** 2 3 3

In the above program a = 4 now we understand the pre and post increment/decrement.
b = --a → (1) a = a-1[→( a =3);] (2) b=a→[(b =3)]; i.e. In prefix decrement first decrease and then assign.

c=a-- → (1) c = a [c = 3]; (2) a = a-1[ a = 2]; i.e. In postfix decrement first assign and then decrease.
so finally a = 2, b = 3, c = 3 and gets printed through printf().

**5.** int a =4,b =3,c;
c = a-- -b;
printf("\n%d%d%d",a,b,c);

**Output:-** 3 3 1

Here at first a = 4; and in the exp. c = a- - -b; postfix decrement op. is used with a means first a is use in exp and then decrease i.e.→(1) c = a-b;[c = 4-3]→[c = 1]  (2) a = a-1;[a = 4-1]→[3] and b still remain same so finally a = 3, b = 3, c = 1 and gets printed through printf().

**6.** while('a'<'b')
printf("\n malyalam is a palindrome");

**Output:-** "malyalam is a palindrome" printed indefinitely.

Because condition 'a'<'b' never

condition is checked becomes false because a = -1 that is not greater or equal to 0 and jumps out of the loop.

**11.** int a = 4, b = 0,c;
while( a>=0)
{
        if(a = =b)
            break;
        else
            printf("\n%d  %d",a,b);
        a--;
        b++;
}
**Output:-** 4  0
          3  1

Here a = 4 and b = 0 and when condition in loop is checked it becomes true and then control jumps to the else block because a!=b and gets printed the value of a and b that is 4 and 0 respectively. and then a is decreased by 1 and b is increased by 1 so a = 3 and b = 1.Again when repeatedly when loop condition is checked it becomes true and control executes the body of loop and control print out the value of a and b that is 3 and 1 from the else block because condition becomes false and now a = 2 and b = 2 and loop condition will be again true and when comparison  a = = b gives true control execute the if block and jumps out of the loop because of "break" statement.

**12.** int i;
for(i = 1;i<=5;printf("\n%d",i));
         i++;
**Output:-** 1 will printed indefinitely no. of times.

Here ";" is used after the loop means loop contain NULL statement and i++ is not in the body of the loop because no braces is used. In first i is initialize with 1 and when condition is checked becomes false and every time it execute the body of loop that print the above massage "malyalam is a palindrome".

**7.** int i;
```
while(i =15)
{
        printf("\n%d",i);
        i++;
}
```
**Output:-** print 15 indefinitely.

Because in the statement while(i = 15), i is not compared with 15. Here i is assigned with 15 that is a non zero value so each time when condition is checked i becomes 15 and condition becomes true and execute the body of loop that first print the value of i means 15 and then increment by 1 and i becomes 16 but again when condition check is encountered then again i becomes 15 and again execute the body of loop as same as previous that cause 15 printed indefinitely.

**8.** float a = 1.1;
```
while( a = =1.1)
{
        printf("\n%d",x);
        x=x-0.1;
}
```

**Output:-** No output

Because in the condition a float variable is compared with double value and control jumps out of the loop.

**Drill Note:** whenever we use floating point constant it is consider a double type value.

it becomes true and gets printed i that is 1 now no increment take place and whenever condition is checked it always becomes true and indefinitely print 1.

**13.** int i = 1,j = 1;
```
for(; ;)
{
        if(i>5)
              break;
        else
              j+=i;
        printf("%d\t",j);
        i+=j;
}
```
**Output:-** 2    5

In this program in first i = 1 and j = 1; And whenever there is no condition in the for loop by default it is assume true and execute the body and when i>5 is executed control jumps to the else block because condition is false and then j+=i [j = j+i] that gives j =2 and than j is printed through printf(). Now next statement i+=j gives i =3 and from the ending braces of loop control jumps to the loop and check for the condition that is true because missing and again i>5 is checked that becomes false and control execute the else block that cause j =5 (3 + 2) and gets printed now i will be 8 and now when the next time i>5 condition is checked it will be true and control jumps out of the loop because of the "break" statement.

100

# Lab Exercise -

Print the n terms of the following series.

1.      1, 3, 5, 7, 9, .........

2.      2, 4, 6, 8, 10, ........

3.      1, 4, 9, 16, 25, .......

4.      1, 8, 27, 64, 125, .....

5.      1, -1, 1, -1, 1, ......

6.      1, 1, 2, 4, 7, 13, 24, ... (Lucas series)

7.      $1 + x^2/2! + x^3/3! + x^4/4! + x^5/5!$ .......... ($e^x$)

8.      $x - x^3/3! + x^5/5! - x^7/7! + x^9/9!$ .......... (sinx)

9.      $1 - x^2/2! + x^4/4! - x^6/6! + x^8/8!$ .......... (cosx)

10.      $x - x^2/2 + x^3/3 - x^4/4 + x^5/5$ .............. (log(1+x))

11.      WAP to print the table of n.

12.      WAP to calculate the factorial of n.

13.      WAP to calculate the power p of a number n.

## WAP to print the following-

| | | | |
|---|---|---|---|
| **16.** | 1<br>21<br>321<br>4321<br>54321 | **25.** | 1<br>121<br>12321<br>1234321<br>123454321 |
| **17.** | 12345<br>1234<br>123<br>12<br>1 | **26.** | 123454321<br>1234321<br>12321<br>121<br>1 |
| **18.** | 54321<br>4321<br>321<br>21<br>1 | **27.** | \*<br>\*\*\*<br>\*\*\*\*\*<br>\*\*\*\*\*\*\*<br>\*\*\*\*\*<br>\*\*\*<br>\* |
| **19.** | 1<br>22<br>333<br>4444<br>55555 | **28.** | \*\*\*\*\*\*\*\*\*<br>\*      \*<br>\*      \*<br>\*\*\*\*\*\*\*\*\* |
| **20.** | \*<br>\*\*<br>\*\*\*<br>\*\*\*\*<br>\*\*\*\*\* | **29.** | 4<br>434<br>43234<br>4321234<br>43234<br>434<br>4 |
| **21.** | 1<br>123<br>12345<br>1234567<br>123456789 | **30.** | 1<br>232<br>34543<br>4567654<br>567898765<br>67890109876 |
| **22.** | 987654321<br>7654321<br>54321<br>321<br>1 | | |
| **23.** | 1<br>12<br>123<br>1234<br>12345 | **31.** | a<br>aba<br>abcba<br>abcdcba<br>abcdedcba |

32. WAP to find the average of the values read from the input. The sequence of values in the input is terminated by -1.

33. WAP to find the maximum, second maximum, position of maximum and position of second maximum from the sequence of n numbers.

34. WAP to print all the ASCII values and their equivalent characters using a while loop. The ASCII values vary from 0 to 255.

35. WAP to print out all Armstrong numbers between 1 and 500. If sum of cubes of each digit of the number is equal to the number itself, then the number is called an Armstrong number. For example,

    153=(1*1*1)+(5*5*5)+(3*3*3).if the number is in two digits then we square the digit of the number.

36. WAP to print all prime numbers from 1 to 300.

37. WAP to fill the entire screen with a smiling face. The smiling face has an ASCII value 1.

38. WAP to add first seven terms of the following series using for loop:
    1/1!+2/2!+3/3!+......

39. WAP a program to generate all combinations of 1, 2 and 3 using for loop.

40. According to a study, the approximate level of intelligence of a person can be calculated using the following formula:

    i=2+(y+0.5 x)
    WAP, which will produce a table of values of i, y and x, where y varies from 1 to 6 , and for each value of y, x varies from 5.5 to 12.5 in steps of 0.5.

41. WAP to print all the prime numbers between two given numbers.

42. WAP to count the number of digits in a given number.

43. WAP to print the sum of all the digits of a given number.

44. WAP to check whether a given number is palindrome or not.

45. WAP to count all the vowels, consonants, digits, spaces, special symbols from a given text typed by the user, terminated by the enter key.

46. WAP to find the sum of first n prime numbers.

47. WAP to determine whether a specified value is prime or not in a given sequence of values. The sequence of values to be read from the input is terminated by 0.

48. Print the sum of following series.
$$1 \times 2 + 2 \times 3 + 3 \times 4 + 4 \times 5 + \text{.......} + (n-1) \times n.$$

49. Print the sum of following series.

50. $e^{-x}$  $1 - x + x^2/2! - x^3/3! + x^4/4! \text{.....}$

51. WAP to read n numbers and count even and odd numbers.

$$1 + 1/2 + 1/3 + 1/4\text{......} + 1/n$$

52. WAP to compute the volume $(4/3pir^3)$ and surface area $(4pir^2)$ of a sphere of any radius r.

53. WAP to compute the perimeter p and area a of a triangle of sides a, b and c where
p = a+b+c
a = sqrt(s(s-a)(s-b)(s-c))
and  2s = a + b+ c

54. WAP to read a positive integer and determine and print its binary equivalent.

55. WAP to print the sum of n numbers , sum of squares of first n even numbers and sum of the cube of first n odd numbers.

56. WAP to calculate net pay of n employees. Net pay is basic + da + hra cca - pf (da is 39% of the basic, hra is 15% of basic less than or equal to rs 8000/- and 30% of the basic above rs 8000, cca is fixed to rs 800 and pf deduction is rs 600).

57. Write a program to calculate overtime pay of 10 employees. Overtime is paid at the rate of rs. 12.00 per hour for every hour worked above 40 hours. Assume that employees do not work for fractional part of an hour.

58. While purchasing certain items, a discount of 10% is offered if the quantity purchased is more than 1000.if quantity and price per item are input through the keyboard, write a program to     calculate the total expenses.

**59.** WAP to check whether a given sequence of values is sorted in increasing order. The sentinel value for the sequence is -1.

**60.** WAP to find the sum and average of values appearing at the positions divisible by 3 in the given sequence of n values.

**61.** WAP to input the marks of n students and count the number of students who have obtained a, b, c,d and f grades. The grades are awarded according to the following rules.

| Marks | Grade |
|-------|-------|
| >= 80 | A |
| >= 70 | B |
| >= 60 | C |
| >= 50 | D |
| < 50  | F |

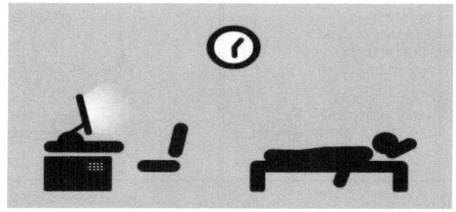

# CHAPTER

# ∞ 5 ∞

## (One Dimensional Array)

## Introduction-

**ARRAY –**

Array is a collection of similar data items or elements. Or we can say that array is a collection of homogeneous data elements stored continuously under a single name.

**Need for an array –**

When the number of variables of same type and nature are more then it is difficult to handle them. So we need an array. Let us understand the use of array with an example:

```
int i,a;
for(i=1;i<=5;i++)
{
        printf("Enter the no.");
        scanf("%d",&a);
}
```

In the above program as soon as the new value is assigned to the variable a the old value is lost.

Thus all the variables that we have used so far are not able to hold more than one value at a time. But sometimes we wish to store more than one value for a variable.

For example if we wish to arrange the marks of 10 students in ascending order.

**There are two ways for it:**

(i) Use of 10 different variables so that each variable can store marks of a single student.

(ii) Use a single variable which can store the marks of all students.

Obviously the second option looks better because it is easier to handle them. A single variable which can store more than one value at a time is called an Array.

**Drill Note-**

It is a collection of homogeneous data elements stored continuously under a single name. Array declaration:-

int a[6];

Here a is the name of the array, int is the data type of values which the array will store, 6 is the size of array and [] are called as subscript operator. The size of array must be a constant. The most important thing is that all the values in the array should be of the same type.

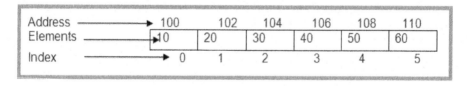

10, 20, 30, 40, 50 are the elements of the array. To use the elements of the array we refer to the index. The array index starts from 0 i.e. if the size of the array is 6, so the indices of the array will be from 0 to 5.

In the definition we also said that the elements of the array are stored continuously, i.e. if the element at 0 index has address 100 then the next elements will have addresses 102, 104, 106, 108, 110 if the array is an integer array because an integer occupies only 2 bytes. But if it was a float array the addresses will have been 100, 104, 108, 112, 116, 120 since a float number occupies 4 bytes.

If there are more than one array of the same size are to be used in a program then another type of declaration can be used.

**For Example,**

If the percentage of the students of a class is to be calculated and the marks of all the students is input in arrays. Then all the arrays should be of same size.

**So** this type of declaration can be used:

```
#define SIZE 10
main()
{
        int maths[SIZE], hindi[SIZE],english[SIZE];
}
```

**Drill Note-** Here **SIZE** is a global or symbolic constant.

**Array Initialize:**

| int a[5]; | /*This array will contain garbage values*/ |
|---|---|
| int a[5]={10,20,30,40,50}; | /*This array will contain 10,20,30,40,50 values*/ |
| int a[5] = {0,0,0,0,0}; | /*This array will contain 0,0,0,0,0 values*/ |
| int a[5] = {0}; | /*This array will contain 0,0,0,0,0 values*/ |
| int a[5] = {1}; | /*This array will contain 1,0,0,0,0 values*/ |
| int a[5] ={10, , 30}; | /*This array will contain 10,0,30,0,0 values*/ |
| int a[ ] = {10,20,30}; | /*The size of this array will be assumed as 3*/ |
| int a[3] = {10,20,30,40}; | /*Too many initializes error.*/ |
| static int a[5]; | /*This array will contain 0,0,0,0,0 values*/ |

**Drill Note –**

If the size of the array is missing but the values are given then the size of the array formed will be equal to the number of initializes.

**Drill Note –**

If the number of initializes is more than the size of the array then the error of too many initializes is given.

## Limitations of array -

1. The array formed will be *homogeneous*. That is in an integer array only integer values can be stored, while in a float array only floating values and character array can have only characters. Thus no array can have values of two data types.

2. While declaring the array passing *size* of the array is *compulsory*, and the size must be a constant. Thus there is either shortage or wastage of memory.

3. Insertion or deletion of elements in an array will require shifting.

4. The array does not check its boundaries: In C there is no check to see if the values entered in the array are exceeding the size of the array. Data entered with the subscript exceeding the array size will be simply placed outside the array, probably on the top of the data or the program itself.

   This will lead to unpredictable results, to say the least, and there will be no error message to warn the programmer of going beyond the array size. In some cases the program may hang. Thus the following program can give undesired result:

```
int a[10],i;
for(i=0;i<=20;i++)
a[i]=i;
```

## SOME SOLVED PROGRAMS-

1. Write a program to print the average of n numbers.

```
int a[50],n,i,sum=0;
float avg;
printf("Enter the number of elements in the array: ");
scanf("%d",&n); /*input & sum of array*/
for(i=0;i<n;i++)  /*the first element in the array is numbered
                    as 0, so the last element is one less than the
                    size of the array*/
{
        printf("Enter number %d",i+1);
        scanf("%d",&a[i]);
        sum + = a[i];
}
avg=(float)sum/n;      /*typecasting sum from interger to float*/
printf("average = %f",avg);
```

110

2. WAP to insert an element in 1-d array(unsorted) at the given position.

```
#define SIZE 20
main()
{
        int n,i,a[SIZE],item,pos;
        printf("enter the no. of elements in the array: ");
        scanf("%d",&n);                          /*Input in array*/
        for(i=0;i<n;i++)
    {
        printf("Enter the element %d: ",i+1);
scanf("%d",&a[i]);
}
printf("Enter the item and its position of insertion: ");
scanf("%d %d",&item,&pos);
pos--;                             /*Array index starts from 0*/
for(i=n-1;i>=pos;i--)
        a[i+1]=a[i];               /*insertion*/
        a[pos]=item;               /*Output*/
for(i=0;i<n+1;i++)
        printf("\n%d",a[i]);
}
```

3. **WAP** that will read an array of integers. The program should display the elements appearing at even and odd subscript position separately.

```
        int even,odd,i,n,a[50];
        printf("Enter the number of terms: ");
        scanf("%d",&n);
        /*input*/
        for(i=0;i<n;i++)
        {
                printf("Enter number %d: ",i+1);
                scanf("%d",&a[i]);
        }
        printf("\nOdd\tEven\n");
        for(i=0;i<n;i++)
        {
        if(i%2==0)             /*array index starts from 0*/
                printf("\n%d\t",a[i]);
        else
                printf("%d\t",a[i]);
        }
```
4. **WAP** that reads a float array and reverse this array.

```c
float a[10];
int n,i;
printf("Enter the number of terms: ");
scanf("%d",&n);
/*input*/
for(i=0;i<n;i++)
{
        printf("Enter the number %d",i);
        scanf("%f",&a[i]);
}
for(i=n-1;i>=0;i--)
{
        printf("%.2f, ",a[i]);
```

5. Some repeated random numbers are given, write a program to print them in increasing order with their frequency.

```c
#define SIZE 100
main()
{
    int a[SIZE],b[SIZE],freq[SIZE],i,j,k,n,found,t;
    printf("Enter how many numbers");
    scanf("%d",&n);
    /*input array*/
    for(i=0;i<n;i++)
    {
            printf("enter element %d ",i+1);
            scanf("%d",&a[i]);
    }
    for(i=0,k=0;i<n;i++)
    {
            found = 0;
            for(j=0;j<k;j++)
            {
                    if(a[i] == b[j])
                    {
                            freq[j]++;
                            found = 1;
                            break;
                    }
            }
            if(found == 0)
            {
                    b[k] = a[i];
                    freq[k++] = 1;
            }
    }
    for(i=0;i<k-1;i++)
```

```
            for(j=i+1;j<k;j++)
                    if(freq[i] < freq[j])
                    {
                            t = b[i];
                            b[i] = b[j];
                            b[j] = t;
                            t = freq[i];
                            freq[i] = freq[j];
                            freq[j] = t;

                    }
        for(i=0;i<k;i++)
                printf("%d\t%d\n",b[i],freq[i]);
}
```

**6.** WAP to merge two array a and b into third array c.

```
#define SIZE 20
main()
{
int n1,n2,i,j,k,a[SIZE],b[SIZE],c[SIZE];
/*input in first array*/
printf("Enter the no. of elements in the first array: ");
scanf("%d",&n1);
for(i=0;i<n1;i++)
{
        printf("Enter the element %d: ",i+1);
        scanf("%d",&a[i]);
}

/*input in second array*/

printf("\nEnter the no. of elements in the second array: ");
scanf("%d",&n2);
for(i=0;i<n2;i++)

{
        printf("Enter the element %d: ",i+1);
        scanf("%d",&b[i]);
}

/*merge*/

for(i=0,j=0,k=0;i<n1&&j<n2;k++)
{
        if(a[i]<b[j])
                c[k]=a[i++];
        else
                c[k]=b[j++];
```

```
}

/*remaining of first list*/

while(i<n1)
        c[k++]=a[i++];
/*remaining of second list*/

while(j<n2)
        c[k++]=b[j++];
/*output*/
for(i=0;i<(n1+n2);i++)
        printf("%d\n",c[i]);
}
```

**7.** WAP to find the k$^{th}$ smallest number from a given list of numbers:

```
int a[20], i, j, n,t,k;
printf("Enter the number of elements in the list: ");
scanf("%d",&n);

/*input in the array*/

for (i=0;i<n;i++)
{
        printf("Enter the number %d: "i+1);
        scanf("%d",&a[i]);
}

/* loop to sort the array*/

for(i=0;i<n-1;i++)
{
        for(j=i+1;j<n;j++)
        {
                if(a[i]>a[j])
                {
                        t=a[i];
                        a[i] = a[j];
                        a[j]=t;
                }
        }
}
printf("Enter the position of element:" );
scanf("%d",&k);
printf("the %d smallest element  of the list is %d",k, a[k-1]);
```

114

# What would be the output of the following programs?

**1.** int num[26],temp;
num[0] = 100;
num[25] = 200;
temp = num[25];
num[25] = num[0];
num[0] = temp;
printf("\n%d %d",num[0],num[25]);
**Output:** 200 100

Here in first two statements after declaration the first and last element is assigned with 100 and 200 respectively and the in next three statements swap both of them. So num[0] = 200 and num[25] = 100.

**2.** int array[26],i;
for (i = 0; i<=25;i++)
{
  array[i] = 'A' + i;
  printf("\n%d %c",array[i], array[i]);
}
**Output:**    65 A
               66 B
               -----
               -----
               90 Z
In the above program first time array of i will be 65 because i =0 and 'A' gives 65 so array[0] = 65 that gets printed through printf( ) in integer and character format. And each time when i increment by 1 the array will contain 66,67,68 on successive position and will print through printf( ) in integer and character format.

**3.** int sub[50],i;
for( i = 0; i <= 48; i++);
{
        sub[i] = i;
        printf("\n%d",sub[i]);
}
**Output:** 49

**5.** int b[ ] = {10,20,30,40,50};
int i, *k;
k = b;
for (i = 0; i<= 4; i++)
{
        printf("%d ",*k);
        k++;
}
**Output:-** 10 20 30 40 50
In the above program the base address of b is assign to the k through k = b statement. Because when we use the name of array it tells the base address of array. And loop runs 5 times in the above program and each time k deference the respective element and print it. And we know when pointer is incremented it moves the required bytes(in the above program moves 2 byte because it points to int array) and point the next element. Here first time k contains 0th element address and print it by deference and by increment it points to next element and because loop runs 5 times so five times pointer incremented and point the value starting from base address so it print all the array element.

**6.**      main( )
         {
            int a [ ] = {2,6,4,8,10};
            int i;
            change( a, 5);
            for(i = 0;i<= 4;i++)
               printf("%d ",a[i]);
         }
         change(int *b, int n)
         {
            int i;
            for(i = 0;i <n;i++)
            *(b+i) = *(b+i)+5;
         }

Because of ";"(Null statement) the loop will execute till 48 without executing any statement and when i's value will be 49 the condition becomes false and control jumps out of the loop and execute the next statement that will sub[i] = i→sub[i]→49. and the value of sub[i] gets printed through printf( ) that is 49.

**4.** int b[ ] = {10,20,30,40,50};
int i;
for (i = 0; i<=4; i++)
        printf("%d ",*(b+i))

**Output:-** 10 20 30 40 50

Compiler understand *(b + i) as b[i]. In the above program i vary from 0 to 4 and through printf( ) value of b[i] gets printed each time that will 10 20 30 40 50 successively.

**7.** static int a[5];
int i;
for( i = 0; i<=4; i++)
        printf("%d ",a[i]);

**Output:-** 0 0 0 0 0
Because here array's storage class is static and in static array all the elements will assigned with 0 and when we print the array 5 times 0 will gets printed.

**Output:-** 7 11 9 13 15
Here pointer b receive the base address of a and 5 is passed to n. and in the change( ) each time b[i] is replaced by b[i] +5. and loop will runs form 0 to 5. so firstly b[0] = b[0] + 5(2+5→7) and similarly the next four element are changed and the value will be in array b 7 11 9 13 15 and gets printed in main( ).

**8.** int a[ 5] = {5,1,15,20,25};
int i,j,k = 1,m;
i = ++a[1];
j = a[1]++;
m = a[i++];
printf("\n%d %d %d",i,j,m);
**Output:-** 3 2 15

Here in the third statement i = ++a[1]. Here we know the index of array is start from 0 so a[1] = 1. now in the above statement prefixed increment op. is used so the value of a[1] is increment first and will be 2 and then assign so i will be 2 so a[1] = 2 and i = 2. Again in the next statement j = a[1]++ postfix increment op. is used so first the value of a[1] is assign j so j will be 2 and then increment so a[1] = 3. now in the next statement m = a[i++]. First a[i] is assigned in m because i = 2 so a[i] (a[2]) = 15 and assigned in m and then i is incremented and becomes 3. so finally i = 3 j = 2 and m = 15.

# Point out the errors, if any, in the following program segments:

**1.**
```
int char mixed[10],i;
    for( i = 0; i< 10; i++)
    {
        scanf("%d",&mixed[i]);
    }
```
**Output:-** Error.
Because mixed datatype cannot be used.

**2.**
```
int SIZE;
scanf("%d",&SIZE);
int a[SIZE];
for( i = 1; i<=SIZE ;i++)
{
    scanf("%d",a[i]);
    printf("%d",a[i]);
}
```
**Output:** Error.
Because the size of array must be constant but, here SIZE is a variable that is used as size of array.

**3.** main( )
```
{
        int i, a = 2, b = 3;
        int a[2+3];
        for( i = 0; i< a+b; i++)
    {

    scanf("%d",&a[i]);

    printf("\n%d",a[i]);
    }
    }
```
**Output:** No error.

**4.** Assume that array begins at 1200
```
main()
{
    int a[ ]= {2, 3, 4, 1, 6};
printf("%d %d", a, sizeof(a));
}
```
**Output:** 1200 10

**6.**
```
        main( )
{
        int a[6] =
{10,20,30,40,50};
        int i;
        for(i = 0; i<=25; i++)

    printf("\n%d",a[i]);
}
```
**Output:** No error.
Because if we cross the bounds of the array the garbage stored in the next position in memory will be displayed. But a warning will be display "array bounds are being exceed."

**7.** main( )
```
{
    int s[50];
    for( i = 1; i<=50; i++)
    {
        s[i] = i;
        printf("\n%d",s[i]);
    }
}
```
**Output:** No Error.
Here array size is 50 and because array index is start from 0 the last index will be 49 but in this program array is access from 1to 50. So same as the previous program no error will encounter but a warning will display "array bounds are being exceed."

**8.** Assume that the array begins at 65486?
```
main()
{
    int a[ ]= {12, 14, 15, 23, 45};
    printf("%u %u", a, &a);
}
```
**Output:** 65486 65486

| 5. Assume that the array begins at 65486?<br><br>```<br>main()<br>{<br>    int a[ ]= {12, 14, 15, 23, 45};<br>    printf("%u %u", a+1, &a+1);<br>}<br>```<br>**Output:**65488 65496 | ```<br>main()<br>{<br>float a[ ]= {12.4, 2.3, 4.5, 6.7};<br>    printf("%d", sizeof(a)/sizeof(a[0]));<br>}<br>```<br><br>**Output:** 4 |

## Multiple choice.

**1. An array is a collection of –**

a) Different data types scattered throughout memory.
b) The same data type scattered throughout memory.
c) The same data type placed next to each other in memory.
d) Different data types placed next to each other in memory.

**Output: c)** The same data type placed next to each other in memory

**2. Which element of the array does this expression reference?**
num[4]

    a) first element.
    b) last element.
    c) fourth element.
    d) Fifth element.

**Output: d)** Fifth element

**3. What is the difference between the 5's in these two exexpressions?**
    int num[5];
    num[5] = 11;
a) First is particular element, second is type.
b) First is array size, second is particular element.

**7. What would happen if you assign a value to an element of an array whose subscript exceeds the size of the array?**
a) The element will be set to 0
b) Nothing, it's done all the time.
c) Other data may be overwritten
d) Error message from the compiler.

**Output: c)** Other data may be overwritten

**8. When you pass an array as an argument to a function, what actually gets passed?**
a) Address of the array.
b) Values of the elements of the array.
c) Address of the first element of the array.
d) Number of elements of the array.
**Output: a)** Address of the array.

**9. Which of these are reasons for using pointers?**
a) To manipulate parts of an array
b) To refer to keywords such as for and if
c) To return more than one value from a function
d) To refer to particular programs more conveniently
Output: a) c)

118

**c)** First is particular element, second is array size.
**d)** Both specify array size.

**Output: b)** First is array size, second is particular element.

**4.** Are the following array declarations correct?
        **a)** int a(25);
        **b)** int size = 10, b[size];
        **c)** int c = {0,1,2};

**Output:** all are wrong.

In (a) these brackets"( )" are not allowed in array dimension.

In (b) array size is variable.

In (c) a simple integer variable is assigned with three value that is only possible in array variable.

**5.** What would happen if you try to put so many values into an array when you initialize it that the size of the array is exceeded?

**a)** Nothing
**b)** Possible system malfunction
**c)** Error message from the compiler
**d)** Other data may be overwritten
**Output: b)** Possible system malfunction

**6.** What would happen if you put too few elements in an array when you initialize it?
a) Nothing
b) Possible system malfunction
c) Error message from the compiler
d) Unused elements will be filled with 0's or garbage
**Output: d)** Unused elements will be filled with 0's or garbage

**10.** If you don't initialize a static array, what would be the elements set to?
**a)** 0
**b)** An undetermined value
**c)** A floating point number
**d)** The character constant'\0'

**Output: a)**

**11.** main()
        {
            int a[5]={2,3};
            printf("%d
    %d",a[2],a[3],a[4]);
        }
    a.  garbage value
    b.  2 3 3
    c.  3 2 2
    d.  0 0 0

**Output: 0 0 0**

**Explanation:** when an array is partially initialized, the remaining array elements are initialized to 0.

## State wheather the following statements are True or False:

1. The array int num[26] has twenty-six elements.

2. The expression num[1] designates the first element in the array.

3. It is necessary to initialize the array at the time of declaration

4. The expression num[27] designates the twenty-eighth element in the array.

5. Address of a floating-point variable is always a whole number.

## Answers:

| | | | |
|---|---|---|---|
| 1. False | 2. False | 3. False 4. True | 5. True |

1. If a[i]=i++ is undefined, then by the same reson i=i+1 should also be undefined. But it is not so. Why?

   **Answer:** If an object is to be modified within an expression then all accesses to it within the same expression must be for computing the value to be stored in the object. The expression a[i]=i++ is disallowed because one of the accesses of i ( the one in a[i]) has nothing to do with the value that ends up being stored in i.

   In this case the compiler may not know whether the access should take place before or after the incremented value is stored.

   The expression i=i+1 is allowed because I is accessed to determine i's final value.

2. Does mentioning the array name gives the base address in all context?
   Answer: No, it is said that the array name has its base address in it. But the array does not give its base address in two situations:

A. *When array name is used with sizeof operator.*
B. *When the array name is an operand of the & operator.*

3. Are the expressions *a* and *&a* for an array of 10 integers?

   **Answer:** No, Even though both the expressions give the same result in the above question they mean two different things. *a* gives the address of the first *int*, whereas *&a* gives the address of array of *ints*. Since these happen to be same the results of the expressions are same.

120

# Lab Exercise – WAP- Write a Program.

1. WAP to sort a 1-d array using bubble sort technique.

2. WAP to sort a 1-d array using selection sort or linear sort technique.

3. WAP to sort a 1-d array using insertion sort technique.

4. WAP to search an element in 1-d array using linear search method.

5. WAP to search an element in 1-d array using binary search method.

6. WAP to insert an element in 1-d sorted array.

7. WAP to delete  an element from 1-d array(unsorted) from the given positions.

8. WAP to delete an element from 1-d sorted array.

9. WAP that will read an array of integers and print even and odd element separately.

10. WAP to find sum of element appearing at even and odd subscript position of an array of integers.

11. WAP to find maximum and the minimum values from a set of values stored in an array, along with their positions in the array.

12. WAP to read 6 digits and find out if they are in a strictly ascending order. For example, the sequence 5,6,7,9,11,14 is in strict ascending order whereas the sequence 5,5,6,7,9,11 is not in a strict ascending order. Display an appropriate message.

13. WAP to read a set of height and find  out  the  average  height. The program should then calculate the deviation of  each height from the average. The deviation d, is defined as: d=m(i)-a. Where  a  represents the  average  height, and  m(i) represents the height.

14. WAP that will read 10 integers into an array and then display their averages.

15. WAP that will display the maximum and it position in an array of integers. If the maximum occurs more than once its last position should be displayed.

16. WAP that will display the max and min and their respective positions in an array. If the max and min occurs more than once their first position should be displayed.

17. WAP that will read roll no. And marks of 10 students in two different arrays. Program will print the marks of students whose roll no. Is provided by user.

18. WAP that will read 2 array, sum their individual element in third array and display the third array.

19. WAP that will read an array of integers. after reading array, the program should check if there any duplicate value in the array. The program should display the appropriate message.

20. WAP that will read 2 arrays. Sum individual elements of both arrays in reverse order and stores it in third array. Display the third array.

21. WAP that will read an array and insert an integer at the end of array.

22. WAP to insert an integer at the beginning of an array.

23. WAP to insert an array at the end of another array.

24. WAP to insert an array at the beginning of another array.

25. WAP to insert an array into another array at a positions specified by user.

26. WAP to find whether a array is palindrome or not.

27. WAP to send all the negative elements of an array to the end without altering the original sequence. for e.g. If array contains 5 -3 2 6 8 -4 7 -6 9 -1 then the resultant array should be 5 2 6 8 7 9 -3 -4 -6 -1 .you may use two arrays.

28. WAP to delete an array element present at the beginning.

29. WAP to left rotate an array by one element.

30. WAP to right rotate an array by one element.

**31.** WAP to left rotate an array by n elements, where value of n will be provided by user.

**32.** WAP to right rotate an array by n elements, where value of n will be provided by user.

**33.** WAP that will read an array, replaces multiple occurrence of any element by 0 and then display the resultant array. For eg. If input is 1 1 2 2 3 4 2 1 5 4 output is 1 0 2 0 3 4 0 0 5 0 .

**34.** WAP to shift multiple occurrence of element in the following manner. for eg. If input is 1 1 2 2 3 4 2 1 5 4 output is 1 2 3 4 5 0 0 0 0 0 .

**35.** WAP to delete the multiple occurrence of elements in an array.

**36.** WAP to replace any nth element of an array at the first position, the (n+1)th element at second position etc.

**37.** WAP to rearrange $k^{th}$ elements of an array so as to replace the elements at the odd suffixes with the elements at even suffixes. for eg, 1 2 3 4 5 6 7 8 should be changed to as: 1 3 5 7 2 4 6 8

**38.** WAP to sort an array in descending order.

**39.** WAP to store any ten numbers in an array and print the LCM and HCF of all the numbers.

**40.** WAP to store any ten numbers in an array number and print the smallest, The largest and the average.

**41.** WAP to store any 100 numbers in an array. Arrange the first fifty numbers in ascending order and last fifty numbers in descending order and print the sorted array.

**42.** WAP which accepts a positive decimal integers input from the keyboard converts the integer into its binary equivalent and outputs the integer with its binary equivalent.

**43.** WAP to create a matrix age[20] to store any twenty ages and print the sum of all even and odd ages respectively.

**44.** 25 numbers are entered from the keyboard into an array. WAP to find out how many of them are positive, how many are negative , how many are even and how many are odd.

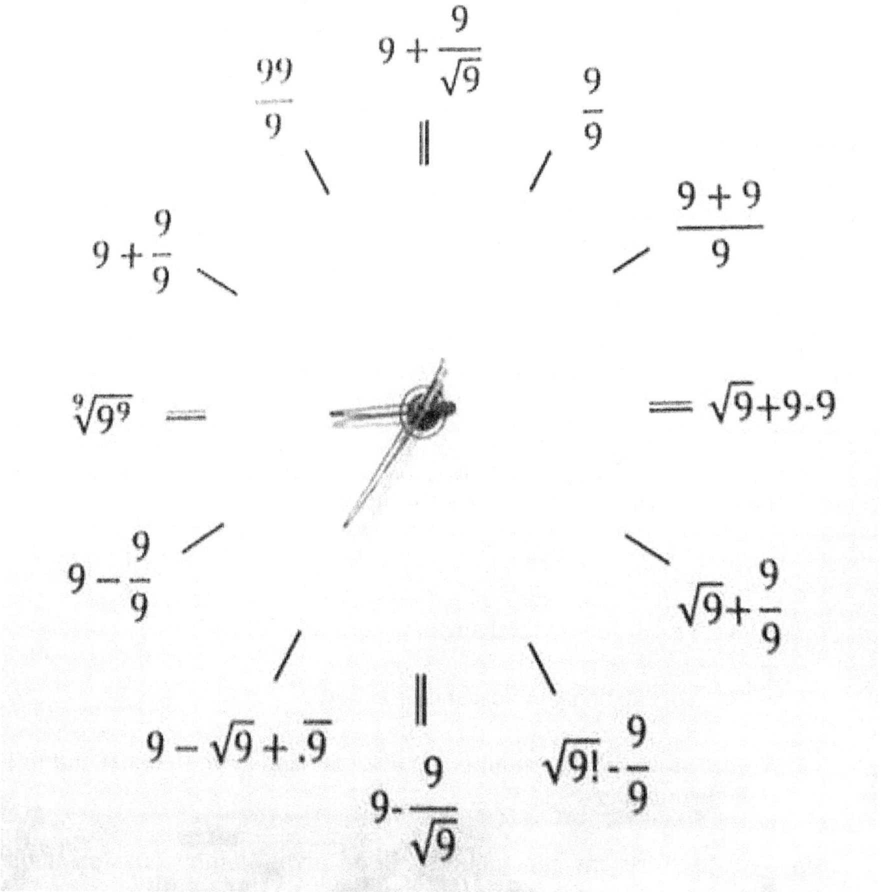
$9+\frac{9}{\sqrt{9}}$
$\frac{9}{9}$
$\frac{9+9}{9}$
$=\sqrt{9}+9-9$
$\sqrt{9}+\frac{9}{9}$
$\sqrt{9!}-\frac{9}{9}$
$9-\frac{9}{\sqrt{9}}$
$9-\sqrt{9}+.\overline{9}$
$9-\frac{9}{9}$
$\sqrt[9]{9^9}$
$9+\frac{9}{9}$
$\frac{99}{9}$

**C Programmers Thinks like it !!**
**Think Different LoL !!!!!!!!!!!**

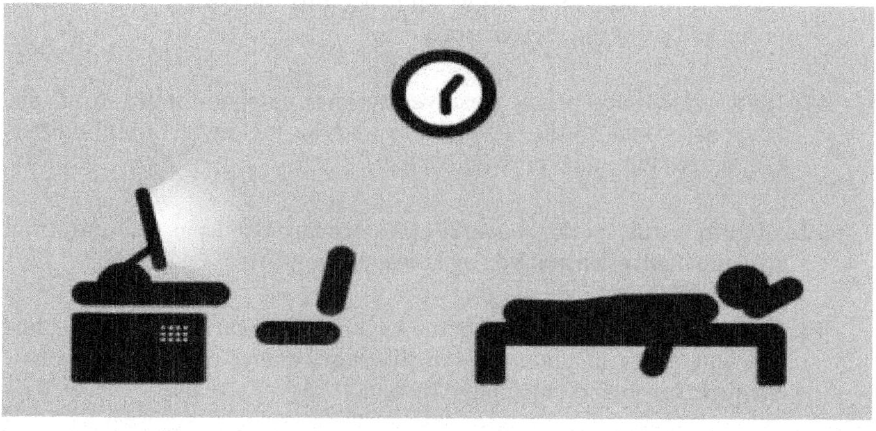

# CHAPTER
## ∞ 6 ∞
## (Two Dimensional Array (Matrix))

# Introduction-

Two dimensional array is popularly known as tables or matrix and can be easily visualized as having rows and columns. Matrix can also be thought of as arrays of arrays.

*To create a two dimensional array, specifying both dimensions i.e. rows and columns in square brackets.*

**For e.g.** the following declaration creates a matrix of 4 rows and 5 columns.

```
int mat[4][5];
or
#define MAXROW 4
#define MAXCOL  5
int mat[MAXROW][MAXCOL];
```

|   | 0   | 1   | 2   | 3   | 4   |
|---|-----|-----|-----|-----|-----|
| 0 | 0,0 | 0,1 | 0,2 | 0,3 | 0,4 |
| 1 | 1,0 | 1,1 | 1,2 | 1,3 | 1,4 |
| 2 | 2,0 | 2,1 | 2,2 | 2,3 | 2,4 |
| 3 | 3,0 | 3,1 | 3,2 | 3,3 | 3,4 |

Array are stored in row order, thus the expression mat[0] represents the first row of 5 values, mat[1]represents second row, mat[2]represents third row, and so on.

Similarly the expression mat[0][0] refers to the upper left value in the matrix, mat[2][3] represents the fourth value in third row.

**Matrix initializes:-**

      **1.** int mat[4][3];
      **2.** int mat[4][3]={{10,20,30,40},{50,60,70,80},{90,100,110,120}};
      **3.** int mat[4][3]={10,20,30,40,50,60,70,80,90,100,110,120};
      **4.** static int mat[4][3];

**Drill Note** - int mat[ ][ ] is invalid because dimensions are not specified.

**Drill Note** - int mat[ ][ ]={1,2,3,4,5,6} is invalid because it is not possible to decide the row & column of the matrix.

**Drill Note** - int mat[ ][3]={1,2,3,4,5,6} is valid

**Drill Note** - int mat[2][ ]={1,2,3,4,5,6} is invalid as column is compulsory in matrix declaration.

**Memory map of a multi dimensional array:**

Let us see the arrangement of array elements in a two dimensional array

|   | 0 | 1 | 2 | 3 |
|---|---|---|---|---|
| **0** | 10 | 5 | 6 | 7 |
| **1** | 36 | 94 | 56 | 29 |
| **2** | 83 | 67 | 12 | 69 |
| **3** | 39 | 55 | 13 | 29 |

The array arrangement in the above figure is only conceptually true. This is because memory doesn't contain rows and columns.

In memory whether it is a one dimensional or a multi dimensional array the array elements are stored in one continuous chain. The arrangement of array elements of the given two dimensional array in memory is shown below:

| [0][0] | [0][1] | [0][2] | [0][3] | [1][0] | [1][1] | [1][2] | [1][3] | [2][0] | [2][1] | [2][2] | [2][3] | [3][0] | [3][1] |
|---|---|---|---|---|---|---|---|---|---|---|---|---|---|
| 10 | 5 | 6 | 7 | 36 | 94 | 56 | 29 | 83 | 67 | 12 | 69 | 86 | 39 |
| 100 | 102 | 104 | 106 | 108 | 110 | 112 | 114 | 116 | 118 | 120 | 122 | 124 | 126 |

# SOME SOLVED PROGRAMS -

1. WAP to transpose a 2-d array.

```c
#define maxrow 10
#define maxcol 10
    main()
    {
        int m[maxrow][maxcol],i,j,row,col;
        clrscr();
        printf("Enter number of rows and columns in the matrix: ");
        scanf("%d %d",&row,&col);
        for(i=0;i<row;i++)
        {
            for(j=0;j<col;j++)
            {
            printf("Enter element %d,%d: ",i+1,j+1);
            scanf("%d",&m[i][j]);
            }
        }
        /*To print the matrix as input by the user*/
        printf("Matrix input:\n\n");
        for(i=0;i<row;i++)
        {
            for(j=0;j<col;j++)
            printf("%d\t",m[i][j]);
            printf("\n");
        }       /*transpose*/
        printf("\n\nTransposed matrix\n\n");
        for(i=0;i<col;i++)
        {
            for(j=0;j<row;j++)
            printf("%d\t",m[j][i]);
            printf("\n");
        }
        getch();
    }
```

2. Input a 3 * 3 matrix using keyboard, write a program to convert it in to 4 *4 matrix by adding corresponding row and columns.

```c
int mat1[3][3],mat2[4][4]={0},i,j;        /* Input */
        for(i=0;i<3;i++)
        for(j=0;j<3;j++)
    {
    printf("Enter element [%d,%d] ",i+1,j+1);
    scanf("%d",&mat1[i][j]);
    }
/* Convert 3 * 3 matrix into 4 * 4 matrix */
```

```
for(i=0;i<3;i++)
for(j=0;j<3;j++)
        {
                mat2[i][j] = mat1[i][j];
                mat2[i][3] += mat1[i][j];
                mat2[3][j] += mat1[i][j];
                mat2[3][3] += mat1[i][j];
        }
                /* Output */
        for(i=0;i<4;i++)
        {
                for(j=0;j<4;j++)
                printf("%d\t",mat2[i][j]);
                printf("\n");
        }
```

3.  Write a program to find if a square matrix is symmetric.

```
        int m[10][10], i, j, r,c;
        printf("Enter number of rows & columns of the Matrix:");
        scanf("%d%d",&r,&c);
        if(r !=c)
        {
                printf("Symmetric matrix must be a square matrix");
                getch();
                exit(1);
        }               /*Matrix input*/
        for(i=0; i<r; i++)
        {
                for(j=0; j<c; j++)
                {
                        printf("Enter element %d,%d",i+1,j+1);
                        scanf("%d",&m[i][j]);
                }
        }               /* Check for symmetry*/
        for(i=0; i<r; i++)
        {
                for(j=0; j<c; j++)
                {
                        if(m[ i ][ j ] != m[ j ][ i ])
                        {
                        printf("The matrix is not a symmetric");
                                getch();
                                exit(0);
                        }
                }
                printf("The matrix is a symmetric");
```

128

# Lab Exercise -

1. WAP to find row sum and column sum of a matrix.

2. WAP to prepare a one-dimensional array $a[n^2]$ from a 2 dimensional array $m[nxn]$ that will have all the elements of array m if they are stored in row-major form and a one-dim array $b[n^2]$ in column-major form. for example for the following array—

   ```
    1  2   3  4
    5  6   7  8
    9 10  11 12
   13 14  15 16
   ```

   The resultant array a will be 1 2 3 4 5 6 7 8 9 10 11 12 13 14 15 16,
   and the resultant array b will be 1 5 9 13 2 6 10 14 3 7 11 15 4 8 12 16

3. WAP that will read 2 matrices, add their individual elements and display the resultant matrix.

4. WAP that will read 2 matrices, multiply the matrices and display the resultant matrix.

5. WAP that will transpose a 2-d array but the array is stored as 1-d array.

6. WAP to create a square matrix and print the first and the second diagonal elements on a clear screen. Also find the sum of all the elements lie on either diagonal.

7. WAP to extract the maximum and the minimum elements from a matrix.

8. WAP to double all the elements of the matrix.

9. WAP to print all those elements of a matrix are not diagonal elements.

10. WAP to sort all the elements of a matrix.

11. WAP to obtain the determinant value of a matrix.

Yehhhh,....!! After a long time, finally my C- Code is running....

# CHAPTER
## ∞ 7 ∞
## (String (Character array))

## Introduction-

A string is an array of characters. Any group of characters (except double quotes) enclosed between double quotes is called a string constant.

A string is a one-dimensional array of characters terminated by null ( \0 ).

**For e.g.**

char s[10] = {'s','h','i','v','a','m','\0'};

| S | H | I | V | A | M | \0 | p | o | H |
|---|---|---|---|---|---|----|---|---|---|

Each character in the array occupies one byte of memory and the last character is always a '\0'. This '\0' is called a null. It defines the end of the string. Because of the presence of this character the various functions working on the string are able to know the end of the string.

Thus it can be said that the input given to the string gets terminated at null'\0'. And the remaining array contains garbage values.

**Drill Note:** the null '\0' looks as if two characters are typed but the compiler treats it as a single character. It is an escape sequence.

Also remember that '0' is different from '\0'. ASCII of 0 is 48 while ASCII of '\0' is 0.

**Character array initialization -**

1.   char s[10];
2.   char s[7] = {'s','h','i','v','a','m','\0'};
3.   char s[7] = {'s','h','i','v','a','m'};
4.   char s[7] = "shivam";
5.   char s[ ] = {'s','h','i','v','a','m','\0'};

## Let us observe a few important aspects of string -

1.   In the last declaration null character is missing i.e. a '\0' is added automatically the compiler at the end of the string.

2.   The size of the string should be equal to the maximum number of characters in the string plus one.

3.   The initialization of the string without the mentioning of size is also permitted, as in the integer array. In such case the array size will be automatically based on the number of elements initialized.

## String input -

The common function used for input is *scanf.* This function can also be used to input the string using format specifer %s.

**For e.g.**
        scanf("%s",name);

While inputting the string the **&** (address of operator is not required).

A problem with the scanf function is that it ends the input on the first white space it finds (a white space includes blank, tabs, carriage return, form feed, new line character.)

Therefore if the following line is typed as input--
**Shivam Kumar**

Then only the string "Shivam" will be taken as input into the variable name, because the blank space after word "Shivam" will end the string.

Many times it is required to read the entire line of text, and it is not possible using the scanf. This can be achieved by using the getchar function.

This function reads a single character at a time and store the character in the array. So we have to use this function repeatedly using a loop until the user types the null character or a new line character.

**Another** function which can be used to input the string is called as gets(). And is used as:

> char name[10];
> gets(name);

This function can also read the blank spaces and thus take a line as input in one go.

**String output -**

The commonly used output function printf() can be used for string also using the format specifer %s to display the string on the screen.

> printf("%s",name);

**Drill Note -** Also the function puts() can be used.

> puts(name);
> The precision of the string can also be specified **%10.3**

Indicates that the first three characters are to be printed in the field width of 10 columns. 7 spaces will be printed before the string. But if the specification is (%-10.4) then the string will be printed as left justified and all the 7 spaces will printed towards the right.

1. **Remember** that if the field width is less than string length then string equal to string length will be printed. printf("%3.4s",name); will print 4 characters not 3.

2. The integer value typed to the right side of the decimal point specifies the number of characters to be printed.

3. If the number of characters to be printed is specified as 0 then nothing is printed.

   char name[10]="Shivam Kumar";

   printf("%s",name);

   printf("%6s",name);

   printf("%12.6s",name);

   printf("%-12.6s",name);

   printf("%.2s",name);

# SOME SOLVED PROGRAMS -

1. WAP to sort the names in a given list in ascending order.

```
#include<string.h>
main()
{
    char names[10][20], t[20];
    int i=0,j=0,n;
    printf("Enter how many names");
    scanf("%d",&n);
    /*Input names*/
    for(i=0;i<n;i++)
    {
            printf("Enter name %d ",i+1);
            gets(names[i]);
    }
    /*Sorting*/
    for(i=0;i<n-1;i++)
    {
            for(j=i+1;j<n;j++)
            {
                    if(strcmp(names[i],names[j]) > 0)
                    {
                            strcpy(t,names[i]);
                            strcpy(names[i],names[j]);
                            strcpy(names[j],t);
                    }
            }
    }
    /*Output*/
    for(i=0;i<n;i++)
    {
            printf("%s\n",names[i]);
    }
    getch();
}
```

2. Input a string through keyboard write a program to print a string in reverse order as per word:

**e.g.** How Are You = You Are How.*/

```
main()
{
        char s1[50],t1[50],t2[50]="";
        int i=0,j=0;;
        printf("Enter a string");
```

134

```
gets(s1);
strcat(s1," ");
while(s1[i]!= '\0')
{
        if(s1[i] == ' ')
        {
                t1[j++] = ' ';
                t1[j] = '\0';
                strcat(t1,t2);
                strcpy(t2,t1);
                j = 0;
        }
        else
                t1[j++] = s1[i];
        i++;
}
puts(t1);
getch();
}
```

3.  WAP to input a text and replace an entered string occurring within the text with equal number of "*",at all occurring.

```
char ch;
printf("Enter text: ");
while((ch=getch())!='\r')
        printf("*");
```

4.  Write a program that converts a string like "124" to an integer 124.

```
char str[6];
int num= 0, i;
printf("Enter a string containing a number:");
scanf("%s",str);
for(i=0; str[i]!='\0'; i++)
{
        if(str[i]>=48 && str[i]<=57)
                num = num*10+(str[i]-48);
        else
        {
                printf("Not a valid string");
                getch();
                return;
        }
}
printf("\nThe numer is: %d\n",num);
```
**Drill Note:** *Function **atoi** also converts string to integer.*

# What would be the output of the following programs?

**1.**
```
char c[2]= "A";
printf("%c",c[0]);
printf("%s",c);
```
**Output: A A**

From first printf( ) 'A' gets printed because the array size is 2 so 'A' is stored on the 0ᵗʰ position and '\0'(NULL) is stored on the first position. And by using second printf( ) the output will be 'A' because the whole string will gets printed that is "A".

**2.**
```
char s[ ] = "Get organized! learn
          c!!";
printf("\n%s",&s[2]);
printf("\n%s",s);
printf("\n%s",&s);
printf("\n%c",s[2]);
```
Output: t organized! learn c!!
Get organized! learn c!!
Get organized! learn c!!
t

**Through first printf( )** "t organized! learn c!!" gets printed because we put &s[2] for printing the string so the printing will start from the 3ʳᵈ character of string because when we use only name of string it contain the base address and string printing will start from base character.

**Through second printf( )** the whole string will gets printed because string name is used there.

**Through third printf( )** the whole string will gets printed because the address of string(base address because no subscript or index is used) is passed that will be same as second printf( ).

**Through last printf( )** only third character is printed because here %c format specifier is used and in printing list s[2] that refer the third character is used.

**7.**
```
char str1[ ] = {'H','e','l','l','o',0};
char str2[ ] = "Hello";

printf("\n%s",str1);
printf("\n%s",str2);
```
**Output:      Hello**
**            Hello**

Because in the first string the last character is 0 that is the ASCII of NULL(\0) character and when srr1 gets printed it will print the whole string "Hello" and similarly str2 is also gets printed.

**8.**
```
printf(5+"Good Morning");
```
**Output: Morning.**

Here compiler will understand the above printf that the string should be print starting from the 5ᵗʰ character of the string.

**9.**
```
printf("\n%d %d
%d",sizeof('3'),sizeof("3"),sizeof(3) );
```
**Output: 2 2 2**

Because first sizeof contain character but in C the character will convert with its ASCII value and compiler understand it as int so it occupy 2bytes. The second sizeof is a string that contains only single character but C compiler automatically puts null character at the end of the each string so the above string will contain 2 character that occupy 2 bytes. And the 3ʳᵈ sizeof contains 3 that's an integer value and occupy 2 bytes.

**10.**
```
char a[8] ="Rhombus";
int i;
for( i = 0; i<=7; i++)
printf("\n%d",*a);
a++;
```
**Output:** Error.

136

**3.** printf("%c","Harry"[4]);

**Output: y.**

Because when we print s[4] then it print the 5th character of string here we use string "matrix" in the place of s and similarly of s it will print the 5th character of string that is r.

**4.** char a[ ] = {'M','A','T','R','I','X'};
int i;
for( i = 0; i<=5;i++)
printf("\n%c",a[i]);

**Output: No Error.**

Each time the ith of array gets printed till condition is true because the counter is start from 0 so the printing will start from 0th element and gets printed till 5 so each character of string "MATRIX" gets printed and separated by the line.

**5.** main()
{
    char s[7]= "Strings";
    printf("%s",s);
}

**Output:** Unpredictable. Here s[ ] has been declared as a 7 character array and into it a 8 character string has been stored. This would result into overwriting of the bytes beyond the seventh byte reserved for the array with a "\0".there is always a possibility that something important will be overwritten which would be unsafe.

**6.** How would you output \n on the screen?

**Output: "\\n"**

Because array 'a' can't be incremented.

**11.** main()
{
    char string[ ]= "Author Harry";
        int a=5;
            printf("a>10?"%20s":
                "%s",string);

**Output: Author Harry**

**12.** main()
{
        printf(5+ "Computers");
}

**Output: ters**

**13.** main()
{
            char s1= "Matrix";
            char s2=
        "Computers";
            if(s1= = s2)

            printf("Equal");
            else

            printf("Unequal");
}

**Output:Unequal**

**14.** main()
{
            printf("%c",
        "Matrix"[4]);
}

**Output: i**

**15.** Which is more appropriate for reading in a multi-word string?
gets( )        printf( ) scanf( ) puts( )
**Output:** gets( )

# Fill in the blanks:

1. "A" is a _____whereas 'A' is a _____.
2. A string is terminated by a _____which is written as ___.
3. The array char name[10] can consist of a maximum of____ characters.
4. The array elements are always stored in _____memory locations.

## Answers:

| | | |
|---|---|---|
| 1. string character | 2. null character \0 | 3. 9 |
| | 4. consecutive | |

## Lab Exercise -

1. WAP to concatenate two strings.

2. WAP that compares two strings

3. WAP to read a line of text from the keyboard and display the following information on the screen:

    a. number of words

    b. number of characters.

4. WAP to count the length of string inputted by user.

5. WAP to copy one string into another.

6. WAP to concatenate two strings in a third string.

7. WAP to copy a string into another in reverse order.

8. WAP to check whether string inputted by user is palindrome or not.

9. WAP to change the string into lowercase.

10. WAP to remove all the leading blanks in a string inputted by an user.

11. WAP that will print out all the relations of a string typed into it. for eg, the rotations of word " space " are: space paces acesp cespa espac

12. WAP to input any string and print the same in reverse.

13. WAP to input a string and a character to be searched within string. Print the frequency of the character within the string.

14. WAP to input a string and print the character which occurs the maximum number of times within the string.

138

15. WAP to input any string and print the frequency of each character within the string. The character with multiple frequencies should be displayed only once in the output, with the frequency value.

16. WAP to display the biggest name in an entered string. (with maximum length).

17. WAP to enter any name and print the same as per the following format: input:shruti

    **output:**       s
                      sh
                      shr
                      shru
                      shrut
                      shruti

18. WAP to input any sentence and arrange the characters of each word in alphabetical order separately and the print the sentence. For eg , input: computer program in basic.
    **output:** cemoprtu agmoprr in abcis.

19. WAP to take as inputs from the user by using a single subscripted variable, the marks in computer science of 40 students and then print those marks in ascending order in a column.

20. WAP to take a proverbial statement(like "failures are the pillars of success.") As an input from the user and then output the frequency of the vowels occurring in the statement.

21. A city hotel has 10 floors ranging from 1 to 10,each having 60 rooms. Make use of a single dimensional array for the name of the occupant and a 2-d array place(a, b),where a and b represent the floor and the room number respectively.WAP to allocate room for an occupant after inputting the name of the occupant and the room number.

22. WAP to input a text and print the word containing the maximum number of vowels.

23. WAP that replaces two or more or consecutive blanks in a string by a single blank. For e.g., if the input is: grim return to the  planet  of apes!! The output should be :grim return to the planet of apes!!

"You want to discuss the glitches in the software I sent you? No, Tuesday's out - how about never - is never okay?

# CHAPTER
## ∞ 8 ∞
## (Your Brain On Functions)

## Introduction-

Function is a small program which take some input and give us some output. Function allow a large program to be broken down into a number of smaller self contained components, each of which has a definite purpose. It avoids rewriting the code over & over. Breaking down of logic into separate functions make the entire process of writing & debugging easier.

Or another hand you can say Function is a self contained block of statements that is used to perform some task. A function is assigned some work once and can be called upon for the task any number of times. Every C program uses some functions, the commonly used functions are printf, scanf, main, etc.

Functions can be library functions or user defined functions. Library functions are those functions which come along with the compiler and are present in the disk. The user defined functions are those which the programmer makes by himself to make his program easier to debug, trace.

### Drill Note-

**printf ()**, **scanf()**, **exit()**, **pow()** are library functions. Every library function has a header file. *There are a total of 15 header files in C*. main() is a user defined function.

Every program must have a main function. This main function is used to mark the beginning of the execution. It is possible to code any program using only the main program but this leads to many problems. It becomes too large and complex thus difficult to trace, debug and test.

But if the same program is broken into small modulus coded independently and then combined into a single unit then these problems can be solved easily. These modulus are called as functions. Thus a function can be defined as a small program which takes some input and gives us some output.

**Drill Note-** I am not going to type header files again and again, so when writing programs please don't forget to start your programs with header files.

**Function to calculate the sum of two numbers:**

```
int sum(int, int);          /* Function Prototype or Declaration*/
main()
{
        int a,b,ans;
        printf("Enter two numbers: ");
        scanf("%d %d",&a,&b);
        ans= sum(a,b);   /*Function Call*/
        printf(" sum is %d", ans);
        getch();
}
int sum( int x, int y)      /*Function Definition or Process*/
{
        int z;
        z = x + y;
        return(z);
}
```

**Now let us see some of the features of this program:**

1.      The first statement is the declaration of the function which tells the compiler the name of the function and the data type of the arguments passed.

2.      The declaration is also called as prototype.

3.      The declaration of a function is not necessary if the output type is an integer value. In some C compilers declaration is not required for all the function.

4. The function call is the way of using the function. A function is declared once, defined once but can be used a number of times in the same program.

5. When the compiler encounters the function call, the control of the program is transferred to the function definition the function is then executed line by line and a value is returned at the end.

6. At the end of the main program is the definition of the function, which can also be called as process.

7. The function definition does not terminate with a semicolon.

8. A function may or may not return any value. Thus the presence of the return statement is not necessary. When the return statement is encountered, the control is immediately passed back to the calling function.

9. While it is possible to pass any number of arguments to a function, the called statement returns only one value at a call. The return statement can be used as:

    **return;**
    **or**
    **return(value);**

    The first return without any value, it acts much as the closing of the braces of the function definition.

10. A function may have more than one return statement. It can be used as :

    **if (a!=0)**
    **return(a);**
    **else**
    **return(1);**

11. All functions by default return int. But if the function has to return a particular type of data the type specifiers can be used along with the function name.

    **long int fact(n)**

12. If function main() calls a function sum() then main() is the **calling function** and sum() is **called function**.

**No arguments and no return values:**

Some functions do not receive any value from the calling function. Thus the function prototype will be as:

prn( ) i.e. no arguments will be passed. This can also be achieved as prn(void) And similarly the calling function does not get any value from the function. This is made possible by using the keyword void before the function name. to illustrate this point let us consider the following program:

```
void prn( );        /*declaration can also be made as void prn(void);*/
main( )
{
        prn( );
        prn( );
        prn( );
}
void prn( )
{
        printf("Hello");
}
```

**Argument Passing Mechanism -**

- **(i) Call by value -**

When arguments are passed by value then the copy of the actual parameters is transferred from calling function to the called function definition in formal parameters.

Now any changes made in the formal parameters in called function definition will not be reflected in actual parameters of calling function. Like in the above function to calculate the sum of two numbers the calling statement was written as:

ans = sum(a, b);

Here the values of variables a, b are passed from the main function to the calling function's definition.

In the definition variables x, y accept the values of a, b respectively. Here, the variables a, b are called the actual arguments while x, y will be called the formal arguments.

The scope of the actual and formal arguments is different so any change made in the formal arguments will not be seen in the actual arguments.

**e.g:**

```
void swap(int, int);
main()
{
        int a,b;
        printf("Enter 2 numbers");
        scanf("%d%d",&a,&b);
        swap(a,b);       /*In this call statement a,b are the actual parameters*/

printf("%d\t%d"a,b);
        }
void swap(int x,int y)   /*In this function definition x & y are the formal parameters */
        {
                int t;
                t=x; x=y; y=t;
        }
```

**Drill Note –**
    In the above e.g.: changes made in x, y will not be reflected in a,b.

## (ii) Call by reference -

    When arguments are passed by reference then the address of the actual parameters is transferred from calling function to the called function definition in formal parameters.

    Now any changes made in the formal parameters in called function definition will be reflected in actual parameters of calling function.

    Sometimes it is not possible to pass the values of the variables, for example while using an array it will not be possible to pass all the values of the array using call by value.

    So, another type of function calling mechanism is used call by reference where the *address of the variable is passed.*

    Here the definition would work by reaching the particular addresses. This method is generally used for the *array and pointers.*

**e.g.:**

```
main()
{
        int a,b;
        printf("Enter 2 numbers");
        scanf("%d%d",&a,&b);
        swap(&a, &b);            /*In this call statement address
                                   of a, b gets transferred*/
        printf("%d\t%d"a,b);
}
void swap(int *p1, int *p2)      /*In this function definition p1 & p2
                                   are the pointers which receive the
                                   address of a, b*/
{
        int t;
        t=*p1; *p1=*p2; *p2=t;
}
```

**Drill Note –**
In the above e.g.: changes made in p1, p2 will be reflected in a, b automatically.

**Drill Note –**
   Arrays are also passed by reference. When we pass the name of the array then only the base address is transferred in the function definition.

**Type of Functions -**

1.    **Library Functions -** Functions defined previously in the library are called as library functions.

**e.g.**

```
#include<math.h>

main()

{
        int n, p, ans;

        printf("Enter number and its power");

        scanf("%d%d",&n,&p);

        ans = pow(n,p);

        printf("%d",ans);

        getch();

}
```

146

# Common Library Functions:

## stdio.h functions-

| | |
|---|---|
| fclose( ) | Closes a stream |
| fcloseall() | Closes all open streams |
| feof() | Tests if end-of-file has been reached on a stream |
| fflush() | Flushes a stream |
| fgetc() | Gets a character from a stream |
| fgetpos() | Gets the current file pointer position |
| fsetpos() | Positions the file pointer of a stream |
| fgetchar() | Gets a character from stdin |
| fgets() | Gets a string from a stream |
| fopen() | Opens a stream |
| fprintf() | Sends formatted output to stream |
| fputc() | Outputs a character to a stream |
| fputs() | Outputs a string to a stream |
| fread() | Reads data from a stream |
| fscanf() | Scans and formats input from a stream. |
| fseek() | Sets the file pointer to a particular position. |
| ftell() | Returns the current position of the file pointer. |
| fwrite() | Writes to a stream. |
| getc() | gets one character. |
| getchar() | gets a character from stdin. |
| gets() | Get a string from stdin. |
| getw() | gets an integer from stream. |
| printf() | Sends the formatted output to stdin. |
| putc() | Outputs a character to stdout. |
| putchar() | Outputs a character on stdout. |
| puts() | Outputs string and appends a newline character. |
| putw() | Outputs an integer on a stream |
| remove() | Removes a file |
| rename() | Renames a file |
| Rewind() | Brings the file pointer to stream's beginning |
| scanf(). | Scans and formats input from stdin. |

## conio.h

| | |
|---|---|
| clrscr() | Clears text mode window |
| getch() | gets a character from console but does not echo to the screen |
| getche() | gets a character from console, and echoes to the screen |
| putch() | Oututs character to the text window on the screen |
| cgets() | Reads string from console |
| getchar() | Inputs a character from stdin. |

## stdlib.h

| | |
|---|---|
| itoa() | converts an integer to a string. |
| atoi() | Converts string of digits to integer. |
| Random() | Returns a random number between 0 and number – 1 |
| randomize() | initializes random number generator. |
| exit() | Terminates the program. |
| min() | Returns the smallest of two numbers. |
| max() | Returns the largest of two numbers. |
| ltoa() | converts a long to a string |
| ultoa() | converts an unsigned long to a string |
| atof() | converts a string to a floating point |
| _atold() | converts a string to a long double |

## math.h

| | |
|---|---|
| abs() | gets the absolute value of an integer |
| acos() | Calculates the inverse of cos Accepts the angle value in radians |
| asin() | Calculates the inverse of sin Accepts the angle value in radians |
| atan() | Calculates the inverse of tan Accepts the angle value in radians |
| ceil() | Returns the largest integer in given list. |
| cos() | Calculates the cosine Accepts the angle value in radians |
| cosh() | Accepts the angle value in radians |

| | |
|---|---|
| exp() | Calculates the exponent |
| floor() | Returns the smallest integer in given list. |
| log() | Calculates the natural logarithm |
| log10() | Calculates the log of base 10 |
| pow() | Calculates the power of a number |
| sin() | Calculates the sine value of an angle. Accepts the angle value in radians |
| sqrt() | Calculates the square root of a number |
| tan() | Calculates the tangent value of an angle. Accepts the angle value in radians |
| tanh() | Calculates the tangent hyperbolic value. |

## string.h                          string.h

| | |
|---|---|
| strcat() | Function to concatenate(merge) strings. |
| strcmp() | Function to compare two strings. |
| strcpy() | Function to copy a string to another string |
| stricmp() | Function to compare two strings ignoring their case. |
| strlen() | Function to calculate the length of the string |
| strlwr() | Converts the given string to lowercase |
| strrev() | Function to reverse the given string. |
| strupr() | Converts the given string to uppercase |
| strdup | Duplicates a string. |
| strnicmp() | Compares the first n characters of one string to another without being case sensitive. |
| strncat() | Adds the first n characters at the end of second string. |
| strncpy() | Copies the first n characters of a string into another. |
| strchr() | Finds the first occurrence of the character. |
| strrchr() | Finds the last occurrence of the character. |
| strstr() | Finds the first occurrence of string in another string. |
| strset() | Sets all the characters of the string to a given character. |
| strnset() | Sets first n characters of the string to a given character. |

## 2. User Defined Functions -

Functions defined by us are known as User Defined Functions. main() function is also user defined function because the definition of main() is defined by us.

**e.g.**

```
int power(int, int);
main()
{
        int n, p, ans;
        printf("Enter number and its power");
        scanf("%d%d",&n,&p);
        ans = power(n,p);
        printf("%d",ans);
        getch();
}
int power(int n, int p)
{
        in ans=1, i;
        for(i=1;i<=p;i++)
        {
                ans = ans * n;
        }
        return(ans);
}
```

## Function whose argument is a two dim array:-

```
void mat_sum(int m1[ ][10], int r1, int c1, int m2[][10], int r2, int c2, int m3[][10])

{
        int i,j;
        if(r1 != c1 && r2 != c2)
        {
                printf("Can't sum");
                exit();
        }
        for(i=0;i<r1;i++)
                for(j=0;j<c1;j++)
                        m3[i][j] = m1[i][j] + m2[i][j];

}
```

The above function can be called from main() as mat_sum(m1,r1,c1,m2,r2,c2,m3);

150

## Recursion -

A function is called recursive if a statement within the body of a function calls the same function. Sometimes called as 'circular definition', recursion is a function calling itself in the definition. A recursive function should have two parts recursive statement & a termination condition.

Suppose we want to calculate the factorial of an integer. As we know, the factorial of a number is the product of all the integers between 1 and that number. Factorial of 4 can be expressed as 4! = 4 * 3! Where ! stands for factorial. Thus the factorial of a number can be expressed in the form of itself. Hence this can be programmed using recursion.

**e.g.:**

```
int fact (int);                    /*function definition */
main()
{
int n,ans;
printf("Enter a number: ");
scanf("%d",&n);
ans = fact(n);                     /*function call */
printf("factorial = %d",ans);
getch();
}
int fact(int n)
{
        if(n= =0)                  /*terminating condition*/
        return (1);
        return (n*fact(n-1));      /*recursive statement*/
}
```

## Now let us evaluate this program:

Assuming the value of n is 3 when the control of the program is passed from the main() function the function fact. Since n is not equal to 0 so the condition is false and the recursive statement is executed.

3*fact(2)

now fact(2) is the calling function and thus the control of the program again reaches the beginning of the definition. Still the terminating condition is false so the recursive statement is executed.

2*fact(1)

Again fact(1) is the calling function and thus the control of the program again reaches the beginning of the definition. Still the terminating condition is false so the recursive statement is executed.

1 * fact(0)

Now the condition is true so the answer to the calling function(fact(0)) will be 1 and so on. Thus the sequence of acts will be:

fact(3)=3 * fact(2)
fact(2)=2 * fact(1)
fact(1)=1 * fact(0)

When we use a recursive program a stack is used to organize the data. Stack is a Last In First Out (LIFO) data structure. This means that the last item to be stored (push operation) in the stack will be the first one to come (pop operation) out.

In the above program when the fact(2) is called the value 3 will be stored in the stack. Similarly when fact(1) is called the value 2 will be stored at the top of 3 on the stack.

Now when the fact(0) returns 1. it will be multiplied to the first value in the stack i.e.

1. This result will be multiplied to the second waiting value of the stack i.e. 2 and so on.

When a function in its definition calls another function it is called *chaining*. Recursion is a special type of chaining where a function calls itself.

**e.g.:**

```
main()
{
        printf("Harry\n");
        main();
}
```
when executed the program will give the output as :
Harry
Harry
Harry

–

–

152

The execution of any recursive function can continue indefinitely so to bring the execution to the end a terminating condition is applied.

Use of recursive functions is to solve the problem where the solution is expressed in terms of successively applying the same solution to subsets of problems.

**But there are also some disadvantages of the recursive functions:**

1.    These functions are more time consuming, so the execution speed of the program is slow.

2.    More memory space is occupied due to the formation of stack to keep the waiting values.

## Fill in the blanks -

1.  Function returns the control to the calling function on the final _or _.

2.  To not return anything to the calling function, _____can be used.

3.  List of the parameters passed to a function are separated using _____.

4.  The default return type of a function in C is _____.

5.  In C all the arguments passed in a function are by _____.

6.  Call–by–reference  can be achived through _____.

7.  main is a _____ function.

8.  _____ are mandatory in a function.

9.  _____ is the ability of a function to call by itself.

10.  The point at which a program stops recursion is called _____

11.  Recursion uses _____ memory than iterative method.

### Answers -

1.  } or return statement.
2.  void
3.  ,
4.  int
5.  call-by-value

6.  pointers
7.  user defined
8.  arguments
9.  recursion
10. terminating condition

11. more

## Solved programs -

1. **WAP** to calculate the power p of a number n by user defined function.

```
int pow(int,int);/*declaration*/
main()
{
        int n,i,ans,p;
        printf("Enter two numbers: ");
        scanf("%d %d",&n,&p);
        ans=pow(n,p);/*call*/
        printf("%d to the power %d is %d",n,p,ans);
}
int pow(int n,int p)/*defination*/
{
        int i,ans=1;
        for(i=1;i<=p;i++)
                ans=ans*n;
        return(ans);
}
```

2. **WAP** to calculate the Greatest common divisor of two numbers using recursive function.

```
int gcd(int, int);
main()
{
        int n,m;
        int ans;
        printf("\n Enter two integer numbers");
        scanf("%d %d",&n,&m);
        ans = gcd(n,m);
        printf("GCD of %d and %d is %d",n,m,ans);
}
int gcd(int n, int m)
{
        if(n >= m && n%m == 0)
                return(m);
        else
                return gcd(m,n%m);
}
```

154

3. **WAP** to calculate the Greatest common divisor of two numbers using non- recursive function.

```
int gcd(int,int);
main()
{
        int n,m,ans;
        printf("Enter two integers");
        scanf("%d %d",&n,&m);
        ans = gcd(n,m);
        printf("GCD of %d and %d is %d", n,m,ans);
}
int gcd(int n, int m)
{
        int t;
        while(m!=0)
        {
                t = m;
                m = n % m;
                n = t;
        }
        return (n);
}
```

4. Write a program to search a sub-string using pointers.

```
int strsearch(char [ ],char [ ]);
main()
{
        char s1[50],s2[10];
        int ans=0;
        printf("Enter a string");   /*input of string */
        gets(s1);
        printf("Enter a string");   /*input of substring to search*/
        gets(s2);
        ans = strsearch(s1,s2);   /*function call*/
        if(ans == -1)                    /*using the returned value*/
                printf("String is not found");
        else
                printf("String is found at pos %d ",ans+1);
}
int strsearch(char s1[ ],char s2[ ])/*definition*/
{
        int i,j;
        i=j=0;
        while(s1[i] != '\0')
```

```
        {
                if(s1[i] == s2[j])
                {
                        while(s1[i+j] == s2[j] && s2[j] != '\0')
                                j++;
                        if(s2[j] == '\0')
                                return (i);
                        j=0;
                }
                i++;
        }
        return (-1);
}
```

5. **WAP** to calculate the determinants of a matrix*/

```
#define MAXROW 4
#define MAXCOL 4
int det_mat(int [ ][MAXCOL],int,int);
main()
{
        int mat[MAXROW][MAXCOL]={0};
        int r,c,i,j,sum;
        printf("Enter dimension of matrix");
        scanf("%d%d",&r,&c);
        /*Input Matrix */
        for(i=0;i<r;i++)
                for(j=0; j<c;j++)
                {
                        printf("Enter element %d %d", i+1, j+1);
                        scanf("%d",&mat[i][j]);
                }
        /*function call*/
        sum = det_mat(mat,r,c);
        /*output*/
        printf("%d",sum);
}
int det_mat(int mat[ ][MAXCOL], int r, int c)
{
        int i,j,k,sign,sum,a;
        int mat2[MAXROW][MAXCOL]={0};
        sign = 1;
        sum = 0;
        if(c = = 1)
                return(mat[0][0]);
```

```
for(i=0 ; i<c; i++,sign *= -1)
{
        for(j=1; j<r; j++)
        {
                for(k=0; k<c; k++)
                {
                        if(k == i)
                                continue;
                        if(k>i)
                                mat2[j-1][k-1]=mat[j][k];
                        else
                                mat2[j-1][k]=mat[j][k];

                }
        }

        sum = sum + mat[0][i] * sign * det_mat(mat2,r-1,c-1);
        }
        return (sum);
}
```

## Fill in the blanks –

The return statement returns only _____.

An _____ can be assigned initial values by including appropriate expressions by transferring control to some other part of program.

An automatic variable does not retain _____ once the control is transferred out of its defining function.

An extern variable declaration must begain with storage class specifiers _____.

If the line int sp;
        Occurs outside any function, it _____ the external variable sp.

if the line
static char buffer[max];
Appears in one file of a program, then the variable name will not conflict with the same name in _____ of the same program.

An external variable definition must not begin with storage class specifies ____.

# What would be the output of the following program?

**1.**
```
main( )
{
printf("\n welcome in c:");
    display( );
}
display( )
    {
    printf("History of C:");
        main( );
    }
```

**Output:** Both massage will get printed indefinitely.

Because when main( ) calls display control jumps to the display and because in the body of display main is again call then control again jumps to the main and this process will be repeat repetedly.

**2.**
```
main( )
{
    float area;
    int radius = 1;
    area = circle (radius);
    printf("\n%f",area);
}
circle( int r)
{
    float a;
    a = 3.14*r*r;
    return(a);
}
```
**Output:** 3.000000

Because in function definition there is no explicit return type and default return type is int so when we return *a* that is 3.14 will demote to 3. And when 3 is printed as float it will promote in floating point format and gets printed 3.000000.

**5.**
```
main( )
{
    int i = 40,c;
    c = check(i);
    printf("\n%d",c);
}
check(int ch)
{
    if(ch>=40)
        return(100);
    else
        return(10*10);
}
```
**Output:** 100
Because the value of i is passed to ch that is 40. and when condition is checked in function definition it becomes true so if block is executed and returns 100.

**6.**
```
main( )
{
    int i = 5, j = 2;
    hello (i, j);
    printf("\n%d %d",i,j);
}

hello(int i, int j)
{
    i = i*i;
    j = j*j;
}
```
**Output:** 5 2
The function here is call by value so any change in the formal argument will not effect the actual argument. So in main( ) function i and j are still same.

**7.**
```
main( )
{
    int x = 5, y = 2;
    hello(&x ,&y);
    printf("\n%d %d",x,y);
```

```
3.  main( )
    {
        printf("\n Go for Matrix:");
        main();
    }
```
**Output:** The massage will print indefinitely.

Because main again call main( ) that will be recursive call without any terminating condition,so massage gets printed indefinitely.

```
4.  main( )
    {
        static int i = 0;
        i++;
        if ( i<=5)
        {
            printf("%d\t",i);
            main( );
        }
        else
            exit( );
    }
```
**Output:** 1  2  3  4  5

Here first i++ is executed and each time the value of i increment by 1. now for the first time it will be 1 and condition becomes true and gets printed the value of i that is 1 now again main function is called and we know i is declared as static so it's value will not again initialize and now this time when increment take place it becomes 2 and in this way until i will not be 5, i gets printed and call main function repeatedly but when i becomes 6 condition will be false and control jumps to the else block and because of exit( ) it stops the program.

```
    }
    hello(int *i,int *j)
    {
        *i = *i * *i;
        *j=*j * *j;
    }
```
**Output:** 25  4

In the above program because function is call by reference and the address of x any y is passed to i and j and by dereference [*i = *i * *i] becomes [x = x*x] that gives 25 and similarly next statement gives 4. because here function is called by reference so it will change the actual argument and then x =25 and y = 4 gets printed through printf( ).

```
8.  main( )
    {
        int i = 5, j = 3;
        calc( &i , j);
        printf("\n %d %d",i,j);
    }
    calc( int *i, int j)
    {
        *i =*i * *i;
        j = j*j
    }
```
**Output:** 25  3

Here to argument is passed to the called function first the address of i and second the value of j so when we dereference i. it change the actual argument but the operation on j doesn't effect to actual argument so the value of j remains same and i gets change.

**Point out the errors, if any, in the following programs:**

```
1.  main( )
    {
        int a = 3,b = 4, c,k;
        c = summult(i,j);
        d = summult(i,j);
        printf("\n%d  %d",c,d);
    }
    summult(int x, int y)
    {
            int a1, b1;
            a1= x+y;
            b1 = x*y;
            return(a1,b1);
    }
```
**Output:** Error. More than one value can't be returned by a function.

```
2.  main( )
    {
        int x;
        x = massage( );
    }
    message( )
    {
        printf("\n your computer
can be effected by Viruses:");
            return;
    }
```
**Output:** No Error.

Because here no explicit return type is prefixed in function definition so default return type is int and here return statement is also exist in function definition so it will return a garbage integer value. But if there will be void type in function definition then error is encounterend.

```
3.  main( )
    {
        float a = 185.5;
        char ch = 'C';
        display(a,ch);
```

```
7.  main( )
    {
        message( );
        message( );
    }
    messae( )
    {
        printf("Whole world is
                    waiting for you:");
    }
```
**Output:** Error. Function definition must not be present immediately after the function definition.

```
8.  main( )
    {
        matrix( )
        {
        printf("Welcome in the world
            of computer:");
        }
    }
```
**Output:** Error. One function can't be defined into the body of another function.

```
9.  main( )
    {
        Matrix(computer( ));
    }
    void computer( )
    {
        printf("Beginning with C:");
    }
```
**Output:**
```
9.  main( )
    {
        int i = 135, a = 135, k;
        k = demo( i , a);
        printf("\n %d",k);
    }
    demo(int j, int b)
    int c;
    {
```

160

```
        }
    display(a,ch)
    {
        printf("\n%f %c",a,ch);
    }
```
**Output:** Error.
Formal argument don't have any data type in function definition.

**4.** main( )
```
    {
        int a = 35,b;
        b = check (a);
        printf("\n %d",b);
    }
    check( m)
    {
        int m;
        if( m>40)
            return(1);
        else
            return(0);
    }
```
**Output:** Error. The variable m must be declared before the braces.The formal argument can be declared by two following ways:
**(a)**Check(int m)
```
    {

    }
```
**(b)**check( )
```
    int m;
    {

    }
```
**5.** main()
```
        {
            display();
        }
        void display()
        {
            printf("Matrix");
        }
```
**Output:** Error of redeclaration

```
        c = j + b;
        return (c);
    }
```
**Output:** Error. The declaration int c should be inside the body of demo( ).

**10.** main( )
```
    {
        int p = 23,f = 24;
        out(&p, &f);
        printf("\n%d %d",p,f);
    }

    out (int q, int g)
    {
        q = q + q;
        g = g + g;
    }
```
**Output:** Error. The variable q and g in function definition should be declared as integer pointer.

**11.** main( )
```
    {
        int i = 35, *z;
        z = fun( &i);
        printf("\n%d",z);
    }

    fun( int *m)
    {
        return(m + 2);
    }
```
**Output:** Unpredictable Output.
Here in the above program the address of i(&i) suppose 2005 is passed to m so m contains the address of i and returns m+2 is equal to 2007. so this function return 2007 to the main( ) that will store in z and z gets printed through printf( ). Here address is assume by the compiler so we can't say what will be the output but there will print an int value.

**13.** main()
```
    {
```

because display() is called before it is defined. In such cases the compiler assumes that the function display() is declared as **int display ();** that is, an undeclared function is assumed to return an int and accept an unspecified number of arguments. Then when we define the function the compiler finds that it is returning void hence the compiler reports the discrepancy.

6. 
```
main()
{
    int a=1;
    while(a<=5)
    {
        printf("%d",a);
        if( a>2)
            goto abc;
    }
}
fun()
{
    abc:
    printf("Author Harry");
}
```
**Output:** goto cannot take control to a different function.

```
main()
{
    int a=10;
    void f();
    a=f();
    printf("%d",a);
}
void f()
{
    printf("Hello");
}
```
**Output:** The function has been declared as void but still the program is trying to collect the value returned by f() in variable *a*.

```
    int a,b;
    a=sumdig(123);
    b=sumdig(123);
    printf("%d %d",a,b);
}
sumdig(int n)
{
    static int s=0;
    int d;
    if(n!=0)
    {
        d=n%10;
        n=(n-d)/10;
        s=s+d;
        sumdigit(n);
    }
    else
        return (s);
}
```
**Output: 6 12**

14. 
```
f(int a, int b)
{
    int a;
    a=20;
    return a;
}
```
Output: Error The variable *a* is redeclared

15. 
```
main()
{
    int b=10;
    b=f(20);
    printf("%d",b);
}
int f(int a)
{
    a>20?return(10):return(20);
}
```
**Output:** return statement cannot be used as shown with the conditional operators. Instead the following can be used:
```
return(a>20?10:20);
```

162

# State whether the following statements are True or False:

1. The variables commonly used in C functions are available to all functions in a program.

2. To return the control back to the calling function we must use the keyword return. The same variable names can be used in different functions without any conflict.

3. Every called function must contain a return statement.

4. A function may contain more than one return statement.

5. Each return statement in a function may return a different value.

6. A function can still be useful even if you don't pass any arguments to it and the function doesn't return any value back.

7. Same names can be used for different functions without any conflict.

8. A function may be called more than once from any other function.

9. It is necessary for a function to return some value.

10. A function can have several declarations but only one definition.

11. A function cannot be defined inside another function.

12. Will the following function work:
```
main()
{
    f1(int a, int b);
{
    return(f2(20));
}
f2 (int a)
{
    return(a*a);
}
```

13. In a function two return statements should never occur.

14. In a function two return statements should never occur successively.

15. In C all functions except main() can be called recursively.

16. Usually recursion works slower than loops.

17. Too many recursive calls may result in stack overflow.

# Answers:

| | | | |
|---|---|---|---|
| 1. False | 2. False | 3. True | 4. False |
| 5. True | 6. True | 7. True | 8. False |
| 9. False | 10. True | 11. True | 12. True |
| 13. False | 14. True | 15. False | 16. True |
| 17. True | | | |

# Answer the following:

1. When we mention the prototype of a function we are defining or declaring the function?

   **Output:** declaring

2. There is a mistake in the following code, add a statement to remove it.

```
main()
{
        int a;
        a=f(10,3,14);
        printf("%d",a);
}
f(int aa, float bb)
{
        return((float)aa+bb);
}
```

   **Output:**
   The declaration of the function f is missing add the following above main()
   
```
          float f(int,float);
```

3. What are the two notations of defining functions commonly known as:

```
int f( int a, float b)
{
        /*some code*/
}
int f(a,b)
int a;
float b;
{
        /*some code*/
}
```

   **Output:**
           The first one is known as ANSI notation and the second is known as Kernighan and Ritchie or simply K&R notation.

164

# Lab Exercise –

1. Write a function which takes to integer as argument and return there sum. WAP to test this function.

2. Write a function which takes to integer as argument and return there average in float. WAP to test this function.

3. WAP that uses a function that converts a lowercase character to its uppercase.

4. WAP that uses a function that calculates factorial of a given number.

5. WAP that uses a function power that calculates the power of a given number.

6. WAP that uses a function that finds the largest of three integer quantities.

7. WAP that receives any year from the keyboard and uses a function to determine whether the year is a leap year or not.

8. WAP that uses a function which receives a float and an int from main(),finds the product of these two and returns the product which is printed through main().

9. WAP that uses a function to calculate the sum of n odd integers.

10. WAP that uses a function to calculate the sum of n even integers starting from a given even integer.

11. WAP that uses a function to determine whether a given positive integer is a prime number or not.

12. WAP that uses a function to determine whether a given positive integer is a fibonacci number or not.

13. WAP that uses a function that finds the length of the largest monotonically increasing subsequence in a sequence of real numbers.

14. WAP that uses a function for finding the absolute value of the integer parameter passed to it (do not use any library function).

15. WAP that uses a function that takes two  arguments: a character and an integer and prints the character given number of times. if however the integer is missing the function prints the character twice.

16. WAP that uses a function to sum n natural numbers starting from a given number.

17. WAP that uses a function that takes a character argument and prints it number of times equal to number of times that function has been called to the input.

18. WAP that uses a function which takes a real number as its argument and returns the sum of digits(complete including fraction parts) of this number.

19. WAP that uses a function that checks whether the given number is divisible by 11 or not by using the algorithm which states that a number is divisible by 11 if and only if the difference of the sums of digits at odd positions and even positions is either zero or divisible by 11.

20. WAP that uses a function isdigit which should return a non-zero if the given number is a digit and 0 if not.

21. WAP that uses a function isalpha which should return a non-zero if the given number is a alphabet and 0 if not.

22. WAP that uses a function isalnum which should return a non-zero if the given number is a alpha numeric and 0 if not.

23. WAP that uses a function isupper which should return a non-zero if the given number is a uppercase character and 0 if not.

24. WAP that uses a function toupper which accepts a character argument and return its equivalent uppercase character.

25. WAP that uses a function that returns the gcd(greatest common divisor) of two integers.

26. WAP that invokes a function satis() to find whether four integers a, b, c, d sent to satis() satisfy the equation $a^3+b^3+c^3=d^3$ or not. The function satis() returns 0 if the above equations satisfied with the given four numbers otherwise it returns -1.

27. WAP that uses a function called carea() to calculate area of a circle. The function carea() receives radius of float type and returns area of double type. the function main() gets radius value from the user, calls carea(),and displays the result. the function carea() is local to main().

28. WAP that uses various functions to sum following series:
a) $(1)+(1+2)+(1+2+3)+(1+2+3+4)+$_____ upto n terms

**b)** $(2^2)+(2^2+4^2)+(2^2+4^2+6^2)+(2^2+4^2+6^2+8^2)+$_____ upto n terms

**c)** $1+1/3+1/5+1/7+1/9+$_____ upto n terms

**d)** $1+1/x+1/(x^2)+1/(x^3)+1/(x^4)+$_____ upto n terms

29. WAP that receives a positive number from the keyboard and uses a functions to obtain the prime factors of this number. for eg, prime factors of 24 are 2,2,2,and 3,whereas prime factors of 35 are 5 and 7.

30. WAP that uses a function that can compute sum of any geometric series.

31. WAP that uses a function that generate every third integer, beginning with i=1 and continuing for all integers that are less than 100. Calculate sum of those integers that are evenly divisible by 5.

32. WAP that uses a function for calculating volume and surface area of a sphere given diameter of the sphere.

33. WAP to print the largest element of an array using a function.

34. WAP that uses a function that takes a double array name and an array size as arguments and that SWAP the first and last value in that array.

35. WAP that uses a function which will accept an array of integers as an argument. it should find and return the smallest element in the array after sorting it. the calling program requires the sorted array. The size of the array can be defined to be a global constant.

36. WAP that uses a function that receive an int array, its size and a character '+' or '-'.by default the character should be '+'.for the character '+',the function returns the sum of positive numbers stored in the array and for the character '-',the function returns the sum of negative numbers stored in the array.

37. WAP that reads a float array having 15 elements. the program uses a function reverse() to reverse this array. make suitable assumptions wherever required.

38. WAP that uses various functions to express the following algebraic formulas in a recursive form:

**a)** $y=(x1+x2+x3+$_____$+xn)$

**b)** $y=1-x+(x^2)/2-(x^3)/6+(x^4)/24+$_____$+(-1)nx^n/n!$

**c)** $p=(f1*f2*f3*$_____$*ft)$

**39.** WAP that uses a function that takes a decimal number as a parameter and returns its octal equivalent.

**40.** WAP that uses a function that takes a decimal number as a parameter and returns its hexadecimal equivalent.

**41.** WAP that uses a function that takes a six digit integer as a parameter. if the number is even, then adds up its digits else multiply the individual digits and returns the result.

**42.** WAP that uses a function to send all -ve elements of an array to the end without altering the original sequence i.e. if array contains 5,-4,3,-2,6,-11,12,-8,9 then the return array will be 5,3,6,12,9,-4,-2,-11,-8

**43.** WAP that uses a function for the binary search algorithm without using recursion technique.

**44.** WAP that uses a function to print the length of a string.

**45.** WAP that uses a function to copy a string into another string.

**46.** WAP using following functions to reverse a string:
a) func1() to reverse string using another array.
b) func2() to reverse string without using another array.

**47.** WAP that uses a function to concatenate two strings.

**48.** WAP that uses a function to a string into uppercase.

**49.** WAP that uses a function to find the first occurrence of a string into another string.

**50.** WAP that uses a function to find the last occurrence of a string into another string.

**51.** WAP that uses a function to compares two strings and returns 0 if the strings are equal and -1 if the strings are unequal.

**52.** WAP that uses two functions, code() and decode(),that accepts a string for an argument. the code() function should modify the argument string adding 1 to all characters in it except the null terminator. the decode() function restores the coded string to its original form. this program should accept a string on the command line, print the string coded, and then print it decoded. if no string is specified on the command line, prompt for none.

53. WAP that uses a function that accept two strings as the arguments and compare them to find the length of the greatest common substring between the two.

54. WAP that uses a function for analyzing a line of text by examining each of the characters and determining into which of several different categories it falls. In particular, we want to count the number of vowels, constants, digits, white space character and other characters.

55. WAP that uses a function that will read characters in a character type array and write the characters backwards into another character array. assume that text contains 80 characters.

56. WAP that uses a function to sort all the elements in an array between the position lb and ub (ib is the lower bound and ub is the upper bound).

57. WAP that uses a function that takes a string as a parameter and returns the frequency, of each character, in that string.

58. WAP that uses a function that takes two strings consisting of maximum 80 characters as parameters. examine both these strings and remove all the common characters from both these strings. display the resultant string in the main function.

59. WAP that uses a function that takes two strings as parameter and return the position of the first occurrence of the first string in the main string and null if not present.

60. WAP that uses function that takes a string as a parameter and replace one or more blank between words by a single blank.

61. WAP that uses function that takes a string as a parameter and set the string such that every sentence should start with an upper case character.

62. WAP that uses function that takes two strings as parameters and compares these strings lexicographically. the function should return -1 or 0 or 1 depending on whether str1 is lexicographically "less than" or "equal to" or "greater than" str2.

63. WAP that uses a function to search for a given word in a dictionary. The dictionary is a lexicographically sorted array of characters strings. use binary search method. you can make use of the standard c library function to compare two strings.

64.  WAP that uses a function that will accept a set os strings and output them in increasing order of lengths of the strings and sorted alphabetically.

65.  WAP that uses a function that takes a string and replace all occurrence of the string "and" in the text by "or" and the modified text should be print by main() function.

66.  WAP that uses a function that will accept a set of names separated by newline and check whether they are written properly. a name should begin with an upper case alphabet, following which each string in a name should begin with an upper case letter. the only non-alphabetic character allowed in a name are "." And '-' (period and hyphen).

67.  WAP that uses that recognizes whether a telephone number is valid or not by checking for the following criterion. a telephone number is a 10 digit string whose first digit is a '0' followed by 2 digits          lying within 1-4.the remaining positions may be occupied by any digit from 0-9,other than the 4th position which can be occupied by any digit from 1-9.

68.  WAP that uses a function called pr_rev() that reads a string input from the keyboard and prints it in reverse. for example, hello would be printed olleh.

69.  WAP that uses a recursive function called print_num() that has one integer argument. it will print the number from 1 to n on the screen, where n is the value of the argument.

70.  WAP that uses a function that calculates factorial of a given number using recursion method.

71.  WAP that uses a function that calculates multiplication of two given numbers using recursion method.

72.  WAP that uses a function that prints the nth element of fibonnicci series using recursion method.

73.  WAP that uses a function that prints the entered string in reverse order using recursion method.

74.  WAP to solve the tower of hanoi problem.

75.  WAP to sort the array using quick sort using recursion technique.

76. WAP that uses a recursive function to convert given decimal number into its binary equivalent.

77. WAP that uses a function for the binary search algorithm using recursion technique.

78. WAP that uses a function to find the determinant value of a matrix.

79. A positive number is entered through the keyboard. Write a function to obtain the prime factors of this number. For e.g., prime factors of 24 are 2,2,2 and 3,whereas prime factors of 35 are 5 and 7.

80. A 5 digit positive integer is entered through the keyboard, write functions to calculate sum of digits of the 5-digit number:

    **1)** without using recursion.
    **2)** using recursion.

81. WAP to use the suitable function to obtain the prime factors recursively.

82. WAP to use the suitable function to generate the first n terms of the fibonnicci sequence recursively.

83. WAP to use the suitable function to find the binary equivalent of a given decimal integer and display it.

84. WAP to use a function that compute the binomial coefficient $n!/((k!)(n-k)!)$

85. WAP to use the function that compute the distance between two points and use it to develop a function that will compute the area of the triangle whose vertices are $a(x1,y1)$, $b(x2,y2)$,and $c(x3,y3)$.use these function to develop a program which returns a value 1 if the point $(x,y)$ lies inside the triangle abc, otherwise a value 0.

86. Given three variables x,y,z write a function to circularly shift their values to right. in other words if x=5,y=8,z=10 after circular shift y=5,z=8 and x=10.call the function with variables a,b,c to circularly shift their values.

The biggest
mistake by most
human beings:
"listening half
,understanding
quarter , telling
double".

# CHAPTER

## ∞ 9 ∞

# (Your Brain on Pointers)

## Introduction-

A pointer is a special variable that is used to store the address of some other variable. A pointer can be used to store the address of a single variable, array, structure, union, or even a pointer.

**Pointers - Why ?**

### Using Pointers allows us to –

- **Achive** call by reference (i.e write functions which change their parameters)

- **Handle** arrays efficiently.

- **Handle** structures (Record) efficiently.

- **Create** linked lists, trees, graphs etc.

- **Put** data onto the heap.

- **Create** tables of functions for handling windows events, signals etc.

- **Already** been using pointers with **scanf()**

- **Care** must be taken when using pointers since there are no safety features.

As **C Programming** is such a low level language it is difficult to do anything without pointers. We have already seen that it is impossible to write a function which alters any of its parameters

**Mind Wash Drill –**

Pointers can also able to writing of linked lists and other such data structure.

The standard library, together with the windows, windows 95 and windows NT

Programming environments use pointers to functions quite extensively.

*Problems with pointers-*

One problem is that pointers have a bad reputation. they are supposed to be difficult to use and difficult to understand.

**The concept of pointers -**

Every variable is stored in the memory, and each memory location has a numeric address. The declaration of the variable-

int a = 5;

Here a is the name of the variable, the value of the variable is 5 while the address of the variable is 100 (assumed).

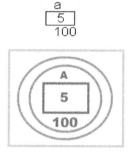

**Mind Wash Drill Table –**

| Declaring Pointers |
| --- |
| 1. Pointers are declared by using star sign **"*"** |
| 2. Declare an integer:   **int I;** |
| 3. Declare a Pointer to an integer: **int *p;** |
| 4. There is some debate as to the position of the **"*"**   **int* p;** |

The first step is to know how to declare a pointer. This is done by using C's multiply character "**\***" (which obviously doesn't perform a multiplication).

The "**\***" is placed at some point between the keyword int and the variable name. Instead of creating an integer, a pointer to an integer is created.

**Mind Wash Drill Table –**

*Both above and below tables will help you to understand the concept of pointers on your fingertips.*

| int | *pi; | /* **pi** is a pointer to an **int** */ |
| long int | *p; | /* **p** is a pointer to a **long int** */ |
| Float* | pf; | /* **pf** is a pointer to a **float** */ |
| char | c, d, *pc; | /* **c** and **d** are a char and **pc** is a pointer to char */ |
| double* | pd, e, f; | /* **pd** is pointer to a double, **e** and **f** are double */ |
| char* | start; | /* **start** is a pointer to a **char** */ |
| char* | end; | /* **end** is a pointer to a **char** */ |

**The declaration of the variable tells the compiler to -**

1.  Reserve space in the memory to hold the integer value.
2.  Associates the name "a" with this memory location.
3.  Stores the value 5 at this location.

**Pointer and the indirection operator –**

*The two fundamental operators used with the pointers are:*

1.  Address operator **&**
2.  Indirection operator **\***

```
main()
{
        int a = 5;
        int *p;             /*pointer declaration*/
        p= &a;              /*copying address of variable a to the pointer p*/
        *p = 10;            /*indirection or use of pointer to
                            change the value of variable a*/
        printf("%d", a);
        printf("%d",*p);
        printf("%d",*(&a));
        }
```

**Mind Wash Drill** - All the printf statements in the above program will give the output as 10. Since the variable p is not an ordinary variable like any other integer variable.

It is A variable which stores the address of some other variable (a in this case). Since p is a variable, the compiler must provide memory to this variable also. Any type of pointer gets two bytes in the memory.

> int *p1;
> float *p2;
> char *p3;
> All pointers p1, p2, p3 get 2 bytes each.

## Memory and pointer -

Suppose if three pointers are declared for int, float, char. All the three pointers will occupy 2 bytes in the memory. This is because all the memory addresses are integer values ranging from 0 to 65536. Thus we can say that a pointer irrespective of its type is storing the addresses as integer values and each integer requires only two bytes.

```
main()
{
        int a = 5,*p1;
        float b=2.5,*p2;
        char c='a',*p3;
        p1= &a;
        p2 = &b;
        p3=&c;
        printf("%d",sizeof(p1));
        printf("%d",sizeof(p2));
        printf("%d",sizeof(p3));
}       output: 2 2 2
```

## Pointers and addresses -

```
main()
{
        int a = 5;
        int *p;
        p= &a;
        *p = 10;
printf("%d", p);  /*prints the address in pointer p as integer */
printf("%u",p);   /*prints the address in pointer p as unsigned integer */
printf("%x",p);   /*prints the address in pointer p as hexadecimal */
printf("%x",p);   /*prints the address in pointer p as hexadecimal */
}               output: -12, 65524, fff4, FFF4
```

176

Let us evaluate the output. The first answer is a negative value this is because the range of pointers is from 0 to 65536 and the variables are allocated memory from top to bottom i.e. from 65536 then 65535, 65534 and so on until 0.

The variable a is stored at address 65524 and if we print the address of variable a which is stored in pointer p using format specifer %d a negative value is printed because the address exceeds the int limit.

if %u is used the address is printed in the form of unsigned integer. %x or %X is used to print the address in hexadecimal form, the only difference is that %x will use alphabets in lowercase while %X will use uppercase alphabets.

**Pointers Expression:-**

Like any other variables, pointer variables can be used in expressions. In a program all the following operations are valid.

1.      C allows us to add or subtract integers from pointers.
         sum= sum +*p1;

2.      Also short hand operators are allowed
         sum+=*p1;
         ans = *p1++;

This will cause the pointer p1 to point to the next value of its type and the dereference the value.

**Let us use an e.g. to illustrate the point:**

```
main( )
{
int a[5]={10,20,30,40,50},*p;
p=a      /*address of array can be pointed into the pointer without
           the use of & operator*/
printf("%d,",*++p);        /*dereferencing the next address*/
printf("%d",++*p);         /*dereferencing the address and adding 1 to
                             the element */

}
```

**output: 20, 21**

**3.**   As well as to subtract one pointer from another.

```
*p1--;
main( )
        {
int a[5]={10,20,30,40,50},*p;
p=a;
printf("%d,",*++p);       /*dereferencing the next address i.e. index 1*/
printf("%d",*p--);        /*dereferencing the index 1 and then the postfix will
                            affect*/
printf("%d",*p); /*dereferencing the pointer*/

}
```
**output:** 20, 20, 10

**4.**   If p1 and p2 are both pointers to the same array, then p2-p1 gives the number of elements between p1 and p2

$$*p3 = *p2 - *p1;$$

**5.** Two pointers can also be compared such as --
          p1>p2
          p1= = p2
          p1! = p2.
These comparisons are useful only while using string or arrays.

**6.** Two pointers cannot be multiplied divided or added.

## Mind Wash Drill –

A *null pointer* is a special pointer value that is known not to point anywhere. It means that no other valid pointer, to any other variable or array cell or anything else, will ever compare equal to a null pointer.

Another way to use a null pointer is, by using any one of the standard header files, including <stdio.h>, <stdlib.h>, and <string.h>. To initialize a pointer to a null pointer, you might use code like-

```
#include <stdio.h>
int *p = NULL;
```

And to test it for a null pointer before inspecting the value pointed to you might use code like -

```
if(p != NULL)
printf("%d\n", *p);
```

It is also possible to refer to the null pointer by using a constant 0, and you will see some code that sets null pointers by simply doing

int *p = 0;

Furthermore, since the definition of "true"' in C is a value that is not equal to 0, you will see code that tests for non-null pointers with abbreviated code like -

```
if(p)
    printf("%d\n", *p);
```

This has the same meaning as our previous example; if(p) is equivalent to if(p != 0) and to if(p != NULL).

## Pointers to pointers –

Pointers store the address of a variable, similarly the address of a pointer can also be stored in some other pointer.

```
main ( )
{
int a=5;
int *p1;               /*pointer to an integer*/
int **p2;              /*pointer to pointer to an integer*/
int ***p3;             /*pointer to pointer to pointer to an integer*/
        p1= &a;
        p2= &p1;
        p3 =&p2;
        printf("%d",a);        /*output = 5*/
        printf("%d",*p1);      /*output = 5*/
        printf("%d",**p2);     /*output = 5*/
        printf("%d",***p3);    /*output = 5*/
        printf("%u",*p2);      /* address of p1 will be printed*/
}
```

## Pointers and Array:

When an array is declared, the compiler allocates a base address and sufficient amount of storage to contain all the elements in the array in continuous locations.

The base address is the location of the first element (index 0) of the array. Suppose we declare the array a as follows:

static int a[5]={10,20,30,40,50};

Suppose the base address of the array a is 100 and because the integers require two bytes each.

| [0] | [1] | [2] | [3] | [4] |
|-----|-----|-----|-----|-----|
| 10  | 20  | 30  | 40  | 50  |

100   102   104   106   108

The name a is defined as a constant pointer pointing the first element a[0] and therefore the value of a is 100, the location where a[0] is stored.

That is a is equal to &a[0] is equal to100.

If we declare the pointer p as an integer pointer, then we can make the pointer p to point to the array a –

p= a;

or

p = &a[0];

Now we can access every value of this array a using p++ to move from one element to another. The relationship between p and a is shown below:

p   is equals to &a[0];   (=100)

p+1 is equals to &a[1];   (=102)

p+2 is equals to &a[2];   (=104)

p+3 is equals to &a[3];   (=106)

p+4 is equals to &a[4];   (=108)

When handling an array we can either use the array index or pointers to access array elements. Thus we can point to the third element of the array as:

a[2] or *(p+2)   (remember the array index starts from 0).

**Pointers and Functions-**

As discussed earlier the function passing the array as a parameter uses call by reference mechanism.

**WAP (Write a program) to swap two numbers.**

| Using call by value: | Using call by reference: |
|---|---|
| ```c
void swap(int ,int);
main( )
{
    int a,b;
    printf("Enter two numbers");
    scanf("%d %d",&a,&b);
    swap(a,b);
    printf("%d %d",a,b);
    getch( );
}
void swap( int, int)
{
    int x,y,t;
    t=x;
    x=y;
    y=t;
}
``` | ```c
void swap(int * ,int*);
main( )
{
    int a,b;
    printf("Enter two numbers");
    scanf("%d %d",&a,&b);
    swap(&a,&b);
    printf("%d %d",a,b);
    getch( );
}
void swap( int * p1, int * p2)
{
    int t;
    t=*p1;
    *p1=*p2;
    *p2=t;
}
``` |

**In the call by reference-**

- The function prototype is declared as pointers.
- The dereference pointers are used in function definition.
- When the function is called, the addresses are passed as actual arguments.

**Common Errors -**

A pointer contains garbage address until it is initialized. If we try to dereference this pointer then it will not give any error, but it will jump to that address and assign the value in that address. This is a logical error which a compiler can not detect.

**Memory Allocation -**

1. Static Memory Allocation.
2. Dynamic Memory Allocation.

The conventional way to use an array is by declaring the array with its size and since the size of array must be a constant so it leads to either wastage or shortage of memory because the array is allotted memory at the time of compilation of the program.

**Mind Wash Drill –**

The memory allocated at the time of compilation is called static memory. These problems can be overcome by the use of pointers. Pointers can be used to allocate memory at the time of execution of the program, *called dynamic memory.*

Thus *dynamic memory* can be described as *the process of allocating memory at run time.* C does not inherently have this facility but they can be included in the program using the header file *alloc.h*

| Functions | Task |
|---|---|
| malloc( ) | Allocates the requested number of bytes and returns the starting address to a pointer. |
| calloc( ) | Allocates the requested number of bytes, initializes them with zero and returns the starting address to a pointer.It allocates the non continous memory. |
| realloc( ) | Reallocates the size by increasing or decreasing the no. of bytes and returns the starting address to a pointer. |
| free() | Frees previously allocated space. |

**Allocating a block of memory(malloc) -**

A block of memory may be allocated using the function malloc. The malloc function reserves a block of memory of specified size and returns a pointer of type void. This means we can assign the base address of the block to any type of pointer. The general syntax of malloc is:

P= (cast type*) malloc(byte size);
    Now let us see an e.g.:

P=(int*)malloc (10 * sizeof(int));

**Here** the function malloc returns an integer type pointer p to an area of memory which has the capacity to store 10 integer numbers. Similarly, the statement

P=(char*)malloc(10*sizeof(char));
          **Or**
P=(char*)malloc(10);                    /*remember each charcter uses one byte*/

182

Allocates 10 bytes of space for the pointer p of character type.

This can be illustrated as:

*Space to store 10 characters*

*Address of first byte*

**malloc** can be used to allocate the space for complex data types such as structure:

> str_p= (struct store *)malloc(sizeof(struct store));
> where str_p is a pointer of type struct sore.

## Mind Wash Drill –

malloc is used allocate the memory of contiguous bytes. The request can fail if the memory space is not sufficient to satisfy the request. If it fails, it returns a NULL.

## Allocating multiple blocks (calloc) -

**Calloc** is also a memory allocation function which is generally used to allocate memory for array and structure. malloc is used to allocate a single block of storage space, calloc allocates multiple blocks of storage, each of same size and initializes them with zero. The general syntax of calloc is:

> P= (cast type*) calloc(n, array size);

Now let us see an **e.g.:**

> P=(int*)calloc (10 , sizeof(int));

The above statement allocates contiguous space for 10 blocks, each of size 2 bytes(since int requires two bytes).

All the bytes are initialized to zero and a pointer gets the starting address of the block allocated. Like malloc here also if the memory request cannot be fulfilled a **NULL** is returned.

**Altering the size of block -**

It is likely that we discover later, that the previously allocated memory is not sufficient and additional space would be required or the allocated memory is quite large than that needed.

In both these cases the size of the block has to be altered this can be achieved by using function realloc (reallocating memory). The general syntax of relloc is:

P= relloc(P, new size);

**Mind Wash Drill –**

**The** new size can be larger or smaller than the previous one. Now let us see an **e.g.** suppose the block for storing 10 integers was allocated using the malloc as :

P=(int*)malloc (10 * sizeof(int));

Now to alter the size so that 5 more numbers can be stored the statement would be:

P= relloc(P, 15);

The function allocates a new memory space of size 15 to the pointer P and returns a pointer to the first byte of the new block.

**Mind Wash Drill –**

Also remember that the new memory block may or may not begin at the same place as the old one.

In such a case it creates a new memory space at some other place, copies all the old data there and returns the block address to the pointer.

**Releasing the used space:**

If the variables are declared at compile time they are destroyed according to their storage classes, but if the dynamic allocation is used it is the duty of the programmer to release the space if not in use.

It is also necessary if the storage space is limited. We can release the memory space if the data at that space is not required by using the function free as: free(p);

1. **WAP** to extract a substring from a string.

```c
#include<stdio.h>
#include<conio.h>
#include<string.h>
main()
{
        char str[20], news[20];
        char *s, *t;
        int pos, n, i;
        printf("Enter the string:");
        scanf("%s",str);
        printf("Enter the position and number of characters to
extract:");
        scanf("%d%d",&pos,&n);
        s=str;
        t=news;
        if(n= =0)
                n=strlen(str);
        s=s+pos-1;
        for(i=0;i<n;i++)
        {
                *t=*s;
                s++;
                t++;
        }
        *t='\0';
        printf("The substring is: %s\n",news);
        getch();
}
```

2. Write a program to sort all the elements of a 4x4 matrix.

```c
int mat[4][4], *arr, i, j, k, t;

printf("Enter the elements of 4x4 matrix:");
/*matrix input*/
for(i=0; i<4; i++)
{
        for(j=0; j<4; j++)
        {
                printf("Enter element %d %d",i+1,j+1);
                scanf("%d",&mat[i][j]);
        }
}
```

```
          /*sort the elements of the matrix*/
    arr = mat; /*Base address of the matrix array*/
    /* Print the matrix as entered using pointer*/
    printf("\nThe matrix formed is...\n");
        for(i=0; i<15; i++)/*number of passes*/
        {
            for(j=i+1; j<16; j++)
            {
                    if(*(arr +i)>*(arr+j))
                    {
                            t = *(arr+i);
                            *(arr+i)= *(arr+j);
                            *(arr+j)=t;

                    }
            }
        }
        /*print the sorted matrix*/
        printf("\n The sorted matrix is:\n");
        for(i=0; i<4; i++)
        {
            for(j=0; j<4; j++)
                    printf("%d",mat[i][j]);
                    printf("\n");
    }

        printf("\n\nPress any key to exit...");
        getch();
    }
```

3.    **WAP** to input any string and delete the extra blanks spaces present in the same.

```
    #include<stdio.h>
    #include<conio.h>
    #include<string.h>
    main()
    {
        static char s1[50];
        char s2[50];
        char *s, *t;
        int i, l;
        printf("Enter a string");
```

```
gets(s1);
s=s1;
t=s2;
l=strlen(s);
for(i=0;i<=l-1;i++)
{
        if(*s= = ' ')/*check for a blank*/
        {
                if(*(s+1)!=' ')
                {
                        *t=*s;
                        t++;
                }
                s++;
        }
        else
        {
                *t=*s;
                t++;
                s++;
        }
}
*t='\0';
printf("Original Statement:%s\n",s1);
printf("Modified Statement:%s",s2);
getch();
}
```

4. Write a program to concatenate 2 strings using pointers. Donot use strcat function.

```
main()
{
        char s1[20],s2[20],*p1,*p2;
        /* Input 1st string*/
        printf("Enter 1st string");
        gets(s1);
        /*Input 2nd string*/
        printf("Enter 2nd string");
        gets(s2);

        /*Assigning address of strings in two pointers*/

        p1 = s1;
        p2 = s2;

        /*Moving pointer 1 to the end of 1st string*/
```

```
        while(*p1 != '\0')
               p1++;
```

/* Adding 2nd string to the end of 1st string*/

```
        while(*p2 != '\0')
               *p1++ = *p2++;
```

/* Adding NULL to the end of string*/

```
        *p1 = '\0';
```

```
        /*Output string after concatenation*/
        puts(s1);
        getch();
}
```

**5. WAP** that receives the month and year from the keyboard as integers and prints the calendar in the following format.

```
        static char *months[ ]= {
                               "January",
                               "February",
                               "March",
                               "April",
                               "May",
                               "June",
                               "July",
                               "August",
                               "September",
                               "October",
                               "November",
                               "December"
                               };
        main()
        {
               static int
        days[12]={31,28,31,30,31,30,31,31,30,31,30,31};
               long int ndays, ldays, tydays, tdays;
               int d, i,   m, fday, y;
               char ch;
               clrscr();
        printf("Enter year(1900 onwards)& month (number):");
        scanf("%d %d",&y,&m);
               ndays = (y-1)*365;
               ldays = (y-1)/4-(y-1)/100+(y-1)/400;
               tdays = ndays+ldays;
```

188

```c
        if((y%100==0&&y%400)||(y%4==0&&y%100!=0))
                days[1]=29;
        else
                days[1]=28;
        d= days[m-1];
        tdays = 0;
        for(i=0; i<m-2; i++)
                tydays = tydays + days[i];

        tdays = tydays + tdays;
        fday = tdays%7;
        cal(y, m, fday, d);
}
cal(int yr, int mo, int fd, int da)
{
        int i, r, c;
        char a;

        clrscr();
        gotoxy(25,2);
        printf("%s %d",months[mo-1],yr);
        gotoxy(5,5);
        printf("--------------------------------------------------");
        gotoxy(10,6);
        printf("Mon Tue Wed Thu Fri Sat Sun");
        gotoxy(5,7);
        printf("--------------------------------------------------");

        r = 9;
        c=11+6*fd;
        for(i=0; i<=da; i++)
        {
                gotoxy(c,r);
                printf("%d",i);
                if(c<=41)
                        c=c+6;
                else
                {
                        c=11;
                        r=r+1;
                }
        }
        gotoxy(5,15);
        printf("--------------------------------------------------");
        printf("\n\n\n\n\nPress any key to exit...");
        getch();
}
```

**6.** Write a program that will read a line and delete from it all occurrences of the word 'the'.

```
main()
{
    char str[80], str2[80];
    char *s,*q,*p;
    int i;
    clrscr();
    printf("\nEnter a sentence not more than 80 chars long:\n");
    gets(str);
        s = str; /*Base address of the string*/
        p = str2; /*Base address of new string*/
    while(*s)
    {
            q = s;
            if(*s=='t'|| *s=='T')
            {
                    s++;
                    if(*s=='h')
                    {
                            s++;
                            if(*s=='e')
                            ;
                            else
                            {
                                    for(i=0; i<=2;i++)
                                        *p++=*q++;
                            }
                    }
                    else
                    {
                            *p++=*q++;
                            s--;
                    }
            }
            else
                    *p++=*s;
                    s++;
    }
        *p='\0';
            printf("\n\nSentence after deleting all occurrences of
    'the' is:\n");
        puts(str2);
    getch();
}
```

# What would be the output of the following program:

**1.**
```
char far *s1,*s2;
printf("%d
%d",sizeof(s1),sizeof(s2));
```
**Output:** 4 2

**2.** Are the expressions *p++ and ++*p same?
**Output:** No.
*p++ increments the pointer and not the value pointed by it, whereas ++*p increments the value being pointed by p.

**3.** Can there be another statement which does the same job as ++*p?

**Output**: (*p)++

**4.** What would be the equivalent pointer expression for referring the same element as a[i][j][k][l]?
**Output:**\*(*(*(*(a+i)+j)+k)+l)

**5.** What would be the output of the following program:
```
int a[]={12, 13, 14, 15, 16};
printf("%d %d %d",
sizeof(a), sizeof(*a),
sizeof(a[0]);
```
**Output:** 10 2 2

**6.** What will be the output of the following program assuming that the array begins at location 1002.
```
int a[3][4]= {1, 2, 3, 4,5, 6, 7, 8,
9, 10, 11, 12};
printf("%u %u %u", a[0]+1,
*(a[0]+1), *(*(a+0)+1));
```
**Output:** 1004 2 2

**7.**In the following program how will you print 50 using p?
```
main()
```

**26.** How would you dynamically allocate 2-D array?
**Output:**
```
#include<alloc.h>
#define MAXROW 10
#define MAXCOL 10
main()
{
    int *p, i, j;
    p=(int *) malloc (MAXROW *
    MAXCOL * sizeof(int));
    /*input in matrix*/
    for(i=0;i<MAXROW;i++)
    {
        for(i=0;i<MAXCOL;i++)
        {
        p[i*MAXCOL+j]=i;
        printf("%d",p[i*MAXCOL+j]);
        }
        printf("\n");
    }
}
```

**27.**How would you dynamically allocate a 2-D array of integers such that we are able to access any element using 2 subscripts, as in a[i][j]?

**Output:**
```
#include<alloc.h>
#define MAXROW 10
#define MAXCOL 10
main()
{
int **p, i, j;
    p=(int **) malloc (MAXROW *
    sizeof(int*));
    for(i=0;i<MAXROW;i++)
    p[i]=(int * )malloc(MAXCOL *
    sizeof(int));
    for(i=0;i<MAXROW;i++)
    {
        for(i=0;i<MAXCOL;i++)
        {
```

```
{
    int a[]={10, 20, 30, 40, 50};
        char *p;
        p=(char*)a;
}
```
**Output:**printf("%d",*((int*)p+4));

**8.**In the following program add a statement in the function *fun()* such that address of *a* gets stored in *j*
```
void fun(int**);
main()
{
        int *j;
        fun(&j);
}
void fun(int **k)
{
        int a=10;
/*add statement here*/
}
```
**Output:** *k=&a;

**9.** How will you declare an array of three function pointers where each function receives two *ints* and returns a *float*?

**Output:** float(*a[3])(int,int);

**10.**Would the following program give a compilation error or warning?
```
        float i=10, *j;
        void *k;
        k=&j;
        j=k;
        printf("%f",*j);
```
**Output:** No. here no typecasting is required while assigning the value to and from k because conversions are applied automatically when other pointer types are assigned to void *.

**11.**Would the following program compile?
```
main()
```

```
        p[i][j] = i;
        printf("%d",p[i][j]);
    }
    printf("\n");
}
}
```

**28.**How would you dynamically allocate a 2-D array of integers such that we are able to access any element using 2 subscripts, as in a[i][j]? Also the rows of the array should be stored in the adjacent memory locations.

**Output:**
```
#include<alloc.h>
#define MAXROW 3
#define MAXCOL 4
main()
{
        int **p, i, j;
p=(int **) malloc (MAXROW *
sizeof(int*));

p[0]=(int *) malloc (MAXROW *
MAXCOL* sizeof(int));

        for(i=0;i<MAXROW;i++)
        p[i]=p[0] + i * MAXCOL;

        for(i=0;i<MAXROW;i++)
        {
                for(i=0;i<MAXCOL;i++)
                {
        p[i][j] = i;
        printf("%d",p[i][j]);
                }
                printf("\n");
        }
}
```
**29.**Would the following code work all the time:
```
        main()
        {
                char *p;
                gets(p);
```

```
        {
                float i=10, *j;
                void *k;
                j=k=&a;
                j++;
                k++;
                printf("%u %u", j,
        k);
        }
```
**Output:** No. An error will be reported in the statement k++ since arithmetic on void pointers is not permitted unless the void pointer is appropriately typecasted.

**12.** Would the following program code compile successfully?
printf("%c", 7["Computer"]);
**Output:** Yes it will print r of Computer.

**13.** What is a null pointer?

**Output:** For each pointer type C defines a special pointer value which is guaranteed not to point to any object or function of that type. Usually, a null pointer constant is used for representing a null pointer is the integer 0.

**14.** Is the NULL pointer same as the uninitialised pointer?

**Output:** No.

**15.** In which header file is the NULL macro defined?

**Output:** In files <stdio.h>

**16.** What is the difference between a null pointer, a NULL macro, the ASCII NUL character and a null string?

**Output:** A null pointer is a pointer which does not point anywhere.

```
                printf("%s",p);
        }
```
**Output:** No, since p is an uninitialised pointer it must be pointing at some unknown location in memory. The string that we type would get stored at the location to which p is pointing thereby overwriting whatever is present at that location.

**30.** The following code is improper though it may work sometimes. How would you improve it:
```
        main()
        {
                char *p1= "Matrix";
                char *p2= "Computers";
                strcat(p1,p2);
                printf("%s",p1);
        }
```
**Output:**
```
        main()
        {
                char p1[25]= "Matrix";
                char *p2= "Computers";
                        strcat(p1,p2);
                        printf("%s",p1);
        }
```

**31.** What would be the output of the second *printf()* in the following program:
```
                #include<alloc.h>
                main()
                {
                        int *p;
                p=(int*)malloc(20);
                printf("%u",p);
                /*suppose it prints 1314*/
                        free(p);
                        printf("%u",p);
                }
```
**Output:** 1314
**32.** To *free()* we only pass the pointer to the block of memory which we want to deallocate. Then how does *free()* know how many bytes it should

A NULL macro is used to represent the null pointer in source code. It has a value 0 associated with it.

The ASCII NUL character has all its bits as 0 but doesn't have any relation with null pointer.

The null string is just another name for an empty string "".

17.What will be the output of the following program?

```
#include<stdio.h>
main()
{
    int a, b=5;
    a= b+NULL;
    printf("%d",a);
}
```
**Output: 5**

18.
```
int a[ ] = {10,20,30,40,50};
int *j;
j = a;
j = j+3;
printf("\n%d",*j);
```
**Output:** 40

19.
```
float a[ ] = {3.24,1.5,2.5,3.5,4.5,5.5};
flaot *j,*k;
j = a;
k = a+4;
j = j*2;
k= k/2;
printf("\n%d %d",*j,*k);
```
**Output:**Error. Because multiplication and division are not allowed on pointers.

20. What will be the output of the following program?
```
#include<stdio.h>
main()
{
    printf("%d %d", sizeof(NULL), sizeof(""));
```

deallocate?

**Output:** In most implementations of *malloc()* the number of bytes allocated is stored adjacent to the allocated block. Hence it is simple for *free()* to know how many bytes to deallocate.

33.What would be the output of the following program:
```
#include<alloc.h>
main()
{
    int *p;
    p=(int*)malloc(20);
    printf("%d",sizeof(p))
;
    free(p);
}
```
**Output: 2**

34.What is the difference between *malloc()* and *calloc()* functions?

**Output:** As against *malloc()*, *calloc()* needs two arguments, the number of elements to be allocated and the size of each element.

**For example,**

```
p=(int*) calloc(10, sizeof(int));
```
would allocate space for a 10 integer array. Additionally, *calloc()* would initialize each element with 0.

35.How much maximum memory can be allocated in a single call to *malloc()*?
**Output:** 64 KB.

36.What should be the output of the following program?
```
main()
{
char a[ ]= "Matrix Computers";
char *b= "Matrix Computers";
```

}
**Output: 2 1**

21.How many bytes are occupied by
*near, far* and *huge* pointers?
**Output:** The *near* pointer is 2 bytes
long and the *far* and *huge* pointers
are 4 bytes long.

22.What would be the output of the
following program:
```
char *f();
main()
{
        char *s;
        s=f();
        printf("%s",s);
}
char * f()
{
char string[30];
strcpy(string, "Matrix Computers");
        return(string);
}
```
**Output:** The output is unpredictable
since string is an auto type of array
and would die when the control goes
back to *main()*. Thus s would be
pointing to an array which no longer
exists.

23.What is the solution of the above
problem?
**Output:**char *f();
```
main()
{
        char *s;
        s=f();
        printf("%s",s);
}
char * f()
{
        static char
string[30];
strcpy(string, "Matrix Computers");
        return(string);
}
```

```
printf("%d %d", sizeof(a), sizeof(b));
printf("\n%d %d", sizeof(*a),
sizeof(*b));
}
```
**Output:16 21 1**

37.For the following statements would
a[3]nd    p[3]    fetch    the    same
character?
        char a[ ]= "Matrix";
        char *p= "Matrix";
**Output:** Yes

38.When are *char a[ ]* and *char *a*
treated as same by the compiler?

**Output:** When using them as formal
parameters while defining a function.

39.    Would the program compile
        successfully:
        main()
        {
        char a[ ]= "Matrix";
        char *p= "Computers";
        a= "Computers";
        p= "Matrix";
        printf("%s %s", a, p);
        }
**Output:** No, because we may assign a
new string to a pointer but not to an
array.

40.What    does    the    following
declaration mean:
        int (*p)[10];
**Output:** p is a pointer to an array of 10
integers.

41.What will be the output of the
following program:
        main()
        {
        char *s[ ]={"Frogs", "Do",
        "Not", Die", "They", "Croak!"};

        printf("%d %d",sizeof(s),

**24.** Does there exist some other solution of the above problem?

**Output:**
```
char *f();
main()
{
        char *s;
        s=f();
        printf("%s",s);
        free(s);
}
char * f()
{
        char *p;
        p=(char*)malloc(30)
        ;
strcpy(p, "Matrix Computers");
        return(p);    }
```

**25.** How would you dynamically allocate 1-D array?

**Output:**
```
#include<alloc.h>
#define SIZE 10
main()
{
int *p,i;
p=(int *) malloc (SIZE *
sizeof(int));
/*input in array*/
        for(i=0;i<SIZE;i++)
                {
                p[i]=i;
        /*printing elements*/
                printf("%d",p[i]);
                }
}
```

```
sizeof(s[0]);
}
```
**Output: 12 2**

**42.** What is the difference in the following declaration:

```
char *p= "Matrix";
char a[ ]= "Matrix";
```

**Output:** Here *a* is an array big enough to hold the string and '\0' following the string. Individual characters within the array can be changed but the address of the array will remain same. On the other hand, *p* is a pointer, initialized to point to a string constant. The pointer *p* may be modified to point to another string, but if you attempt to modify the string at which *p* is pointing the result is undefined.

**43.** If int s[5] is a one-dimensional array of integers, which of the following refers to third element in the array?

a) *(s +2)
b) *(s +3)
d) s + 3
e) s + 2

**Output: a) *(s +2)**

# CHAPTER
## ∞ 10 ∞
# (Your Brain on Structure & Union)
# (Enum, Bit Fields, Typedef)

## Introduction-

Arrays are the preferred method of storing objects of the same data type. In addition to array three more derived data types that can be used to store information: structure, unions, bit fields, typedef and enumerator. Unlike array these can be used to store the data of same or different type.

**Structure -**

A Structure can be defined as a derived data type which can represent several different types of data in a single unit. Each individual data item within the structure is referred to as member.

Structure is the method of packing the data of different types to organize the data in a more meaningful way. A structure definition creates a format that may be used to declare structure variable.

A Structure definition is specified by using the keyword struct. This is followed by braces enclosing the members and there data types.

**e.g.:**

```
struct student              /*definition of structure*/
{
int roll;                   /*members*/
char name [10 ];
float per;
}s1,s2;                     /*objects or variables of the structure student*/
```

The members of the structure are not variables and so no memory is allocated to them. They are allowed space in the memory only when the objects are declared. (e.g. s1 and s2).

**Mind Wash Drill-**

**The keyword struct** declares a structure student which holds three different details namely roll, name, marks. These fields are called *members or elements* of a structure. This structure is named as student, the name is called as *structure tag.*

Variable/Object declaration -
**struct student s1,s2;**

The variables of the structure can be declared along with the definition as :

```
struct student
{
        int roll;
        char name[50];
        float marks;
}s1,s2;
```

**Points to be noted about structure -**

1.    The structure definition ends with a semicolon.

2.    While the entire definition is considered as a statement, each member is declared independently for its name and type in a separate statement inside the definition (also called as template)

3.    The tag name can be declared with the structure definition or even later in the main function.

4.    The memory is allotted to the variables and not to the members of a structure.

## Using the members -

In an array we can access individual elements of the array using a subscript operator [ ].

Structures use a different scheme. It uses a dot or period operator (.). So to refer to marks in the above structure:

### s1.marks

Here the variable name is given before the dot and the name of the member after that.

## Mind Wash Drill-

The elements of a structure are always stored in contiguous memory locations.

```
struct student
{
        int roll;
        char grade;
        int marks;
};
        main( )
{
        struct student s1={2, 'A', 89};
        printf("Address of roll=%u",&s1.roll);
        printf("Address of grade=%u",&s1.name);
        printf("Address of marks=%u",&s1.marks);
}
```

Here the output of the program:

Address of roll=65518

Address of grade=65520

Address of marks=65521

| S1.roll | s1.grade | s1.marks |
|---------|----------|----------|
| 2 | A | 89 |

| 65518 | 65520 | 65521 |

**Structure using array -**

```
struct student
{
        int roll;
        char name[50];
        int marks;
};
        main( )
{
        struct student s1;
        printf("Enter the data for student:");
        scanf("%d %s %d",&s1.roll,s1.name,&s1.marks);
        printf("Rollnumber=%d,\nname=%s\nmarks=%d",s1.roll,
        s1.name,s1.marks);
}
```

In the above structure definition an array is used to store the name of the student. While the scanf always contains & before variable name but the string does not have & operator.

**Array of structures -**

```
struct student
{
        int roll;
        char name[50];
        int marks;
}s[10];
```

The above definition uses an array of objects to store the data of 10 students

**Structure Initialize -**

```
struct student s1={1,"ajay",75.5};
struct student s2[3]={{1,"ajay",75.5}, {2,"vijay",75.5},{1,"akash",75.5}};
```

**Mind Wash Drill-**

If we initialize only some members of a structure then others will be automatically initialized to zero.

**Structures within Structure (Nested Structure) -**

Structure within structure is called nesting of structures. When object of a structure is the member of another structure.

```
struct date
{
        int d;
        int m;
        int y;
};
        struct employee
{
        int id;
        struct date dob;
        struct date doj;
}e1;
        main()
{
        printf("Enter id of a employee");
        scanf("%d",e1.id;
        printf("Enter date of birth");
        scanf("%d%d%d",&e1.dob.d, &e1.dob.m,&e1.dob.y);
        .
        .
        .

}
```

**Mind Wash Drill-** In the above example we can also define the structure date inside the definition of structure employee.

## Structure and Pointers -

```
struct student s1,*p;
p = &s1;
s1.roll = 5;
(*p).roll = 7;
        or
p->roll = 7;
printf("%d",s1.roll);      /* This will print 7.
```

## Mind Wash Drill-

Dot(.) operator is used to when we access a member of a structure through an object. (Object.member)

Arrow(->) operator is used when we access a member of structure through a pointer. (Pointer->member)

```c
struct box
{
        int feet;
        int inches;
};
        void swap(struct box *, struct box *)
        main()
{
        struct box b1,b2;
        clrscr();
        /*Input first object*/
        printf("Enter height in feet & inches of box 1");
        scanf("%d%d",&b1.feet,&b1.inches);
        /*Input second object*/
        printf("Enter height in feet & inches of box 2");
        scanf("%d%d",&b2.feet,&b2.inches);
        swap(&b1,&b2);
printf("After swap height of 1ST box- %d feet %d inches\n",b1.feet, b1.inches);
printf("After swap height of 2ND box- %d feet %d inches\n",b1.feet, b1.inches);
        getch();
}
void swap(struct box *p1, struct box *p2)
{
        int t;
        /*swapping feets*/
        t = p1->feet;
        p1->feet = p2->feet;
        p2->feet = t;
        /*swapping inches*/
        t = p1->inches;
        p1->inches = p2->inches;
        p2->inches = t;
}
```

## Union -

Union are also derived data types. They are also used to group together a number of variables. But the difference is that all the members of the union share the same memory location, therefore only one member of the union is can store valid value at one time. A union is a variable that is used to store data of different types at different times.

The union is much like a structure. The different variables defined in the union are called members of the union. They need not be of the same data type. If one member contains a value and another member is assigned a value then the first value will be overlapped by the second value. The compiler allocates enough memory to hold the largest member of the union. Since the memory space is shared, this is a way to save the memory.

**Syntax:**

```
union <union type name>
{
        <type> <variable names> ;
        ...
} [<union variables>] ;
```

**e.g.:**

```
union data
{
        char c;          /*member declaration*/
        int i;
        long l;
        float f;
}d1,d2;
```

**Mind Wash Drill-**
In the above example d1 and d2 will get 4 bytes each because the highest member of the union is of 4 bytes. If there are more than one highest byte member then only on will be considered.

**Mind Wash Drill-** In the above declaration, union is a keyword.

**Mind Wash Drill-** The dot operator is used to access the members of the union. For e.g. to access the members of the above union

```
d.c= 'a';
d.i= 10;
d.l= 65534;
d.f= 72.456;
```

If you store something in the f member of this union and then access the i member, the value of i is unpredictable.

## Difference between Structure and Union -

|  | Structure | Union |
|---|---|---|
| 1. | Keyword is struct. | Keyword is union. |
| 2. | Object of a structure will get memory equal to the sum of memory of all the members. | Object of a union will get memory equal to the memory of highest member of the union. |
| 3. | All the members can be used simultaneously. | Only one member can store valid value. |

### Enumerated Data Type -

An enumerated data type is a data type with user specified constant values. The syntax is similar to that of structure or union: It is used to define constants. The keyword is enum. It is followed by enumerator type. A list of names that are permissible values for this data type. The values are enclosed in braces and separated by commas.

### Examples –

1.

enum bool{FALSE ,TRUE};    /*false and true are constants with values 0 & 1. this numbering is done automatically*/

enum bool b1,b2;    /*objects of enum bool*/
b1=FALSE;
or
b1=TRUE;

2.

enum dow{SUN,MON,TUE=5,WED,THU,FRI,SAT};
/*automatic numbers will be SUN=0,MON=1,TUE=5,WED=6 & so on*/

3.

/*enum declaration*/
enum color{blue, green, red, yellow};
enum color c1,c2;

/*assigning values*/
c1 = red;
c2 = green;

**4.**

```
/*enum declaration*/
enum color{blue, green, red, yellow}c1,c2;

/*assigning values*/
c1 = red;
c2 = green;
```

**5.**    enum color {blue=10, green=15, red=25, yellow=30};
If we do not want default values 0,1,2… then we can itself assign the values.

Declaring an enumerated type does not allocate storage but only describes the user specified data type and associated integer constants with the values given in the braces. By default, the first value assigned value 0, second value with 1, third value with 3,and so on.

**Mind Wash Drill-** We can give duplicate values also in a union.

**Mind Wash Drill-** We can provide floating numbers in a union.

**Bit Fields -**

If in a program a variable is to store only two values1 or 0, we need only one bit to store it. Similarly if the variable is to store values from 0 to 3, then only two bits are required because the binary of all the numbers from 0 to 3 is of two bits. And if the values vary from 0 to 7, then four bits are required.

But if we store an integer then 2 bytes will be used, thus wasting a lot of memory because there is no data type which deals with the bits. However when there are several variable having values which can be packed into a single memory location, we can use 'bit fields'.

Suppose we want to store the following data about an member of a club. Each member can have following data:

  **1.**   Male or Female.
  **2.**   Married or Un Married or Widow or Divorce.
  **3.**   Have any one of the eight hobbies (Cricket, Football etc.).
  **4.**   Can choose from any of the sixteen schemes (Yearly scheme, monthly scheme, etc.)

If we store 0 or 1 in gender in place of Male, Female then this will save some bytes. In the same way the other values can be converted in numbers.

This means we need one bit to store gender, two bits to store, marital status, three bits to store hobby, four bits to store the schemes. Thus in together we need 10 bits altogether, so we can pack all this above information in two bytes.

Thus the declaration will be a follows:

```
struct employee
{
        int gender:1;
        int mar_status:2;
        int hobbies:3;
        int scheme:4;
};
```

The colon in the above declaration tells the compiler that we are talking about bit fields and the number after it tells the no. of bits allotted to each variable.

## Typedef -

C provides the typedef construct, which lets the programmer provide a synonym (same name) for either a built in or user defined data type. Typedef is like a nick name given to a data type. The program becomes easy to trace and understand. The general use of typedef is:

                typedef oldtypename newtypename;
   **e.g.**
                typedef int age;

Here the age becomes a synonym for int. So we can substitute age for int.

                age a1,a2;
                     **or**
                int a1,a2;

Now age can be used to define the int variable a1 and a2.

## Mind Wash Drill-
In the syntax of typedef. First comes the keyword typedef, then the data type, and last the user provided name for this data type.

A typedef is used only to create a synonym for a data type. In a typedef, no variables may be defined and no storage is allotted.

For eg. it is an error to write:

Typedef int age a1,a2;  /*invalid*/

```
Typedef using structure:
typedef struct student
{
        int roll;
        char name[50];
        int marks;
}st;
main( )
{
        st s1,s2;
            or
        struct student s1,s2;
}
```

The typedef name can be the same as the tagname of the structure.

**Typedef and code portability:**

The typedef can be used to promote code portability.

Suppose that we have an application that assumes that all integers are represented by 16-bit storage cells. On computer system A, an int may use 32 bits, on another system B int may use 16 bits.
Thus,

```
/* on computer system A*/
/*integer has 16 bits*/
typedef short int INTEGER;

/*on computer system B*/
/*integer has 32 bits*/
typedef  int INTEGER;
```

**Throughout** the program we may use INTEGER instead of short int in the declaration of variables. This typedef could be put in a file such as port.h then included in the files that need integer variables.

# Fill in the Blanks -

1. _ is a heterogeneous collection of variables grouped as a single unit.
2. _____ gives a blue print for a structure.
3. Memory is allocated for structure only when the _____ is declared.
4. A member element of a structure can be assessed through ___&___.
5. A pointer to a structure can be declared as _____.
6. structures improve the _____ of the program.
7. structures find their use in _____.
8. size of a structure is _____.
9. A collection of heterogeneous objects that remain unrelated called _.
10. All the members of a union share the same _____.
11. Size of the union is _____ .
12. typedef is used to create _____.
13. syntax of typedef is _____.

## Answers –

| | | | |
|---|---|---|---|
| 1. | structure | 8. | sum of all the data members and sub-members. |
| 2. | struct | | |
| 3. | objects | 9. | union |
| 4. | . (period) or -> (arrow operator) | 10. | memory space |
| | | 11. | largest memory space required by one of its members. |
| 5. | struct      tag_name *ptr_to_pointer | 12. | new data type names |
| 6. | readability | 13. | typedef <name> <new name> |
| 7. | system programming | | |

## Some Solved Problems:-

1. Write a program that compares two given dates. To store a date use a structure that contains three members namely date, month and year. If the dates are equal then display the message as "Equal" otherwise "Unequal".

```
struct date
{
        int day, month, year;
};
int check_date(struct date *dt)
main()
{
        int chkdt;
        /*The dates to be compared*/
        struct date d1, d2;
```

208

```c
            /*input the dates to be compared*/
            printf("\nEnter the dates to be compared:");
            chkdt = check_date(&d1);
            if(chkdt == 0)
                    exit();
            fflush(stdin);
            chkdt = check_date(&d2);
            if(chkdt == 0)
                    exit();
            /* Compare the two structures*/
if((d1.day == d2.day)&& (d1.month == d2.month)&&(d1.year == d2.year))
                    printf("\nDate are Equal");
            else
                    printf("\nDate are Unequal");
            getch();
    }
    /*Function to check the date entered*/
    int check_date(struct date *dt)
    {
            printf("\nEnter date(dd)");
            scanf("%d",&dt->day);
            printf("\nEnter month(mm)");
            scanf("%d",&dt->month);
            printf("\nEnter date(yyyy)");
            scanf("%d",&dt->year);
    if((dt->day >31 || dt->day<0) || (dt->month >12 || dt->month < 0) ||
                    (dt->year > 9999 || dt->year < 1000))
            {
                    printf("\nImproper date entered");
                    return(0);
            }
            else
                    return(1);
    }
```

# What would be the output of the following programs?

## 1) 
```
main( )
{
    struct message
    {
        int n;
        char mess1[50];
        char mess2[50];
    }m;
    m.n = 1;
    strcpy(m.mess1,"you can win");
    strcpy( m.mess2, "If you believe");

    /*assume that the structure is located
    at address 2005*/

    printf("\n%u %u
    %u".&m.num,m.mess1,m.mess2);
}
```
**Output:** The address will gets printed of each structure member variable.

## 2)
```
struct gos
{
    int n;
    char mess1[50];
    char mess2[50];
}m1={2, "If you are driven by
success","make sure that it is a quality
drive" };
    main( )
    {
        struct gos m2,m3;
        m2 = m1;
        m3 = m2;
        printf("\n%d %s
%s",m1.n,m2.mess1,m3.mess2);
    }
```

**Output:** 2 If you are driven to by success make sure it is quality drive. Because the object structure 'm1'is initialize when structure is created. And in the main program two other object m2 and m3 is created and m1 is

## 4.
```
main()
{
    struct emp
    {
        char name[20];
        int age;
        float sal;
    };
    struct emp e={"Matrix"};
    printf("%d %f ",e.age,e.sal);
}
```
1. 0.000000
2. Garbage value
3. Error
4. None of the above

**Soution:0.000000**

**Explanation:** When an automatic structure is partially initialized, the remaining elements of the structure are initialized to 0.

## 5.
```
struct emp
{
    char name[20];
    int age;
}
fun (int aa)
{
    int bb;
    bb=aa*aa;
    return(bb);
}
main()
{
    int a;
    a=fun(20);
    printf("\n%d",a);
}
```
**Explanation:** The semicolon at the end of the structure definition is missing, the compiler believes that the fun() would return

210

| | |
|---|---|
| copied in m2 and then m2 is copied in m3 so m1 is copied in m2 and m3 and when there will be same output as printing member of m1. There will be no effect in output to change the member in printf( ).<br><br>An object can be assign in another but can't used in other operations.<br><br>3　　　main()<br>　　　　{<br>　　　　　　union a<br>　　　　　　{<br>　　　　　　　　int i;<br>　　　　　　　　char ch[2];<br>　　　　　　};<br>　　　　　　union a z=512;<br>printf("%d %d",z.ch[0],z.ch[1]);<br>　　　　　}<br>**Output:0 2　binary of 512**<br>is(00000010 00000000) | something of the type struct emp, where as in reality it is attempting to return an int. this causes a mismatch, hence an error results.<br><br>6.　　　f(struct emp);<br>　　　　struct emp<br>　　　　{<br>　　　　　　char name[20];<br>　　　　　　int age;<br>　　　　};<br>　　　　main()<br>　　　　{<br>　　　　　　struct emp e=<br>　　　　　　{"matrix", 30};<br>　　　　　　f(e);<br>　　　　}<br>　　　　f (struct emp ee)<br>　　　　{<br>printf("%s %d",ee.name,ee.age);<br>　　　　}<br>**Explanation:** Error occurs which can be rectified by declaring the structure before the declration of the function f( ). |

**Question-**What is the similarity between structure, union and enum?
**Answer:** All of them let us define a new data type.

**Question-**Would the following declaration work:

```
typedef struct s
{
        int a;
        float b;
}s;
```
**Answer:**　　　**Yes**

**Question-**Can a structure contain a pointer to itself:
**Answer:** Yes, such structures are known as self referential structures.

**Question-**Point out the error if any in the following code

```
typedef struct
{
```

```
        int data;
        NODEPTR link;
    }*NODEPTR;
```

**Answer:** A *typedef* defines a new name for a type, in this case however the error is that a *typedef* cannot be used until it is defined. in the given code fragment the *typedef* declaration is not yet defined at the point where the link field is declared.

**Question-**How will you eliminate the above problem?
**Answer:** To fix this problem, first a name ( "struct node") must be given to the structure. Then declare the link field as a simple *struct node* * as shown below:

```
    typedef struct node
    {
            int data;
            NODEPTR link;
    }*NODEPTR;
```

**Another way** to eliminate the problem is to disentangle the *typedef* declaration from the structure definition shown below:

```
    struct node
    {
            int data;
            NODEPTR link;
    };
    typedef struct node *NODEPTR;
```

Yet another way to eliminate the problem is to precede the structure declaration with a *typedef,* in which case you should use the NODEPTR *typedef* when declaring the link field as shown below:

```
    typedef struct node *NODEPTR;
    struct node
    {
            int data;
            NODEPTR link;
    };
```

In this case, you declare a new *typedef* name involving *struct node* even though *struct node* has not been completely defined yet; this you are allowed to do.

**Question-**
```
void modify(struct emp*)
{
char name[20];
int age;
};
main()
{
struct emp e= {"Sanjay", 35}
modify(&e);
printf("%s %d", e.name, e.age);
}
void modify(struct emp *p)
    {
strupr(p->name);
p->age=p->age+2;
    }
```
**Answer:** The *struct emp* is mentioned in the declaration of the function *modify()* before defining the structure. To solve the problem just declare the function before after declaration of the structure or just add the statement *struct emp* before the prototype.

**Question-**
Would the following code work:
```
#include<alloc.h>
struct emp
    {
int len;
char name[1];
};
        main()
{
char newname[ ]= "Rahul";
struct emp *p= (struct emp *) malloc(sizeof(struct emp) – 1 +
                                    strlen(newname)+1
                );
p->len=strlen(newname);
strcpy(p->name, newname);
printf("%d %s",p->len, p->name);
}
```
**Answer:** Yes, the program allocates space for the structure with the size adjusted so that the name field can hold the requested name (not just one character as the structure declaration would suggest).

**Question-**Can there be a better way to write the above program?
**Answer:** The best way to implement the problem is to use a character pointer instead of an array as shown below:

```
#include<alloc.h>
struct emp
{
        int len;
        char *name;
};
main()
{
        char newname[ ]= "Rahul";
        struct emp *p= (struct emp *) malloc(sizeof(struct emp));

        p->len=strlen(newname);
        p->name= malloc(p->len)+1;
        strcpy(p->name, newname);
        printf("%d %s",p->len, p->name);
}
```

**Obviously** the "convenience" of having the length and the string stored in the same block of memory has now been lost, and freeing instances of this structure require two calls to the function *free()*.

**Question-**How would you free the memory allocated in above question?
**Answer:**          free(p->name);
                     free(p);

**Question-** What would be the output of the following program?
```
        main()
                {
        struct emp
                {
                char *n;
                int age;
                };
        struct emp e1= { "David", 23};
        struct emp e2=e1;
        strupr(e2,n);
        printf("%s",e1.n);
                }
```
**Answer:** David

        When a structure is assigned, passed, or returned, the copying is done monolithically. This means that the copies of any pointer fields will point to the same place as the original.

        In other words, anything pointed to is not copied. Hence, on changing the name through e2.n it automatically changed e1.n

**Question-** Point out the error if any in the following code:

```
main()
{
        struct emp
        {
                char n[20];
                int age;
        };
        struct emp e1= { "David", 23};
        struct emp e2=e1;
        if(e1= =e2)
                printf("The structures are equal");
}
```

**Answer:** Structures cannot be compared using the built in = = and != operators. This is because there is no single, good way for a compiler to implement structure comparison. A single byte by byte comparison the bits present in unused paddings in the structure (such padding is used to keep the alignment of later fields correct). A field by field comparison might require unacceptable amounts of repetitive code for large structures. Also, any compiler generated comparison could not be expected to compare pointer fields appropriately in all cases; for example, it's often appropriate to compare *char** fields with *strcmp()* rather than with = =.

**Question-**How would you check whether the contents of two structure variables are same or not?

**Answer:** struct emp

```
{
        char n[20];
        int age;
};
main()
{
        struct emp e1= { "David", 23};
        struct emp e2;
        scanf("%s %d",e2.n, &e2.age);
        if(structcmp(e1, e2)= =0)
                printf("The structures are equal");
        else
                printf("Structures are unequal");
}
structcmp( struct emp x, struct emp y)
{
        if(strcmp(x.n, y.n)= = 0)
                if(x.age= = y.age)
                        return(0);
        return(1);
}
```

In short, if you need to compare two structures, you will have to write your own function to do so which carries out the comparison field by field.

**Question-**How are structure passing and returning implemented by the compiler?

**Answer:** When structures are passed as arguments to functions, the entire structure is typically pushed on the stack. To avoid this overhead many programmers often prefer to pass pointers to structures instead of actual structures. Structures are often returned from functions in a location pointed by an extra, compiler supplied 'hidden' argument to the function.

**Question-** How can I read/write structures from/to data files?

**Answer:** To write out a structure we can use *fwrite()* as shown below:

> fwrite(&e, sizeof(e),1,fp);

where *e* is a structure variable. A corresponding *fread()* invocation can read the structure back from a file.

On calling ***fwrite()*** it writes out ***sizeof(e)*** bytes from the address *&e*. Data files written as memory images with *fwrite()*, however, will not be portable, particularly if they contain floating point fields or pointers. This is because memory layout of structures is machine and compiler dependent.

Different compilers may use different amount of paddings, and the sizes and byte orders of fundamental types vary across machines. Therefore, structures written as memory images cannot necessarily be read back in by programs running on other machines (or even compiled by other compilers), and this is an important concern if the data files you're writing will ever be interchanged between machines.

**Question-**If the following structure is written to a file using *fwrite()*, can *fread()* read it back successfully?

```
struct emp
{
        char *n;
        int age;
};
struct emp e = {"Sujay", 15};
FILE *fp;
fwrite(&e, sizeof(e), 1,fp);
```

**Answer:** No, since the structure contains a *char* pointer while writing the structure to the disk using *fwrite()* only the value stored in the pointer *n* would get written (and not the string pointed by it). When this structure is read back the address would be read back but it is quite unlikely that the desired string would be present at this address in memory.

**Question-**Would the following program always output the size of the structure as 7 bytes?

```
struct ex
{
        char ch;
        int i;
        long int a;
};
```

**Answer:**
No, a compiler may leave holes in structures by padding the first *char* in the structure with another byte just to ensure that the integer that follows is stored at an even location.

Also there might be two extra bytes after the integer to ensure that the long integer is stored at an address which is a multiple of 4.

This is done because many machines across values in memory more efficiently when the values are appropriately aligned. Some machines cannot perform unaligned accesses at all data be appropriately aligned.

Your compiler may provide an extension to give you control over the packing of structures ( i.e., whether they are padded), perhaps with a *#pragma*, but there is no standard method.

If you are worried about wasted space, you can minimize the effects of padding by ordering the members of a structure from largest to smallest. You can sometimes get more control over size and alignment by using bitfields, although they have their own drawbacks

**Question-**       main()

```
{
        struct a
        {
                category:5;
                scheme: 4;
        };
        printf("size = %d", sizeof(struct a));
}
```

**Answer**: size= 2

Since we have used bit fields in the structure and the total number of bits is turning out to be more than 8 (9 bits to be precise) the size of the structure is being reported as 2 bytes.

# Lab Exercise – (WAP- Write a Program)

1. WAP to store information of 10 employees and to display information of an employee depending upon the employee number input from the user.

2. WAP to accept and print a student's result using a structure.

3. WAP that uses a function that takes two date (day, month, year) structure objects as arguments and returns the structure with later date.

4. WAP that uses a structure called point(x, y co-ordinates) to model a point. Define three points, and have the user input values to two of them. Then set the third point equal to the sum of the other two, and display the value of the new point. Interaction with the program might look like this: Enter co-ordinates for p1: 2 3 enter coordinates for p2: 6 8 coordinates of p1+p2 are: 8 11

5. WAP to add given number of days to a given date. Make use of structures wherever possible.

6. Give necessary declarations for an array of 20 voter records, each record of which consists of four data values viz. Id-no, name, address, age. Make use of above declarations to write a program segment that prints id-no., name for all those voters whose age exceeds 60. (Assuming suitable data types.)

**Engineering Students True Story**

Our Exam Syllabus : 80GB

We Read : 80 MB

Keeps on Mind : 80 KB

Write on Exam Hall : 80 Bytes

And The Exam Result Will Come On Binary Digit

00, 01, 10, 11......

# CHAPTER
# ∞ 11 ∞
# (Console Input and Output in C)

# Introduction-

### getchar Function (Single character Input) -

getchar( ) is used to enter a single character into the computer. The getchar function is a part of the standard C input/output library. It returns a single character from a standard input device (typically a keyboard). The function does not require any arguments.

**Syntax:-**        Character variable = getchar( );

### putchar Function (Single character output) -

This function is used to transmit a single character to a standard output device (typically monitor).

It is also a part of the standard C I/O library. The character being transmitted will normally be represented as a character-type variable. It must be expressed as argument to the function, enclosed in parentheses, following the word putchar.

**Syntax:-**        putchar(character variable);

## The scanf Function (Entering input data) -

This function can be used to enter any combination of numerical values, single characters and strings. scanf( ) enters data from the standard input device and stores it in the computer's memory. This function returns the number of data items that have been entered successfully. Syntax:- cnt=scanf( "control string", arg1,arg2,arg3......argn);

Where the value of cnt will be number of successful input & Control string is a string for formatting, and arg1,arg2..... are arguments that represent the individual input data items. The arguments are written as variables or arrays, whose types match the corresponding character groups in the control string. Each variable name must be preceded by an ampersand (&).

## The printf Function (Writing Output data) -

This function can be used to output any combination of numerical values, single characters and strings.its purpose is to display data . printf( ) move data from the computer's memory to the standard output device.

**Syntax:-** printf("control string",arg1,arg2.........argn);

**Here control string** refers to a string that contains formatting information, and arg1,arg2. are arguments that represent the individual output data items.

The control string can include a flag, which affects the appearance of the output. The flag must be placed immediately after percent sign(%). Some commonly used **flags are:**

**(-)** :- Data item is left justified within the field (blank spaces required to fill theminimum field width will be added after the data item rather than before the data item)

**(+)** :- A sign (either + or -) will precede each signed numerical data item. Without this flag, only negative data items are preceded by a sign.

**(0)** :- causes leading zeros to appear instead of leading blanks. Applies only to data items tha are right justified within a field whose minimum size is larger than the data item.

**(' ')** **(blank space):-** A blank space will precede each positive signed numerical data item. This flag is overridden by the + flag if both are present.

**(#)** **(with o- and x- type conversion):-** causes octal and hexadecimal data items to be precede by o and ox,respectively.

**#** **(with e-, f- and g- type conversion):-** causes a decimal point to be present in all a floating-point numbers, even if the data item is a whole number.

220

## Optional format specifiers:

1.  The field width specifer tells printf( ) how many columns on the screen should be used while printing a value. **For e.g.**

    int a=5;
    printf("%10d",a);

    would give integer a a field width of 10 columns. Since the value cannot occupy the complete 10 columns, it will be right aligned leaving blank spaces on the left side.

    **Thus output will be:**
                        5
2.  if a minus sign is given with the format specifiers:
    int a=5;
    printf("%-10d",a);
    would mean that the output should be left aligned leaving space at the right. Show that output resulting from each of the following printf statements if the declaration is:
    **float a=2.5, b=0.00005, c=3000;**

**(i)**   printf ("%f %f %f", a, b, c);
                output: 2.500000 0.000050 3000.000000
        **Note** that each float number uses six places after decimal point.

**(ii)**  printf ("%8f %8f %8f", a, b, c);
                output: 2.500000e+00=5.000000e-05 3.000000e+03

**(iii)** printf ("%e %e %e" , a, b, c);
                output: 2.5000e+00   5.0000e-05 3.000e+03

**(iv)**  printf ("%12.4e %12.4e %8.3e" , a, b, c);
                output: 2.500000 +0.000050 %ø8f

**(v)**   printf ("%-8f %+8f %ø8f" , a, b, c);
                output: 2.500000 +0.000050 %ø8f

**(vi)**  printf ("%#8f %8f %8f" , a, b, c);
                output: 2.500000 0.000050 3000.000000

**(vii)** printf ("%g %g %g", a, b, c);
                output: 2.5 5e-05 3000

**(viii)** printf ("%#g %#g %#g", a, b, c);
                output: 2.50000 5.00000e-05 3000.00

**Example:**

Here is a simple program that defines the use of flags with integer and floating-point quantities, decimal, octal ,hexadecimal numbers ?

```
#include<stdio.h>
#include<conio.h>
main( )
{
        int i =123;
        float x=12.0, y=-3.3;
        int p=1234,q = 01777, r=0xa08c;
        printf(":%6d %7.0f  %10.1e:\n\n",i,x,y);
        printf(":%-6d %-7.0f %-10.1e:\n\n",i,x,y);
        printf(":%8u %8o %8x\n\n",p,q,r);
      printf(":%-8u %-8o %-8x\n\n",p,q,r);
}
```
**output:**

| : | 123  | 12   | -3.3e+00: |
|---|------|------|-----------|
| : | 123  | 12   | -3.3e+00: |
| : | 1234 | 1777 | a08c:     |
| : | 1234 | 1777 | a08c:     |

## gets( ) function and puts( ) function:-

These function are used to facilitate the transfer of strings between the computer and the standard input/output devices. Each of these functions accepts a single argument. The argument must be a data item that represents a string. The string may include white space characters.

**Gets( )** is used to get a string from keyboard (standard input).
**Puts( )** is used to put a string on standard output.

**Syntax:**

```
        gets(character_string variable);
        puts(character_string variable);
        #include<stdio.h>
        main( )
        {
                char line[20];
                gets(line);
                puts(line);
        }
```

# What would be the output of the following programs?

1. 
```
main( )
{
    char ch;
    ch = getchar( );
    if( islower( ch))
    putchar(toupper (ch));
    else

    putchar(tolower(ch));
}
```
Output: It will convert small letter to capital and capital to small. Means if you input 'a' the output will be 'A' and if you will 'A' then the output will be 'a'.

2. 
```
main( )
{
    int i = 2;
    float f = 2.5367;
    char str[ ] = "Life is like that";
printf( \n%4d\n3.3f\n%4s",i,f,str);
}
```

Output: ---2(3 spaces before 2 because here i gets printed in 4 columns width) --3.536(2 spaces before the num and num will print with 3 floating places.)

is like that.(because str contains more than 4 character so it will neglect the maximum length and print the whole str.)

3. 
```
main()
{
    int a=250;
    printf("%1d", a);
}
```

Output: 250

6. 
```
main( )
{
    printf("More often than
    \b\b not \r the person
    who \
    wins is the one who thinks
    he can!");
}
```
Output:    the    person    who wins is the one who thinks he can!.
Because control print the message in printf from left to right and when \b is encounter it moves the cursor one character and when the \r is encounter it moves the cursor to the beginning of the current line and the print the next message that will overwrite the previous message.

7. 
```
char p[ ] = "The sixth sick
sheikh's  sixth ship is sick";
    main( )
    {
        int i = 0;
        while(p[i]!='\0')
        {
            putch(p[i]);
            i++;
        }
    }
```
Output:
 The sixth sick sheikh's sixth ship is sick
Because the loop start from 0 and executes successfully till the Null character is encountered so each character of string will gets printed start from beginning.

8. What would be the output of the following program:

printf("%%%%");

Output: %%

| | |
|---|---|
| 4.      main()<br>{<br>     float a = 3.15529;<br>     printf("%6.2f",a);<br>     printf("%6.3f",a);<br>     printf("%5.4f",a);<br>     printf("%2.1f",a);<br>     printf("%0.0f",a);<br>}<br>Output:      _ _3.16<br>           _3.155<br>           3.1553<br>           3.2<br>           3<br><br>5. Point out the error if any in the following program:<br>     char ch;<br>     int i;<br>     scanf("%c", &i);<br>     scanf("%d", &ch);<br>     printf("%c %d",ch, i);<br>Output: You will not get a chance to input a character for the second scanf() statement. Solution to this problem is to precede the second scanf() with the following statement. fflush(stdin);<br>This would flush the enter hit for the previous scanf() to be flushed out from the input stream, i.e. keyboard. | 9.Would the following code work, if yes, what would be the output:<br>     int n=5;<br>     printf("n=%*d",n,n);<br>**Output:**      Yes. n= 5<br><br>* indicates that an *int* value from the argument list will be used for field width. In the argument list the width precedes the value to be printed. In this case the format specifier becomes *%5d*<br><br>10.      Can we specify variable field width in a *scanf()* format string?<br><br>**Output:**<br>No. A * in *scanf()* format string after a % sign is used for suppression of assignment. That is, the current input field is scanned but not stored.<br><br>11.      Out of *fgets()* and *gets()* which function is safe to use?<br><br>**Output:**<br>fgets(), because unlike fgets(), gets() cannot be told the size of the buffer into which the string supplied would be stored. as a result there is always a possibility of overflow of buffer. |

## Point out the errors, if any, in the following program segments:

| | |
|---|---|
| 1.      main( )<br>{<br>     int i;<br>     char a[] = "Hello";<br>     while(a != '\0')<br>     {<br>          printf("%c",*a);<br>          a++;<br>     }<br>}<br>**Output:** Error. "Lvalue required" because array can't increamented. | 5.      main( )<br>{<br>     int dd,mm,yy;<br>     printf("\n Enter day,moth and year\n");<br><br>     scanf("%d %*c %d %*c%d",&dd,&mm,&yy);<br>     printf("The date is:%d-%d-%d",dd,mm,yy);<br>}<br>Output: No Error. |

| 2. | 6. |
|---|---|

```
2.      main( )
        {
            double dual;
            scanf("%f",&dual);
printf("\nDouble Value = %lf",dual);
        }
```

**Output:** No Error but the output will be -0.000000. Because double occupy 8 byte and float occupy 4 byte.

```
3.      main( )
        {
            int evel;
            scanf("%d\n",&n);
printf("\nInterger Value =
%d",evel);
        }
```
**Output:** Error. Undefined symbol n.

```
4.      main( )
        {
            char *mess[5];
            for(i = 0; i<5; i++)
            scanf("%s",mess[i]);
        }
```
**Output:** Error. Undefined symbol i moreover when we are talking about the array of pointer it should not receive any string it can receive the address of any string or character.

```
6.      main( )
        {
            char buffer[50];
            int no = 97;
            double val = 2.34174;
            char name[10] = "Shweta";

            sprintf(buffer,"%d %lf
%s",&no,&val,name);
            printf("\n%d %lf
%s",no,val,name);

            sscanf(buffer, "%4d %2.2lf
%s",&no,&val,name);
            printf("\n%s",buffer);
            printf("\n%d %lf
%s",no,val,name);
        }
```
**No Error.**
Because sprint( ) print the variable into the specified string(e.g. buffer in above example) instead to print the variable to screen. Similarly sscanf( ) read character from a string and to convert and store tem in variables according to specified formats. So in the above program first the value of all the variables is copied in buffer array and when we print out buffer it gives all the copied values. And then with sscanf( ) all the value read from the buffer string and store them in the variable and when variable gets printed it displayed all the above assigned values.

## Answer the following:-

1) To receive the string "We have got the guts, you get the glory!!" in an array char str[100] which of the following functions would you use?
   - a) scanf("%s",str);
   - b) gets(str);
   - c) getche(str);
   - d) fgetchar(str);

   Output: gets(str)

2) Which function would you use if a single key were to be received through the keyboard?
   - a) scanf( )
   - b) gets( )
   - c) getche( )
   - d) getchar( )

   Output: getche( )

3) If an integer is to be entered through the keyboard, which function would you use?
   - a) scanf( )
   - b) gets( )
   - c) getch( )
   - d) getche( )

   Output: scanf( )

4) If a character string is to be received through the keyboard which function would work faster?
   - a) scanf( )
   - b) gets( )

   Output: gets( )

5) What is the different between getchar( ),fgetchar( ),getch( ) and getche( )?

   Output:
   All receive a character from keyboard. There are minor differences in them:
   getchar( ):Receives a character from keyboare, but it is necessary to hit the enter key after the character.
   fgetchar( ): Same as getchar( ). getchar( ) is mecro whereas fgetchar( ) is a function.
   getch( ):Receives a character from keyboard without echoing(displaying) it on the screen.
   getche( ): Receives a character from keyboard and echoes it on the screen.

6) The format string of a printf( ) can contain:
   - a) Character, format specifications and escape sequences
   - b) Character, integers and floats
   - c) Strings, integers and escape sequences
   - d) Inverted commas, percentage sign and backslash character

   Output: a) Character, format specifications and escape sequences

# CHAPTER
## ∞ 12 ∞
## (File handling through C)

## Introduction-

**Until now,** we have used the functions scanf and printf to read and write data. These are console oriented input and output functions which always use the keyboard and screen as the target place. It is fine until the data is small. However in real life problems involve large volumes of data and in such cases the console oriented output and input operations has two major problems:

**A.** It is time consuming to handle a large amount of data.
**B.** The entire data is lost as soon as the program is closed or computer is switched off.To overcome these problems we use file handling. File can be used to store the data in the hard disk so that the data is permanently saved and does not get deleted even if the computer is switched off.

A file can be defined as a place on the disk where a group of related data is stored. A number of functions can be performed on the files:

+ Naming a file.
+ Opening a file.
+ Reading data from a file.
+ Writing data to a file.
+ Closing a file.

# Let us see some of the functions of file

| Function name | Operation |
|---|---|
| fopen() | Creates a new file<br>Or opens an existing file for use. |
| fclose() | Closes a file. |
| fgetc() | Reads a character from file. |
| fputc() | Writes a character from file. |
| fprintf() | Writes a data from file. |
| fscanf() | Reads a data from file. |
| fgetw() | Reads an integer . |
| fputw() | Writes an integer. |
| fseek() | Sets a position to a desired points in the file. |
| ftell() | Gives the current position in the file(i.e number of bytes from the beginning). |
| rewind() | Sets the position to the beginning of the file. |
| fwrite() | Writes data to a file. |
| fread() | Reads data from a file. |
| feof() | Tests if end-of-file has been reached. |
| fflush() | Flushes a stream. |
| Remove() | Deletes the specified file. |
| Rename() | Changes the name or path of file. |
| ferror() | Tests if an error has occurred in the file. |

**Opening a file-**

Before we can read or write information from or to a file on the hard disk we must open the file.

To open the file function fopen( ) is used and a mode which tells the compiler that we would write, read or modify the file. This fopen( ) function performs three tasks:

- Searches the file on the disk.

- Then it loads the file from the disk into the place in memory called buffer.

- It sets a character pointer which will point the first character in the buffer.

**Need of buffer:**

The buffer is the temporary area in the memory of the computer where a file is kept for sometime so that it can be accessed quickly to read or write characters. It would be rather inefficient to every time go to the hard disk and read a character print it on the screen, then again go to the hard disk again to access next character.

Here the buffer comes to use, whenever we open a file the contents of the file get copied to this temporary area and then read character by character from the buffer rather than from the disk and similarly to write characters of the file one at a time on the disk would also be a wastage of time so buffer is used to write the characters and then they are transferred to the disk.

The fopen() gathers information like file name, size of file and the mode to open the file then returns the address of this file to a file pointer called fp. This can be explained as:

```
FILE *fp;
fp=fopen("file_name","mode");
```

here FILE is a constant defined in the header file stdio.h so it is compulsory to use #include<stdio.h>

**Reading a file:**

The function fgetc( ) is used to read the contents of the file which has been brought to the buffer(partly or wholly) from the hard disk. fgetc( ) is used as:
```
ch= fgetc(fp);
```

fgetc( ) is used to read the character from the current position of the pointer. The pointer now moves one place ahead so that it points the next character. The character which was read by the fgetc( ) is assigned to variable ch.

We use this fgetc( )within an infinite while loop, but then the loop has to break at the end of the file. This is done using a special character which is placed at the end of a file. The ASCII of this character is 26. This character is not returned but a marco is returned called EOF. This EOF is also defined in the stdio.h. The fgetc( ) can also be replaced with getc( ).

Sometimes we have to encounter problems while opening a file in the "r" mode, if the file of given name is not present on the disk. Similarly opening a file in "w" mode can also fail due to many reasons like insufficient space in the disk or disk being write protected or damaged disk. Now if the file does not open the fopen ( ) function returns a NULL.(defined in stdio.h and used as # define NULL 0).

**The file opening modes are:-**

"**r**"     open an exiting file for reading only.

"**w**"     open a new file for writing only.

"**a**"     open an exiting file for appending.

"**r+**"     open an exiting file for both reading and writing

"**w+**"     open a new file for both reading and writing.

"**a+**"     open an exiting file for both reading and appending.

**Writing characters to a file:**

**Function fputc( )** is used to print the characters from the screen to the file. And to print a string on the file the function fputs( ) is used.

+ fputc(ch,fp); Here ch is the name of the character and fp the file pointer.
+ fputs(s,fp); Here s is the name of the string and fp the file pointer.

**Let us try a simple program:**

```
#include<stdio.h>
main()
{
FILE *fp;                          /*declaring file pointer*/
fp = fopen("sample.dat","r");   /*opening the file sample.dat in read mode*/

if(fp==NULL)
        printf("file cannot be opened");
            else
        {
            ........
            fclose(fp);
        }
    }
```

**Closing a file:**

When we have finished reading the file, we need to close it. This is done by fclose( ). This is used as; fclose(fp);

To close the file we do not need the filename. The fclose( ) function performs three main tasks.

- The characters in the buffer would be written to the file on the disk.
- At the end of file a character with ASCII value 26 would get written.
- The buffer gets eliminated from the file.

1. Write a program to count the number of characters, spaces, tab, new lines in a file.

```c
#include<stdio.h>
main( )
{
        FILE *fp;
        char ch;
        int lines=0,tab=0,space=0, characters=0;
        fp=fopen("text.c","r");
        while(1)            /* infinite loop*/
        {
                ch = fgetc(fp);
                if(ch= =EOF)
                        break;
                characters++;
                if(ch= = 32)
                        space++;
                if(ch= = '\n')
                        lines++;
                if(ch= = '\t')
                        tab++;
        }
        fclose(fp);
        printf("number of lines = %d\ntabs = %d\ncharacters =
        %d\nspaces =
                %d",lines,characters,spaces);
        getch( );
}
```

2. Write a program to receive some strings from keyboard and print it to a file

```
#include<stdio.h>
main( )
{
        FILE *fp;
        char s[50];
        fp=fopen("text.c","w");    /*opening file*/
        if(fp= =NULL)              /*to check opening errors*/
        {
                puts("file opening error");
                exit();
        }
        printf("Enter some text");
        while(strlen(gets(s))>0)
        {
                fputs(s,fp);
                fputs("\n",fp);
        }
        fclose(fp);
}
```

3. Write a program to read all the strings from file and print it on screen

```
#include<stdio.h>
main( )
{
        FILE *fp;
        char s[50];
        fp=fopen("text.c","r");    /*opening file*/
        if(fp= =NULL)              /*to check opening errors*/
        {
                puts("file opening error");
                exit();
        }
        while(fgets(s,49,fp)!= NULL)
                printf("%s",s);
        fclose(fp);
        getch( );
}
```

# Multiple Choice Questions -

**1.** What values are returned from fclose if the file is closed properly:
- a. zero
- b. one
- c. -1
- d. none

**2.** The function that is used to see an error, if occurred, is
- a. ferror
- b. fiota
- c. fseek
- d. none

**3.** Which mode opens the file for reading and writing mode
- a. r++
- b. i++
- c. w++
- d. r+

**4.** In the following code:
```
FILE *fp;
fp = fopen("trial", "r");
fp points to
```
- a. The first character in the file.
- b. A structure which contains a *char* pointer which points to the first character in the file.
- c. The name of the file.
- d. None of the above.

**5.** Given: FILE file_p;

file_p=fopen("text.dat","a+");
The error in the above is
- a. FILE FILE_p
- b. FILE *filem_p
- c. FILE *file_p
- d. none

**6.** To close a file, we use
- a. fexit(file_p)
- b. fclose
- c. break
- d. fclose(file_p)

**7.** Which condition is used to test the end of file condition-
- a. eof
- b. ferror
- c. feof
- d. none

**8.** Which function takes a file pointer and resets the position to start a file
- a. fseek
- b. rewind
- c. ftell
- d. all the above

## Answers:-

**1 (a)    2 (a)    3 (d)    4 (b)    5 (c)    6 (b)    7 (c)    8 (b)**

## Point out the errors, if any, in the following program segments:

**1.**
```
#include "stdio.h"
main( )
{
    FILE *fp;
    openfile("Myfile.txt",&fp);
    if(fp = = NULL)
    printf("Unable to open file...");
}
openfile( char *fn, FILE **f)
{
    *f = fopen( fn, "r");
}
```

**Output:** No Error. In the above program for opening a file a function openfile( ) is used and two argument is passed first is file name and second one is file pointer. Because file name is a string so a pointer of type character will receive it and to the file pointer f is declared of type FILE. Where FILE is a pre defined structure and because f receive a pointer address so it is declared as double pointer.

**2.**
```
#include "stdio.h"
#include "stdlib.h"
main( )
{
    FILE *fp;
    char c;
    fp = fopen( "Try.c","r");

    if(fp= = null)
    {
    puts("Cannot open file");
        exit( );
    }
    while((c = getc(fp))!=EOF);
        putch(c);
    fclose( fp);
}
```

**Output:** Error. "null" must be in upper case because it is predefined in stdio.h as #define NULL 0.

```
    error");
        exit();
    }
    fclose(fp);
```
**Output :**No error

**7.**
```
#include "stdio.h"
main( )
{
    unsigned char;
    FILE *fp;

    fp = fopen( "trial",'r');
    while((ch = getc(fp))!=EOF)
            printf("%c",ch);

    fclose(*fp);
}
```

**Output: Error.** Type mismatch in parameter '_mode' in call to fopen. Because the mode must be enclosed in double quotes.
**Error.** Undefined symbol ch.
**Error.** Type mismatch in parameter '_stream' in call to 'fclose'. Because there is no need to use * with fp.

**8.**
```
main( )
{
    FILE *fp;
    char name[25];
    int age;
    fp = fopen("yours","r");
while(fscanf(fp,"%s
    %d",name,&age) !=NULL)
            printf("%s
%d\n",name,age);
    fclose(fp);
}
```
**Output: Error.** EOF is used instead of NULL because with fscanf will read the record from the file and when it will to the last record it will meet with EOF.

234

**3.** 
```
main( )
    {
        char fname[ ] =
        "c:\\students.dat";
        FILE *fp;
        fp = fopen( fname ,"tr");
        if (fp = = NULL)
printf("\nUnable to open file...");
    }
```
**Output:** No Error. but remember "stdio.h" must be included.

**4.** 
```
main( )
    {
        FILE *fp;
        char str[80];
        fp = fopen("Try.c","r");
        while(fgets(str,80,fp)! = EOF)
            fputs(str);
        fclose(fp);
    }
```
**Output:** Error. because fputs( ) needs two argument and written as fputs(str,fp) and because we use string in loop so there is NULL in the place of EOF.

**5.** 
```
unsigned char;
FILE *fp;
fp=fopen("matrix", "r");
while((ch=getc(fp))!=EOF)
    printf("%c",ch);
fclose(fp);
```
**Output:** EOF has been defined as *# define EOF-1* in the file "stdio.h" and an *unsigned char* ranges from 0 to 255 hence when EOF is read from the file it cannot be accommodated in *ch*. Solution is to declare *ch* as an *int*.

**6.** 
```
unsigned char;
FILE *fp;
fp=fopen("matrix", "r");
if(!fp)
    {
            printf("file opening
```

**9.** 
```
main( )
    {
        FILE *fp;
        char names[20];
        int i;
        fp = fopen("student.dat",wb);

        for(i = 0; i<10; i++)
        {
            puts("\nEnter name");

            gets(name);
            fwrite(name,size
                of(name),1,fp);
        }
        close(fp);
    }
```

**Output:** Error.Because sizeof should be one word and fclose should be use to close the file.

**10.** 
```
FILE *fp;
fp=fopen("matrix","r");
fseek(fp,20,SEEK_SET);
fclose(fp);
```

**Output:** Instead of 20 use 20L since *fseek()* needs a long offset value.

**11.** 
```
FILE *fp;
char s[80];
fp=fopen("matrix", "r");
while(!feof(fp))
    {
            fgets(s, 80,fp);
            puts(s);
    }
    fclose(fp);
```
**Output:**

The last line of file "matrix" will be read twice. To avoid this, use:
```
while(fgets(s,80,fp)!=NULL)
        puts(s);
```

C - Programmer
Harry.

# CHAPTER

## ∞ 13 ∞

## (Miscellaneous Topics)

## Introduction-

**Macro -**

We already know that **# *define statement*** can be used to define symbolic constants. Thus constants provide a form of shorthand notation. Define statement can be used to define macros, i.e. they can be used to replace these expressions, complete statements or a group of statements.

**Program to find the maximum of two numbers using macro:**

```
#define max (a,b) a>b?a:b          /*declaration of macro*/
main( )
{
        int a,b,ans;
        printf("Enter two numbers");
        scanf("%d %d",&a,&b);
        ans = max(a,b);
        printf("max = %d",ans);
        getch();
}
```

The program contains a macro max, which represents the expression a>b?a:b. when the program is compiled, the expression a>b?a:b will replaces the identifier max.

Macro definitions are customarily placed at the beginning of a file, ahead of the first file function definition. The scope of a macro is global.

A multi-line macro can also be defined by placing a backward slash at the end of each line except the last. This feature permits a single macro to be represented as compound statement.

## Declaration of a variable as a constant:-

We may like that the value of certain variable must not change during the execution of the program. This can be done by declaring the variable with a keyword const at the time of initialization.

**e.g.**    const float PI= 3.14;

This declaration tells the compiler that the value of the variable pi must not change during the execution of the program.

## Declaring a variable as volatile:-

**ANSI standard** defines another qualifier volatile that could be used to tell explicitly the compiler that a variable's value may be changed at any time by some external sources (from outside the program).

volatile int date;

The value of data may be altered by some external factors even if it does not appear on the left hand side of an assignment statement.

When we declare a variable as volatile, the compiler will examine the value of the variable each time it is encountered to see whether any external alteration has changed the value.

## Mind Drill Note-

**Remember that** the value of a variable declared as volatile can be modified by its own program as well.

If we wish that the value must not be modified by the program while it may be altered by some other process, then we may declare the variable as both const and volatile as (volatile const int = 150;).

238

## Defining Symbolic Constants:-

We often use some constants in our program. These constants may appear in the program a number of times. For e.g. the value of pi should always be 3.14. Thus it can be used in the program as

# define PI 3.14

## # is called the preprocessor or compiler directive.

As we already know PI is a constant and so its value must always be the same throughout the program.Symbolic constants are also called as constant identifiers. Following rules apply to the # define statements:

+ To differentiate between variables and symbolic constants the symbolic constants are written in capital.

+ No blank space is given between the # and the word define.

+ A blank space is required between the word define and the symbolic constant.

+ Symbolic names are not declared with the data type.

+ #define statements do not end with a semicolon.

+ #define statements can appear anywhere in the program but before they are used. But usually the are used before the main ( ).

## Pre processor directives:-

The preprocessor, as the name implies, is a program that processes the source code before it passes through the compiler.

## C preprocessors:

The preprocessor is a collection of special statements, which are executed at the beginning of the compilation process. These are called directives.

## Some preprocessor are:

**1. #include.:-** This is used to include header files.

**2 #define :-** This statement is used to define symbolic constants and macros: **i.e.,** single identifires that are equivalent to expressions.

**For example:**

```
#include<stdio.h>
#define area  length*width
main()
{
        int length, width;
        printf("enter length and width");
        scanf(" %d %d",&length,&width);
        printf("\n area is %d",area);
}
```

**3. #if, #elif, #else and #endif** permit conditional compilation of the source program, depending on the value of one or more true/false conditions. They are also used in conjunction with the defined operator.

**For example:**

```
#if defined(FOREGROUND)
        #define BACKGROUND 0
#else
        #define FOREGROUND 0
        #define BACKGROUND 7
#endif
```

**4. #elif :-** #elif is analogous to an else – if clause using in control statements

**5. #else:-**

**6 #endif**

**7 #ifdef :-**    #ifdef is equivalent to #if defined( ).

**8. #ifndef:-**   #ifndef is equivalent to #if!defined. i.e. , "if not defined".

**9. #undef:-**    The #undef directive "undefines" a symbolic constant or a macro identifier; i.e., it negates the effect of a #define directive .

**For example:**

```
#define FOREGROUND 7
#define BACKGROUND 0
main()
{
        .........
        #undef FOREGROUND
        #undef BACKGROUND
}
```

**Mind Drill Note-** *#if, #ifdef, #ifndef must end with #endif.*

240

## Operators:-

The preprocessor also includes two special operators: defined #, and ##.

### Stringizing operator (#):-

It allows a formal argument within a macro definition to be converted to a string. If a formal argument in a macro definition is precede by this operator , the corresponding actual argument will automatically be enclosed in double quotes.

### Token pasing operator (##):-

It causes individual items within a macro definition to be concatenated thus forming a single item.

### Example:

#define display(i) printf(" x" #i "= %f\n",x##i)

Suppose this macro is accessed by writing    display(3);

The result will be:    printf("x3= %f\n", x3);

Thus the expression x##i becomes the variables x3, since 3 is the current value of the argument i.

## Multiple Choice:

| | |
|---|---|
| **1.** What is a preprocessor directive?<br> 1. a message from compiler to the programmer.<br> 2. a message from compiler to the linker.<br> 3. a message from programmer to the preprocessor.<br> 4. a message from programmer to the microprocessor<br><br>**Answer:** 3. a message from programmer to the preprocessor<br><br>**2.** Which of the following are correctly formed #define statements-<br> 1. #define INCH PER FEET 12<br> 2. #define SQR(X) (X*X);<br> 3. #define SQR(X) (X*X) | **4.** A header file is:<br> 1. a file that contains standard library functions.<br> 2. a file that contains definitions and macros.<br> 3. a file that contains user-defined functions.<br> 4. a file that is present in current working directory.<br><br>**Answer:** 2. a file that contains definitions and macros<br><br>**5.** All macro substitutions in a program are done-<br> 1. Before compilation of the program<br> 2. After compilation |

| | |
|---|---|
| **Answer: 3** #define SQR(X) (X*X)<br><br>3. Which of the following is not a preprocessor directive?<br>   1.  #if<br>   2.  #elseif<br>   3.  #undef<br>   4.  #pragma<br><br>**Answer: 2.**#elseif | **3.**  During execution<br>**4.**  None of the above<br>Answer: 1. Before compilation of the program |

## What will be the output of the following program:

**1.**
```
#define sqr(x) (x*x)
main()
{
        int a,b=3;
        a=sqr(b+2);
        printf("%d",a);
}
```
**Output:** 11 because, on preprocessing the expression becomes a=(3+2*2+3).

2.How would you define the sqr macro in above question such that it gives the result of a as 25.

**Output:** #define sqr(x) ((x) *(x))

**3.**  # define cube(x) (x*x*x)
```
main()
        {
        int a,b=3;
        a=cube(b++);
        printf("%d %d",a,b);
        }
```
**Output: 27 6.**
**4.**
```
#define MESS junk
        main()
        {
                printf("MESS");
        }
```
**Output: MESS**

**7.**     main()
```
        {
                #ifdef NOTE
                        /*unterminated
                        comment
                        int a;
                        a=10;
                #else
                        int a;
                        a=20;
                #endif
                printf("%d",a);
```

**Output:** Even though the *#ifdef* fails in this case(Note being undefined) and the if block doesn't go for compilation errors in it are not permitted.

**8.**  Would the following typedef work?
      typedef #include I;
**Output:**No, because *typedef* works only after the preprocessors have finished working.

**9.** #define max(a,b) (a>b?a:b)
```
        main()
        {
                int x;
                x=max(3+2,2+7);
                printf("%d",x);
        }
```
**Output: 9**

242

**5.** 
```
#define PRINT(int)
      printf("%d",int)
   main()
   {
        int x=2,y=3, z=4;
        PRINT (x);
        PRINT (y);
        PRINT (z);
   }
```
**Output: 2 3 4**

6. How would you define the above macro such that it outputs:

        x=2 y=3 z=4
        Output:
        #define PRINT(int)
```
   printf(#int "= %d", int)
   main()
   {
        int x=2,y=3, z=4;
        PRINT (x);
        PRINT (y);
        PRINT (z);
   }
```
The rule is if the parameter name is preceded by a # in the macro expansion, the combination (of # and parameter) will be expanded into a quoted string with the parameter replaced by the actual argument. This can be combined with the string concatenation to print the output desired in our program. On expansion the macro becomes **printf("x" "=%d",x);**
The two strings get concatenated, so the effect is **printf("x =%d",x);**

10. Write a macro PRINT for the following program such that it outputs:
        x=4 y=4 z=5
        a=1 b=2 c=3
```
   main()
   {
        int x=4, y=4, z=5;
        int a=1, b=2, c=3;
        PRINT(x,y,z);
        PRINT(a,b,c);
   }
```
**Output:** #define PRINT(var1, var2, var3)
printf("\n" #var1 "=%d" #var2 "=%d"
#var3 "=%d", var1, var2, var3)

11. Define the macro DEBUG such that the following program **outputs:**
        DEBUG: x=4
        DEBUG: y=3.140000
        DEBUG: ch=A
```
   main()
   {
        int x=4;
        float a=3.14;
        char ch= 'A';
        DEBUG(x, %d);
        DEBUG(a, %f);
        DEBUG(ch, %c);
   }
```
**Output:**#define DEBUG(var,fmt)
printf("DEBUG" #var "="#fmt "\n",var)

12. 
```
   #define str(x) #x
   #define Xstr(x) str(x)
   #define oper multiply
   main()
   {
        char
   *opername=Xstr(oper);
        printf("%s",opername);
   }
```

**Output:** multiply

# Answer the following:

**1.** What is the difference between the following two #include directives:

> #include<conio.h>
> #include"conio.h"

**Answer:**
**#include "conio.h":** This command would look for the file conio.h in the current directory as well as the specified list of directories as mentioned in the search path that might have been set up.

**#incude<conio.h>:** This command would look for the file conio.h in the specified list of directories only.

**2.** Indicate what would the swap macro be expanded to on preprocessing. Would the code compile?

```
#define swap (a, b, c) (c t; t=a; a=b; b=t)
main()
{
    int x=10,y=20;
    swap (x, y, int);
    printf("%d %d",x,y);
}
```

**Answer:**      (int t;t=a,a=b,b=t;);

> This code will not work since declaration of t cannot occur within parenthesis.

**3.** How would you modify the swap macro in the above question such that it is able to interchange two integers?

**Answer:** #define swap(a,b,c) ct;t=a, a=b, b=t;

**4.** In which line of the following program an error would be reported?

```
1.   #define area( r ) (3.14*r *r);
2.   main()
3.   {
4.       float r=1.0, c;
5.       c=area(r);
6.       printf("%f",c);
7.       if(area(r)= =6.28)
8.             printf("Matrix");
9.   }
```

**Answer:** Line number 7, but the real culprit is the semicolon in the line number 1. On expansion line number 7 becomes *if((3.14\*1.0\*1.0);= =6.28)*. Hence the error.

5. What is the type of the variable b in the following declaration?
      #define floatptr float*
      floatptr a,b;

   **Answer:** *float* and not a pointer to a float, since on expansion the declaration becomes:
      float *a,b;

6. Is it necessary that the header files should have .*h*

   **Answer:** No, but traditionally they have been given the .*h* extension to identify them as something different than the .c program files.

7. What do header files usually contain?

   **Answer:** Preprocessor directives like # *define, structure, union and enum* declarations, *typedef* declarations, global variables and external function declarations. One should not write the actual code( i.e. function bodies) or global variable definitions in header files. The *#include* directive should be used to pull in header files, not other .c files.

8. How can a header file ensure that it doesn't get included more than once?

   **Answer:** All declarations must be written in the manner shown below. Assume that the name of header file is FUNCS.H.

      #ifndef_FUNCS
      #define_FUNCS
      #endif

   Now if we include this file twice as shown below, it would get included only once.

9. On inclusion, where are the header files searched for?

   **Answer:** If the header file is included using < > the files get searched in the predefined included path( the path can also be changed). If included with the " " syntax in addition to the predefined path the file is also searched in the current directory(usually the directory from which you invoked the compiler).

# State whether true or false:

a. If the file to be included doesn't exist, the preprocessor flashes an error message.

b. The preprocessor can trap simple errors like missing declarations, nested comments or mismatch of braces.

c. Would it result in an error if the header file is included twice.

d. Would the following program print the message infinite number of times?

```
#define INFINITELOOP while (1)
main()
{
        INFINITELOOP
                printf("\nMatrix");
}
```

e. Would the following program compile successfully?

```
main()
{
        printf("Matrix" "computers");
}
```

**Answer:**

| a. | True | b. | False | c. | False | d. |
|    | True | e. | True  |    |       |    |

# CHAPTER
## ∞ **14** ∞
## (Storage Class)

# Introduction-

Storage class decides the memory location of a variable. Memory location can be –

**1. Main Memory (RAM).**
**2. CPU registers.**

It decides the default value of a variable (Zero value or garbage value). It also decides the scope & lifetime of a variable. Scope indicates the region over which the variable's declaration has an effect or in other words that particular variable can be used.

The four different kinds of scopes are global, function, block and prototype.

**There are 4 storage classes:-**

1.   Automatic storage class (auto)
2.   Static storage class (static)
3.   External storage class (extern)
4.   Register storage class. (register)

## Automatic storage class:-

Variable declared inside a function has by default automatic storage class. It is initialized by garbage value.

The declaration is given as: int a or auto int a;

```
void prn();
main()
{
        int a=5;
        printf("%d ", a);
        prn();
        prn();
        prn();
}
void prn()
{
        int a=10;
        a++;
        printf("%d ",a);
}
```

**Output: 5 11 11 11**

**Here** in the above example the two variables have the same name but they have different scope. Variable *a* in prn() has local scope so every time prn() is called a new copy of *a* will be generated.

## Static storage class:-

Static storage class should be used only when a program requires the value of a variable to persist between different function calls like in recursive function. The variable is declared as: static int b; Static variable will have local scope and global lifetime.

Static variable are defined within individual functions and therefore have the same scope as automatic variables. They are local to the functions in which they are default.

They retain their values throughout the life of the program. Thus if a function is exited and then re-entered at a later time, the static variables defined within that function will return their former values.

```
void prn();
main()
{
        prn();
        prn();
        prn();
}
void prn()
{
        static int a=10;
        a++;
        printf("%d ",a);
}
```
**Output:11 12 13**

In the above example only a single copy of variable *a* will be created and this single copy will be used every time prn() is called, so it will increment the last function call value of variable *a*.

**External storage class:-**

Variable declared outside all the functions have external storage class. Extern storage class should be used for only those variables which are being used by all the functions in the programs, Now there is no need to pass a variable in all the functions.

But it is also not advisable to store all the variables as extern because it will remain active through out the life of the program thus wasting a lot of memory unnecessarily. The external variables are declared as extern int c; It is also used when the variables of one program have to be used in some other programs also **for example:-**

| File1.c | File2.c |
|---|---|
| #include "File2.c"<br>int a;   /*Variable definition */<br>main()<br>{<br>    a= 5;<br>    func();<br>    printf("%d",a);<br>} | extern int a;   /*Variable declaration*/<br>void func()<br>{<br>        a=10;<br>} |
| **Output: 10** Variable *a* will get memory in File1.c. Because it is defined outside the function so it is called as external variable and its scope is global. It can also be used in another file File2.c. variable *a* used in both files is same. But when we compile the File2.c we have to imform the compiler that variable *a* will come from outside so we have declared *a* as extern int a;(no memory allocation at this time), but if we declare it as int a; then compiler will treat it as a new variable. | |

**Register:-**

There are only 14 CPU registers available and even lesser than that can be used by us as the microprocessor is using it. But the CPU registers are accessed by the computer very fast and so the program is executed very fast. So, it will be best used for loop counters which have to be used a number of times. However if a register is not free, auto storage class is used and the execution is carried on. The CPU registers are 2 bytes long. So their maximum range is equal to that of int. float values can not be stored in register. Even if we say register float x, auto is assumed for x. The variable for this class are declared as,

*register int d;*

**Summary:-**

| Storage Class | Memory | Default Value | Scope | Lifetime |
|---|---|---|---|---|
| Auto | Main memory (RAM) | Garbage | Local | Local |
| Static | Main memory (RAM) | Zero | Local | Global |
| Extern | Main memory (RAM) | Zero | Global | Global |
| Register | CPU Registers | Garbage | Local | Local |

# What will be the output of the following-

```
1. int f(int);
     int g(int);
main( )
{
        int x, y, s = 2;
        s *= 3;
        y = f(s);
        x = g(s);
printf("\n%d %d %d",s,y,x);
}
int t =8;
int f( int a)
{
        a += -5;
        t -= 4;
        return(a+t);
}
Int g(int a)
{
        a = 1;
        t += a;
        return(a+t);
}
```

```
4.
main()
{
        static int a[20];
        int i=0;
        a[i]=i++;
        printf("%d %d %d", a[0], a[1],
i);
}
```
**Output:-0 0 1**

```
5.
float x =4.5;
main( )
{
        float y, float f(float);
        x*=2.0;
        y = f(x);
        printf("\n%f %f",x,y);
}
float f(float a)
{
        a+=1.3;
```

250

**Output:- 6 5 6**
First s will be 6 and passed to f( ) and
received by a and after process a will be
1 and t will be 4. because t is a global so
it is available in whole program and
when g( ) is called the a receive again 6
and overlapped by 1 so a=1 and t = t+a
so t = 5 and this function returns a+t so x
will be 6 and finally s = 6, x = 6, y = 5
that will get print through printf( ).

**2.**
```
main( )
{
        static int c = 5;
        printf("\n c = %d",c--);
        if (c !=0)
                main( );
}
```
**Output:- 5 4 3 2 1**
Because c = 5 and first printed and
then decrease by 1 and then call
main( ) but because here c is defined
as static so the control doesn't go to
the initialization and this condition
will be true for five times and each
time c gets printed and then
decrease so c will be 5 4 3 2 1.

**3.**
```
main( )
{
        int i,j;
        for( i = 1; i<5; i++)
        {
            j = g(i);
            printf("\n%d",j);
        }
}
Int g( int x)
{
        static int v = 1;
        int b = 3;
        v+=x;
        return(v+x+b);
}
```
**Output:- 6 9 13 18**

```
        x-= 4.5;
        return(a+x);
}
```

**Output:- 4.500000 14.800000**

**6.**
```
int x = 10;
main( )
{
        int x = 20;
        {
            int x = 30;
            printf("%d ",x);
        }
        printf("\n %d",x);
}
```
**Output:- 30 20**

Because when control executes the
innermost printf it will print 30 because
the local variable gets priority and
when control comes out from this block
the scope will ends and here x =20 and
gets printed.

**7.**
```
main()
{
        extern int i;
        i=20;
        printf("%d",sizeof(i));
}
```

**Output:-** Error extern int i is a
declaration and not definition

**8.**
```
main()
{
        extern int a;
        printf("%d",a);
}
int a=20;
```
**Output:- 20**

# State the True or False:

1. An extern storage class variable is not available to the functions that precede its definition, unless the variable explicitly declared in these functions.

2. The value of an automatic storage class variable persists between various functions invocations.

3. If the CPU registers are not available, the register storage class variables are treated as static storage class variable.

4. The register class variables cannot hold float values.

5. If we try to use register storage class for a float variable the compiler will flash an error message.

6. If the variable x is defined outside all functions and a variable x is also defined as a local variable of some function, then the global variable get preference over the local variable.

7. The default value for automatic variable is zero.

8. The life of static variable is till the control remains within the block in which it is defined.

9. If a global variable is to be defined, then the extern keyword is necessary in its declaration.

10. The address of register variable is not accessible.

## Answers:

| | | | | | |
|---|---|---|---|---|---|
| 1. | True | 2. | False | 3. | False |
| 4. | True | | | | |
| 5. | False | 6. | False | 7. | False |
| 8. | False | | | | |
| 9. | False | 10. | True | | |

252

# CHAPTER
## ∞ 15 ∞
## (Algorithm's)

**I**ntroduction-

**Algorithm No. 1: Sum of two numbers-**

1.      Read A and B.
2.      Set SUM:=A + B.
3.      Write SUM.
4.      Exit.

**Algorithm No. 2: Maximum of two numbers-**

1.      Read A and B.
2.      If A > B, then:
            Set MAX:=A.
        Else:
            Set MAX:=B.
        [End of If structure]
3.      Write MAX.
4.      Exit

**Algorithm No. 3: Maximum of three numbers-**

1.      Read A , B,C.
2.      If A > B, then:
          If A > C, then:
               Set MAX:=A.
          Else:
               Set MAX:=C.
          [End of If structure]
      Else:
          If B > C, then:
               Set MAX:=B.
          Else:
               Set MAX:=C.
      [End of If Structure]
3.      Write MAX.
4.      Exit.

**Algorithm .4**: To input percentage from user and print the grade.(Using Else if)

1.      Read P.
2.      If P>=90, then:
          Set GRADE:='A'.
      Else If P >= 70, then:
          Set GRADE := 'B'.
      Else if P>=50, then:
          Set GRADE:='C'.
      Else:
          Set GRADE:='F'.
      [End of If Else Structure].
3.      Write GRADE.
4.      Exit

**Algorithm No. 5: To print the series 1 to N using *for loop*.**

1.      Read N.
2.      Repeat Step 3 for I:=1 to N:
3.          Write I.
      [End of Step 2 loop]
4.      Exit.

**Algorithm No. 6: To print the series 1 to N using while *loop*.**

1. Read N.
2. Set I:= 1
3. Repeat Step 4 and 5 While I<= N:
4.     Write I.
5.     Set I:=I+1.
   [End of Step 3 loop]
6. Exit.

**Algorithm No. 7: To print the series 1 to N using *do while loop*.**

1. Read N.
2. Set I:=1.
3. Write I.
4. Set I:=I + 1.
5. if I<=N, then: goto step3.
6. Exit.

**Algorithm No. 8: Convert decimal number to binary equivalent.**

1. Read N.
2. Set B:=0.
3. Set I:=0.
4. Repeat step 6 to 9 While N>=0
5. Set N:= N/2.
6. Set B:= B + $10^i$ * Remainder    [this part will take care of reversing the accumulated remainders].
7. Set I:=I+1.
8. Write B.
9. Exit

**Algorithm No. 9:Reverse the digits of given n digit numbers.**

1. Read N.
2. Set REV:=0.
3. Repeat steps 5 and 6 While N>=0.
4. Set N:=N/10.
5. Set REV:= REV *10 + remainder.
6. Print the value of REV.
7. Exit.

**Algorithm No. 10: To verify whether a given number is prime or not.**

1. Read N.
2. Set I:=2 and PRIME =1.
3. Repeat Steps 4 while I<=N/2
4. If(N % I=0)

    Set PRIME:=0. and exit the loop structure.

    Else:

    Set I:= I+ 1.

    [End of If Structure.]

    [End of While loop]
5. If PRIME=1, then:

    Print the number is prime.

    Else

    Print the number is not prime.
6. Exit.

**Algorithm No. 11: Linear search in an array**

**Algorithm No. 12: Calculate factorial using function**

1. Read N.
2. ANS=FACT (N).
3. Write ANS.
4. Exit

**[This procedure is used to calculate the factorial of N]**

1. Set ANS:=1
2. Repeat step 3 for I:=N to 1
3. Set ANS:= ANS* I
4. [End of Step 3 loop]
5. Return ANS.
6. Exit.

# CHAPTER

# ∞ **16** ∞

## (Unsolved Practical Problems)

**I**ntroduction-

1.  A phone number such as (011)711 8802 can be thought of as having three parts: the area code(011), the exchange(711), and the number (8802).write a program that uses a structure to store these three parts of a phone number separately. Call the structure phone. Create an array to store 20 records of its member wherein each record stores the memberno, member name and phone number of phone type. Have the user input the information for all records and then display the entire information on the screen.

2.  Create a structure called volume that uses three variables (length, width, height) of type distance (feet and inches) to model the volume of a room. read the three dimensions of the room and calculate the volume it represents, and print out the result. The volume should be in (feet)$^3$ form i.e., you will have to convert each dimension in to feet and fractions of foot. For instance, the length 12 feet 6 inches will be 12.5 feet.

3.  Declare a structure to represent a complex number (a number having a real part and imaginary part).write a c program to add two complex numbers.

4. Declare a structure to represent a complex number (a number having a real part and imaginary part).write a c program to subtract two complex numbers.

5. Declare a structure to represent a complex number (a number having a real part and imaginary part).write a c program to multiply two complex numbers.

6. Declare a structure to represent a complex number (a number having a real part and imaginary part).write a c program to divide two complex numbers.

7. WAP to record score of a cricket match. one array stores information of batting team such as batsman's name, run scored, indication if out mode by which out along with total runs, overs played, total overs and extras. The other array stores information about bowling team such as bowler's name, overs bowled, maiden overs, runs given and wickets taken. The program reads in the above information and depending upon the user's choice, it displays either the batting team's information or the bowling team's information.

8. WAP to prepare the invoice from the following data: customer number, customer name and address, data of sale, description, quantity, unit price, discount percentage, sales tax percentage.

9. WAP to prepare and print payroll (payslip) of a group of employees for a particular month of the year. the employee information contains the following items: name and designation of employee, basic pay(bp),special pay(sp), contribution to general provident fund(pf),contribution to group scheme(gis),income tax deduction(it),city compensatory allowance(cca)= rs. 250,dearness allowance(da)=114% for basic pay < rs. 3500 85% for basic pay > 3500 and < 6000 74% for basic pay pay > 6000 house rent allowance(hra)=rs. 250.00 for basic pay < rs. 1500 rs. 450.00 for basic pay > 1499 and 2800 rs. 800.00 for basic pay > 2799 and < 3500 rs. 1000.00 for basic > 3499. The program computes the above quantities, gross pay, total deductions net pay and prints in a specified format. (hint: gross=bp+sp+hra+da+cca net=gross-deductions(i.e.,pf+gis+it) make use of structures and arrays in the program.

10. WAP to store 20 records containing country, capital and name of its president. the president name it is a record containing last name, first name, preface(mr, miss, mrs.).the program should display the entire record whenever the country name or capital is given.

11. Suppose a store has a number of items in their inventory and that each item is supplied by almost two suppliers. WAP to store details of 20 items in an array and then print it.

12. An array stores details of 25 students (rollno, name, marks in three subjects).WAP to create such an array and print out a list of students who have failed in more than one subjects. assume 40% as pass marks.

13. WAP to calculate income tax of a group of employee from the following data. Total income, life insurance premiums (lic),unit-linked insurance plan (ulip),provident fund(pf),post-office cumulative time deposit(ctd), national saving certificates(nsc) Assume the following norms for the calculation of income tax: a tax total income slab rates of income tax

| | |
|---|---|
| upto 3500o | nil |
| from 35001 to 60000 | 20% |
| from 60001 to 120000 | 30% |
| 120000 and above | 40% |

b exemptions contributions to lic, gpf, ppf, ulip, nsc, ctd etc, are exempt from paying income tax subject to a maximum of rs. 120000 is admissible.

14. A linear array of size 50 stores following information's: name of the country, country's capital and per capita income of the country. write a complete program in c to do the following:

a) to read a country's name and display capital and per-capita income.
b) to read name of the capital city and displays country's name and displays country's name and per capital income. display an error message incase of an incorrect input.

15. WAP using structure to store price list of 50 items and to print the largest price as well as the sum of all prices.

16. WAP in c using structure to simulate result preparation system for 20 students. the data available for each student includes rollno, name and marks in 3 subjects. the percentage marks and grade are to be calculated from the above information, the percentage marks are the average marks are the average marks and the grade is calculated as

| follows: | % marks | grade |
|---|---|---|
| | < 50 | 'f' |
| | >=50 < 60 | 'd' |
| | >=60 < 75 | 'c' |
| | >=75 < 90 | 'b' |
| | >=90 < 100 | 'a'. |

**17.** WAP a c program to simulate an arithmetic calculator for integers. the program should be able to produce the last result calculated and the number of arithmetic operations performed so far. any wrong operations is to be reported.

**18.** WAP to make a structure named "student" having following as structure member:1) name 2) roll-no 3) marks of three subjects viz. English, hindi, maths. do the following operations using the structure:

**a)** accept name, roll no and marks in three subjects.
**b)** calculate total and percentage.
**c)** show the information on the screen in given below format XYZ school half yearly examination
Name:                    roll no:
Marks in Hindi:
Marks in English:
Marks in Maths:
----------------------------------------
  Total marks:       per:

**19.** WAP to make a structure "contestant" for a beauty contest in which check the following condition & accept details for 5 contestants only if they satisfy following criteria:

**a)** if age is between 18 to 20
**b)** Weight is between 45 to 60
**c)** Qualification is graduate
Structure members are: 1) Name 2) Age 3) Weight 4) Qualifications-->
1. Below graduate 2. Graduate 3. Postgraduate. Now display the details of all 5 contestant in tabular manner.

**20.** WAP to make structure "stock". Accept details of 10 stock items. The structure members are :1)  item_name 2) item_code 3) rate 4) qty_in_ stock 5) amount. now ask of the user item code which he want to see, search it display it if it exit otherwise give appropriate message.

**21.** WAP to create a structure to specify data on students given below: roll number, name, department, course, year of joining assume that there are not more than 450 students in the college. do the following operations using the structure:
a) print names of all students who joined in a particular year.
b) print the data on a student whose roll number is given.

**22.** Create a structure to specify data of customers in a bank. the data to be stored is: account number, name ,balance in account. assume maximum of 200 customers in the bank. do the following operations using the structure:

**a)** to print the account number and name of each customer with balance RS. 100.if a customer requests for withdrawal or deposit, it is given in the form: acct. no, amount,(1 for deposit,0 for withdrawal)
**b)** to give a message, "the balance is insufficient for the specified withdrawal".

23. An automobile company has serial numbers for engine parts starting from aa0 to ff9. The other characteristics of parts be specified in a structure are: year of manufacture, material and quantity manufactured. now, do the following:

> **a)** specify a structure to store information corresponding to a part.
> **b)** WAP to retrieve information on parts with serial numbers between bb1 and cc6.

24. A record contains name of cricketer, his age, number of test matches that he has played and the average runs that he has scored in each test match. create an array of structures to hold records of 20 such cricketers and then write a program to read these records and arrange them in ascending order by average runs.

25. Create a structure to represent a book in a library. It include the following members: book number, book name, author, publisher, price, no. of copies, no. Of copies issued. now do the following operations using the structure:

**a)** to assign initial values.
**b)** to issue a book after checking for its availability.
**c)** to return a book.
**d)** to display book information.

26. Create a structure to represent bank account of 10 customers with the following data members: name of the depositor, account number, type of account (s for saving and c for current account),balance amount. now, do the following operations using the structure:

**a)** To initialize data members
**b)** To deposit money.
**c)** For withdrawal of money after checking the minimum balance(minimum balance is rs. 1000).
**d)** To display the data members.

27. Create a structure to represent batsman in a cricket team. it include the following members: first name, last name, runs made, number of fours, number of sixes. now do the following operations using the structure:

**a)** to assign the initial values.
**b)** to update runs made(it should simultaneously update fours and sixes, if required).
**c)** to display the batsman's information.
make appropriate assumptions about access labels.

28.    Create a structure to represent bowlers in a cricket team. include the following members: first name, last name, overs bowled, number of maiden overs, runs given, wickets taken. now do the following operations using the structure:
**a)** to assign the initial values
**b)** to update the information
**c)** to display the bowler's information.
make appropriate assumptions about access labels.

29.    WAP to manage a room's statistics. the room structure includes the following members: length, width, height. now do the following operations using the structure:

**a)** to assign initial values.        **b)** to calculate area.
**c)** to display information (length, width, height & area).

30.    Modify the above program so that length, width and height become the variable of structure distance that includes: meters, centimeters.

31.    Let itemlist be a linear array of size n ( where n is a user input) where each element of the array contains following fields: item, code, item price, quantity. declare a structure with itemlist as data member and perform the following operations:

**a)** appending an item to the list.
**b)** given the itemcode, delete an item from the list.
**c)** printing the total value of the stock.

32.    WAP to handle 10 account holders. the program should use the structure as defined in q.33.make necessary changes in the class definition - if required.

33.    Write a structure to represent a vector (1-d numeric array).now do the following operations using this structure:

**a)** for vector creation.
**b)** for modification of a given element.
**c)** for displaying the largest value in the vector.
**d)** for displaying the entire vector.
**e)** for adding two vectors and displays the resultant vector.

# WAP using this structure.

**34.** Create two structures mc and fi which store the value of distances. mc stores distances in meters and centimeters whereas fi stores in feet and inches. WAP that reads value for variables of both the structures and can add one variable of mc with an variable of fi.

**35.** Imagine a ticket selling both at a fair. people passing by are required to purchase a ticket. A ticket is priced as RS. 2.50/-. The booth keeps track of the number of people that have visited the booth, and of the total amount of money collected. Model this ticket selling booth with a structure called ticbooth including following members: number of people visited, total amount of money collected. Now do the following operations:

**a)** to assign initial values (assign 0 to both data members).
**b)** to increment only people total in case ticket is not sold out
**c)** to increment people total as well as amount total if a ticket is sold out.
**d)** to display the totals.
**e)** to display the number of tickets sold out(a tricky one).
   WAP to include this structure.

**36.** WAP to perform various operations on a string structure without using language supported built-in string functions. The operations on a structure are:

**a)** Read a string.
**b)** Display the string.
**c)** Reverse the string.
**d)** Copy the string into an empty string.
**e)** Concatenate two strings.

**37.** WAP to process the sales activity for 20 salesman. Each salesman deals in separate product and is assigned an annual target. At the end of the month, his monthly sale is added into the sales till date. At the end of the year, his commission is calculated as follows: if sales made is more than target then the commission is 25% of the extra sales made + 10% of the target if sales made is equal to the target then the commission is 10% of the target. Otherwise commission is zero.

**38.** A bookshop maintains the inventory of books that are being sold at the shop. The list includes details such as author, title, price, publisher and stock position. Whenever a customer wants a book, the sales person inputs the title and author and the system searches the list and displays whether it is available or not. If it is not, an appropriate message is displayed.

If it is, then the system displays the book details and requests for the number of copies required. If the requested copies are available, the total cost of the required copies is displayed, otherwise the message "sorry! These many copies are not in stock" is displayed. Design a system using a structure called stock. This program includes the following operations:

      **a)** The price gets updated as and when required.
      **b)** The stock value of each book should be automatically updated as soon as transaction is completed.
      **c)** The total number of books (titles) sold get displayed (along with total sales (in RS.) As and when required.

**39.** WAP to print the score board of a cricket match in real time. The display should contain the batsman's name, runs scored, indication if out, mode by which out, bowler's score (overs played, maiden overs, runs given, wickets taken).as and when a ball is thrown, the score should be updated.(hint: use separate arrays to store batsman's and bowlers, information).

**40.** WAP to prepare the invoice from the following data: customer name, customer name, customer address, date of sale, item no, item description, quantity sold, unit price of item, discount percentage and sales tax percentage.
note: identify different structures possible here.

**41.** A college maintains a list of its students graduating every year. at the end of the year, the college produces a report that lists the following:
year:
number of working graduates   :
number of non-working graduates :
details of the top-most scorer
     **name**         :
     **age**          :
     **subject**      :
     **average marks**  :

x% of the graduates this year are non-working and n % are first divisioners.

**WAP for it that uses the following structure path:**

person ----->   student ------>         graduate student
(name, age)    (roll no, average marks)  (subject, employed)
the data members of these structures have seen shown in the parenthesis.

**42.** WAP that reads several different names and rearranges the names into alphabetical order, and then writes out the alphabetized list. make use of structure variables within the program.

**43.** Assume that a bank maintains two kinds of accounts for customers, one called as savings account and the other as current account. the savings account provides compound interest and withdrawal facilities but not cheque book facility. the current provides cheque book facility but no interest. Current account holders should also maintain a minimum balance and if the balance falls below this level, a service charge is imposed. create a structure account that stores customer name, account number and opening balance. from this derive the structures current and savings to make them more specific to their requirements. now do the following tasks:

**a)** deposit an amount for a customer and update the balance.
**b)** display the account details.
**c)** compute and deposit interest.
**d)** withdraw amount for a customer after checking the balance and update the balance.
**e)** check for the minimum balance(for current account holders), impose penalty, if necessary, and update the balance.

**44.** WAP defining an union which can hold an "integer" or "float" string. define a variable "union type" to keep track of the type of data stored in the union. write a function to print the value stored in the union.

**45.** WAP to define a union of type "ans" containing two members-an integer quantity and a floating quantity. Compute the average and standard deviation of the numbers and print them.

**46.** WAP for the following: track sales for a used-car business with 12 brands in stock, each with an integer code, and generate a daily report that indicates
**a)** inventory by brand at day's start.
**b)** total cars sold by brand at day's end.
**c)** sales as a percentage of inventory, by brand.
(assume all cars have the same price)
sample input:

| car brand no. | No. Of cars in stock | No. Of cars sold |
|---|---|---|
| 1 | 10 | 0 |
| 2 | 12 | 0 |
| 3 | 13 | 6 |
| --------- | --------- | --------- |
| 12 | 30 | 0 |

Sample output:
Brand #: 1

```
--------
brand #: 3
inventory at day's start: 23
total sales: 6
inventory at day's end: 17
sales as percentage of inventory: 26.086957
-------------
```

**47.** WAP that can maintain the name, roll number and marks of a class of students. the size of the class is variable. include functions to compute the average marks of the class.

**48.** WAP to read in a string and output the frequency, of each character in that string.

**49.** WAP to read in a string and output the frequency of each word in that string.

**50.** A company pays normal wage for work during weeks days from monday to friday and 1.5 times wage for work on saturday and sunday. given data in the following form:

employee number, wage/hour, hours worked on monday, hours on tuesday,.., hours on sunday.
WAP to write out the employee number and weekly wages. use enumerated data type in your program.

**51.** Define a structure for a student having name, roll number and marks obtained in six subjects. assume that "all students" is an array of students. WAP to print the name and roll numbers of the students who have secured highest marks in each subject.

**52.** Define a structure "mca2_oops" which has the members: entry_no, marks, marks_minor, marks_ major, total. WAP for initialize the variables of objects, finding the total marks which is sum of marks_major and marks_minor. This program will handle 30 students and displaying their marks.

**53.** Create a structure of big cities bigcity of india,the data member of the structure are name of the city,std code(say for calcutta std code is 033) etc.WAP which interactively ask the name abd addresss,local phone number of residents and print in the following format:

**1**. Name: s.p.rama rao    **2**. Address:3/2 apc road
**3**. Pincode no.: 700052    **4**. Phone no: (033)-4347270

END.

1. **Java Teach Yourself Core Java in 21 Days. 2014,**
   ISBN- 978-1499643015.
2. **Beginning Programming with Java.: Easy Version. 2014**
   ISBN- 978-1499643039.
3. **Core Java Professional : Learn Java Step By Step With Fun.**
   ISBN - 978-1499651027.
4. **Effective Core Java.: The Complete Core Reference.**
   ISBN - 978-1499642582.
5. **Java Brainstorming.: Special Beginners Edition 2014.**
   ISBN - 978-1499651119.
6. **Java Power To you.: Special Beginner's Edition 2014.**
   ISBN - 978-1499651621.
7. **Java, Brain-Washer.: Special Beginners Edition 2014.**
   ISBN - 978-1499651324.
8. **Thinking in Java.: Special Beginner's Edition 2014.**
   ISBN - 978-1499651478.
9. **Effective Core Java.: The Complete Core Reference.**
   ISBN - 978-1499642582.
10. **JAVA The HARDER BETTER FASTER STRONGER. 978-1499651614**

## Best Java Interview Books

List Search on Amazon.com or Google Play & Google Books. Search with Full
Book Name or ISBN Or Author Name- Harry H Chaudhary.
1. **Cracking The Java Coding Interview Hand Book 2014.**
2. **Java Interview Questions & Answers 2013-2014 Edition.**
3. **Java Interview Made Easy.**
4. **Technical Interview Made Easy.**

## Best Data Structure and Algorithms Books for Beginner's or Students.

List Search on Amazon.com or Google Play & Google Books. Search with Full
Book Name or ISBN Or Author Name- Harry H Chaudhary.

1. **Data Structures And Algorithms.: Made Easy.**
   **ISBN- 978-1495996016**
2. **Algorithms, Professional Edition.: Beginner's Guide.**
   **ISBN- 978-1500137274**
3. **Thinking In Data Structures and Algorithms.:**
   **ISBN-978-1500137281**

# Best C++ Books for Beginner's or Students.

List Search on Amazon.com or Google Play & Google Books. Search with Full Book Name or ISBN Or Author Name- Harry H Chaudhary.

1. **Your Brain On C++ : Learn C++ Very Fast & Very Easy.**
   **ISBN-13: 978-1500349578**

2. **Learning C++ : Fast Track Easy C++ Guide for Beginners.**
   **ISBN-13: 978-1500349509**

3. **C++ for Students : A Beginner's Guide That Makes You C++ Champion. ISBN-13: 978-1500349523**

4. **C++ Without Fear: A Beginner's Guide That Makes You C++ Champion. ISBN-13: 978-1500349530**

5. **C++ How to Program : New Best selling Edition for Beginners.**
   **ISBN-13: 978-1500349547**

6. **Teach Yourself C++ in One Hour Daily (40 Days Champ Course)**
   **ISBN-13: 978-1500339340**

7. **Effective C++ : Easy Beginner's To Experts Edition.**
   **ISBN-13: 978-1500329747**

8. **How to Become a C++ Programmer : Step By Step Beginner's To Experts Edition. ISBN-13: 978-1500329662**

9. **Thinking In C++ Programming : The Definitive Beginner's To Expert's Guide. ISBN-13: 978-1500310790**

10. **C++ Programming Professional. ISBN- 978-1495995552**

# Best C# Programming Books for Beginner's or Students.

List Search on Amazon.com or Google Play & Google Books. Search with Full Book Name or ISBN Or Author Name- Harry H Chaudhary.

1. **How to Become a C# Programmer. ISBN: 978-1500193683.**

2. **Head First C# . ISBN: 978-1500193690.**

3. **Effective C# : ISBN: 978-1500193614.**

4. **C# Professional : ISBN: 978-1500193874.**

## We Want to Hear from You!

For Digital version of each book mentioned above, Search on Google Books or Google play- **Download Digital Edition of these book with 5.99 USD Only** Limited time offer for serious Readers. First Download Free Demo then Purchase with $5.99

As the reader of this book, you are our most important critic and commentator. We value your opinion and want to know what we're doing right, what we could do better, what areas you'd like to see us in correction or publish in, and any other words of wisdom you're willing to pass our way.

You can email or write me directly to let me know what you did or didn't like about this book—as well as what we can do to make our books stronger.

Please note that I cannot help you with technical problems related to the topic of this book, and that due to the high volume of mail I receive, I might not be able to reply to every message. When you write, please be sure to include this book's title and author as well as your name and phone or email address. I will carefully review your comments and share them with the author (Myself) and editors who worked on this book.

One more thing don't forget to give us star Reviews rate comments on Amazon.com **Please** Visit on Amazon.com or other website from where you purchased this book. and Write your own customer Review Rate (Stars) from your heart to our Book and Comments that will help us to improve this book data to make better and better for future

**I did hardwork and I Spent several months to make this book,** atleast I can expect one customer review from you, I hope this book helped you a lot , please share this book with other students and tell your college friends about this book **but please suggest to consider buying your own copy from pothi.com (pdf) or createspace.com store (paperback), lulu.com, smashwords.com, amazon.com (kindle & paperback) or google books (digital) , google Play Store (digital)**

Both Physical Paperback and Digital Editions Are also Available on Amazon.com And Createspace Book Store , but on **google books (digital) , google Play Store (digital)** & pothi.com just Order today **and Get a Discounted digital Copy** with very low price. I would like to suggest you, buy paperback edition for better understanding, search this book's paperback edition on amazon.com with following ISBN Numbers-**ISBN10: 1500533238.** *ISBN-13:* 978-1500533236.

# CHAPTER
# ∞ 17- Part –II ∞
## (Step By Step Chapter Wise Programs)
## (Pumping Brain On C Programming)

### Silent Features of part- II

- 120, C-Programming Practice code examples.
- Creating Library Function's with examples.
- Deleting Library Function's with examples.
- Graphics Programming with examples.
- Intro Operating System Development.
- Live Software Development Project.
- Live Virus Programming.

## 1.Wap To Sum Of Two Variables.

```c
#include<stdio.h>
#include<conio.h>
void main()
{
int a,b,c;
clrscr();
printf("\n\t\t\t I'm Learning C with Harry's Book \n");
printf("\n\n\t\Enter the value of a=");
scanf("%d",&a);
printf("\n\t\t Enter the value of b=");
scanf("%d",&b);
c=a+b;
printf("Sum=%d",c);
getch();
}
```

## 2. Wap To Subtraction Of Two Variables.

```c
#include<stdio.h>
#include<conio.h>
void main()
{
int a,b,c;
clrscr();
printf("\n\t\t\t I'm Learning C with Harry's Book \n");
printf("\n\n\t Enter the value of a=");
scanf("%d",&a);
printf("\n\t Enter the value of b=");
scanf("%d",&b);
c=a-b;
printf("Sub is =%d",c);
getch();
}
```

## 3.Wap To Multiply Of Two Variables.

```c
#include<stdio.h>
#include<conio.h>
void main()
{
int a,b,c;
clrscr();
printf("\n\t\t\t I'm Learning C with Harry's Book \n");
printf("\n\n\t Enter the value of a=");
scanf("%d",&a);
printf("\n\t Enter the value of b=");
scanf("%d",&b);
c=a*b;
printf("Multiply is =%d",c);
getch();
}
```

## 4.Wap To Divide Of Two Variables.

```c
#include<stdio.h>
#include<conio.h>
void main()
{
int a,b,c;
clrscr();
printf("\n\t\t\t I'm Learning C with Harry's Book \n");
printf("\n\n\t Enter the value of a=");
scanf("%d",&a);
printf("\n\t Enter the value of b=");
scanf("%d",&b);
c=a/b;
printf("Divide is =%d",c);
getch();
}
```

## 5.Wap To Find Out Simple Interest, Hence Ask To Enter The Values Of Principle,Rate,Time By User.

```c
#include<stdio.h>
#include<conio.h>
void main()
{
float si,p,t,r;
clrscr();
printf("\n\t\t\t I'm Learning C with Harry's Book \n");
printf("\n\n\t Enter the value of p=");
scanf("%f",&p);
printf("\n\t Enter the value of t=");
scanf("%f",&t);
printf("\n\t Enter the value of r=");
scanf("%f",&r);
si=(p*t*r)/100;
printf("si=%f",si);
getch();
}
```

## 6.wap to read marks of a student in five subjects of a college and calculate his total of marks and also calculate percentage.

```c
#include<stdio.h>
#include<conio.h>
void main()
{
float s1,s2,s3,s4,s5,totel,per;
clrscr();
printf("\n\t\t\t I'm Learning C with Harry's Book \n");
printf("\n\n\t Enter the value subject s1=");
scanf("%f",&s1);
printf("\n\t Enter the value of subject s2=");
scanf("%f",&s2);
```

```
printf("\n\t Enter the value subject s3=");
scanf("%f",&s3);
printf("\n\t Enter the value of subject s4=");
scanf("%f",&s4);
printf("\n\t Enter the value of  s5=");
scanf("%f",&s5);
total=s1+s2+s3+s4+s5;
per=total/5;
printf("\n total=%f  \n per=%f",totel,per);
getch();
}
```

## 7. Wap to swap two variables using third variable.

```
#include<stdio.h>
#include<conio.h>
void main()
{
float a,b,c;
clrscr();
printf("\n\t\t\tI'm Learning C with Harry's Book \n");
printf("\n\n\t Enter the value of a=");
scanf("%f",&a);
printf("\n\n\t Enter the value of b=");
scanf("%f",&b);
c=a;
a=b;
b=c;
printf("\n after swapping a=%f \n\t b=%f",a,b);
getch();
}
```
**Note :** *Swap means interchanging values to each other.*
**Note :** *Here c is a temp. Variable.*

## 8. Wap to swap two variables without using third variable.

```
#include<stdio.h>
#include<conio.h>
void main()
{
float a,b;
clrscr();
printf("\n\t\t\t I'm Learning C with Harry's Book \n");
printf("\n\n\t Enter the value of a=");
scanf("%f",&a);
printf("\n\n\t Enter the value of b=");
scanf("%f",&b);
a=a+b;
b=a-b;
a=a-b;
printf("\n\t\After swapping a=%f\n\n\t\t b=%f",a,b);
getch();
}
```

274

## 9. Wap to calculate area of triangle (Tribhuj).

```
#include<stdio.h>
#include<conio.h>
void main()
{
float a,b,c,s,r,area;
clrscr();
printf("\n\t\t\t I'm Learning C with Harry's Book \n");
printf("\n\n\t Enter the value of a=");
scanf("%f",&a);
printf("\n\n\t Enter the value of b=");
scanf("%f",&b);
printf("\n\t Enter the value of c=");
scanf("%f",&c);
s=a+b+c;
area=s*(s-a)*(s-b)*(s-c);
r=area;
printf("\n\t\t Area=%f",r);
getch();
}
```

## 10. Wap to read time in hour,min,sec and convert it in to total seconds.

```
#include<stdio.h>
#include<conio.h>
void main()
{
int hr,min,sec,totalsec;
clrscr();
printf("\n\t\t\t I'm Learning C with Harry's Book \n");
printf("\n\n\t Enter the value of hr=");
scanf("%d",&hr);
printf("\n\n\t Enter the value of min=");
scanf("%d",&min);
printf("\n\t Enter the value of sec=");
scanf("%d",&sec);
totalsec=(hr*3600)+(min*60)+sec;
printf("\n\t\t Totalsec=%d",totalsec);
getch();
}
```

## 11. Wap to print ASCII code of any character.
```
#include<stdio.h>
#include<conio.h>
void main()
{
char ch;
clrscr();
printf("\n\t\t\t I'm Learning C with Harry's Book \n");
printf("\n\n\t Enter any character =");
scanf("%c",&ch);
printf("\n\t\t ASCII code of =%c is %d",ch,ch);
getch();
}
```

**Mind Drill Note :**

ASCII is a Table (American Standard Code For Instruction Interchange.)

## 12. WAP to find out whether a Entered no. Is Even Or Odd.

```
#include<stdio.h>
#include<conio.h>
void main()
{
int n;
clrscr();
printf("\n\t\t\t I'm Learning C with Harry's Book
\n");printf("\n\n\t Enter any number =");
scanf("%d",&n);
if(n%2==0)
printf("\n\t\t Number is even");
else
printf("\n\t\t Number is odd");
getch();
}
```

## 13. Wap to check that Entered character is capital,small,digit,or a special symbol?

```
#include<stdio.h>
#include<conio.h>
void main()
{
char ch;
clrscr();
printf("\n\t\t\t I'm Learning C with Harry's Book \n");
printf("\n\n\t Enter any character =");
scanf("%c",&ch);
if(ch>=65 && ch<=90)
printf("\n\t\t character is uppercase");
else
if(ch>=97 && ch<=122)
printf("\n\t\t character is smaller case");
else
if(ch>=48 && ch<=65)
printf("\n\t\t character is digit");
else
printf("Character is special symbol");
getch();
}
```

## 14. Wap to find out area by pai.

```c
#include<stdio.h>
#include<conio.h>
void main()
{
float r,area,pi=3.14;
clrscr();
printf("Enter radius");
scanf("%f",&r);
area=pi*r*r;
printf("area=%f",area);
getch();
}
```

## 15. Wap to find out average of two no's

```c
/* average of 2 no*/
#include<stdio.h>
#include<conio.h>
void main()
{
 int a,b;
  float avg;
  clrscr();
  printf("Enter 2 no");
  scanf("%d %d",&a,&b);
  avg=(a+b)/2.0;
  printf("average=%f",avg);
  getch();
}
```

## 16. Wap to Entered total no. Of days and find out in months.

```c
#include<stdio.h>
#include<conio.h>
void main()
{
 int n,m,d;
  clrscr();
  printf("Enter no of days\n");
  scanf("%d",&n);
      m=n/30;
      d=n%30;
  printf("months=%d,days=%d",m,d);
  getch();
}
```

## 17. Wap to swap 3 no. Using third variable.

```c
#include<stdio.h>
#include<conio.h>
void main()
{
int a,b,c,t;
clrscr();
printf("Enter three no");
scanf("%d %d %d",&a,&b,&c);
t=a;
a=b;
b=t;
t=c;
c=b;
b=t;
printf("%d %d %d",a,b,c);
getch();
}
```

## 18. Wap to swap 3 no's without using third variable.

```c
#include<stdio.h>
#include<conio.h>
void main()
{
  int a,b,c;
clrscr();
printf("Enter three no");
scanf("%d %d %d",&a,&b,&c);
a=a+b;
b=a-b;
a=a-b;
b=b+c;
c=b-c;
b=b-c;
printf("%d %d %d",a,b,c);
getch();
}
```

## 19. Wap to calculate profit and loss.

```c
#include<stdio.h>
#include<conio.h>
void main()
{
float sp,cp;
 clrscr();
 printf("Enter cost price and selling price\n");
 scanf("%f %f",&cp,&sp);
 if(cp<sp)
            printf("profit=%.2f Rs",sp-cp);
 else if(sp<cp)
            printf("loss=%.2f Rs",cp-sp);
 else
            printf("no profit no loss");
 getch();
}
```

## 20. Wap for calculate total & percentage then print Grades.

```c
#include<stdio.h>
#include<conio.h>
void main()
{
float p;
  char grade;
  clrscr();
  printf("Enter percentage\n\n");
  scanf("%f",&p);
      if(p>=90)
        grade='A';
      else if(p>=70)
        grade='B';
      else if(p>=50)
        grade='C';
      else
        grade='F';
  printf("grade=%c",grade);
  getch();
}
```

## 21.wap to convert lower case to upper case.

```c
/* lower case to upper case*/

#include<stdio.h>
#include<conio.h>
void main()
{
char ch;
clrscr();
printf("Enter a character\n");
scanf("%c",&ch);
if(ch>=97&&ch<=122)
ch=ch-32;
printf("%c",ch);
getch();
}
```

## 22. Wap to find out large no. Between two no's

```c
#include<stdio.h>
#include<conio.h>
void main()
{
 int a,b;
  clrscr();
  printf("Enter 2 no");
  scanf("%d %d",&a,&b);
      if(a>b)
         printf("%d is greater",a);
      else if(a==b)
         printf("Both are equal");
      else
         printf("%d is greater ",b);
  getch();
}
```

## 23. Wap to find out max no. From four no's

```c
#include<stdio.h>
#include<conio.h>
void main()
{
int a,b,c,d;
  clrscr();
  printf("Enter 4 no");
  scanf("%d %d %d %d",&a,&b,&c,&d);
      if(a>b)
      {
              if(a>c)
              {
                     if(a>d)
                       printf("%d",a);
                     else
                       printf("%d",d);
              }
              else if(c>d)
                  printf("%d",c);
              else
                  printf("%d",d);

      }
      else if(b>c)
              {
                if(b>d)
                 printf("%d",b);
                else
                  printf("%d",d);
              }
      else
              {
                if(c>d)
```

280

```
            printf("%d",c);
            else
            printf("%d",d);
        }
      getch();
}
```

## 24. Wap for Develop mini calculator Using switch with Case.

```c
/* calculator*/
#include<stdio.h>
#include<conio.h>
void main()
{
int a,b,ch;
 clrscr();
 printf("Enter two no\n");
 scanf("%d %d",&a,&b);
 printf("1/t add\n 2/t subtract\n 3/t multiplication\n
4/t divide\n 5/t modulus\n Enter your choice\n");
 scanf("%d",&ch);

 switch(ch)
       {
       case 1:
             printf("sum=%d",a+b);
             break;

       case 2:
             printf("subtraction=%d",a-b);
             break;

       case 3:
             printf("multiplication=%d",a*b);
             break;

       case 4:
             printf("division=%f",(float)a/b);
             break;

       case 5:
             printf("modulus=%d",a%b);
             break;

       default:
             printf("invalid input");
       }

       getch();
}
```

## 25. Wap to for mini calculator using Arithmetic operators each operator perform specific task.

```c
#include<stdio.h>
#include<conio.h>
void main()
{
int a,b;
char ch;
        clrscr();
        printf("Enter two no\n");
        scanf("%d %d",&a,&b);
        flushall();

printf("/n + for add \n - for subtract \n * for multiplication \n / for divide\n Enter your choice\n");

scanf("%d",&ch);

 switch(ch)
        {
        case '+' :
                printf("sum=%d",a+b);
                break;

        case '-' :
                printf("subtraction=%d",a-b);
                break;

        case '*' :
                printf("multiplication=%d",a*b);
                break;

        case '/':
                printf("division=%f",(float)a/b);
                break;

        case '%' :
                printf("modulus=%d",a%b);
                break;

        default:
                printf("invalid input");
        }

        getch();

}
```

## 26. Wap to calculate Factorial of any given no. By user.

```
#include<stdio.h>
#include<conio.h>
void main()
{
Int   n,i,f=1;
   clrscr();
   printf("Hello Guys, I'm Learning C Programming with
Harry's Book ");
printf(" Enter the any no. For factorial");
   scanf("%d ",&n);
for (i=1;i<=n;i++)
f=f*i;
printf("\n factorial is = %d",f);
getch();
}
```

## 27. Wap to calculate power of no.

```
#include<stdio.h>
#include<conio.h>
void main()
{ int n,i,p;
long int ans=1;
clrscr();
printf("Enter a no and its power to be calculated");
scanf("%d %d",&n,&p);
i=p;
        while(i>=1)
        { ans*=n;
        i--;
        }
        printf("%ld",ans);
        getch();
}
```

## 28. Wap to find out how many day in month.

```c
#include<stdio.h>
#include<conio.h>
void main()
{
int a;
clrscr();
printf("Enter a month no");
scanf("%d",&a);

        switch(a)
        {
        case 1:
        case 3:
        case 5:
        case 7:
        case 8:
        case 10:
        case 12:
                printf("There are 31 days in given month");
                break;
        case 2:
                printf("There are 28 days in given month");
                break;
        case 4:
        case 6:
        case 9:
        case 11:
                printf("There are 30 days in given month");
                break;
        default:
                printf("Invalid input");
        }
        getch();2
}
```

## 29. Wap to convert temp from Fahrenheit to centigrade.

```c
#include<stdio.h>
#include<conio.h>
void main()
{
float f,c;
  clrscr();
  printf("Enter Temperature in F");
  scanf("%f",&f);
  c=(f-3.2)/1.8;
  printf("Temperature in C is %f",c);
  getch();
}
```

## 30. Wap to show given year is leap year or not.

```c
#include<stdio.h>
#include<conio.h>
void main()
{    int n;
  clrscr();
  printf("Enter an year");
  scanf("%d",&n);
  if(n%100==0)
        {
        if(n%400==0)
        printf("leap year");
        else
        printf("Not leap year");
        }
  else
        {
        if(n%4==0)
        printf("leap year");
        else
        printf("Not leap year");
        }
  getch();
}
```

## 31. Wap to know is year leap year or not.

```c
#include<stdio.h>
#include<conio.h>
void main()
{
int y;
clrscr();
printf("Enter an year\n");
scanf("%d",&y);
if(y%400==0||y%100!=0&&y%4==0)
printf("Given year is leap year\n");
else
printf("Given year is not leap year");
getch();
}
```

## 32. Wap for weekday.

```c
/* weekday*/
#include<stdio.h>
#include<conio.h>
void main()
{int w;
clrscr();
printf("Enter a weekday\n");
scanf("%d",&w);
    switch(w)
    {
    case 1:
            printf("Sunday");
            break;
    case 2:
            printf("Monday");
            break;
    case 3:
            printf("Tuesday");
            break;
    case 4:
            printf("Wednesday");
            break;
    case 5:
            printf("Thursday");
            break;
    case 6:
            printf("Friday");
            break;
    case 7:
            printf("Saturday");
            break;
    default:
            printf("invalid input");
    }
    getch();

}
```

## 33. Wap to working of telephone bill company.

```c
/* telephone bill*/
#include<stdio.h>
#include<conio.h>
void main()
{
int calls;
float bill;
clrscr();
printf("Enter no of calls");
scanf("%d",&calls);
printf("calls o to 100\t 0Rs\n calls 101-200\t 0.80Rs\n
calls 201-500\t 1.00Rs\n calls >500\t 1.20Rs\n");
if(calls<=100)
       bill=0;
else if(calls<=200)
       bill=(calls-100)*.80;
else if(calls<=500)
       bill=(calls-200)*1.00+80;
else
       bill=(calls-500)*1.20+380;
printf("bill=%.2fRs",bill);
getch();
}
```

## 34. Wap to find out no. Is Armstrong or not.

```c
#include<stdio.h>
#include<conio.h>
void main()
{ int n,sum=0,a,old;
  clrscr();
  printf("Enter a no");
  scanf("%d",&n);
      old=n;
      while(n!=0)
      {
              a=n%10;
              n=n/10;
              sum=sum+a*a*a;
      }
      if(sum==old)
              printf("ARMSTRONG");
      else
              printf("NOT ARMSTRONG");
  getch();
}
```

## 35. Wap to check a no. Is palindrome or not.

```c
#include<stdio.h>
#include<conio.h>
void main()
{ int a;
  long int n,old,rev=0;
  clrscr();
  printf("Enter a no");
  scanf("%ld",&n);
      old=n;
      do
      {
          a=n%10;
          n=n/10;
          rev=rev*10+a;
      }while(n!=0);
      if(old==rev)
          printf("PALINDROME");
      else
          printf("NOT PALINDROME");
  getch();
}
```

## 36. Wap to check whether a no. Is prime or not.

```c
#include<stdio.h>
#include<conio.h>
void main()
{
int n,i,prime=1;
  clrscr();
  printf("Enter a no");
  scanf("%d",&n);
      for(i=2;i<=n/2;i++)
      {      if(n%i==0)
              { prime=0;
                break;
              }
      }
      if(prime==1)
        printf("Prime no");
      else
        printf("Not prime no");
  getch();
}
```

## 37 . Wap to reverse of a given no.

```c
#include<stdio.h>
#include<conio.h>
void main()
{
 int a;
  long int n,rev=0;
  clrscr();
  printf("Enter a no");
  scanf("%ld",&n);
      do
      {
          a=n%10;
          n=n/10;
          rev=rev*10+a;
      }while(n!=0);
  printf("%ld",rev);
  getch();
}
```

## 38. Wap to print table of any no.

```c
#include<stdio.h>
#include<conio.h>
Void main()
{
Int n,i,a;
Clrscr();
Printf("\n Enter any no.");
Scanf("%d",&n);
For(i=1; i<=n; i++)
{
a= n*i;
printf(\n Table is = %d*%d",n,i,a);
}
getch();
}
```

## 39. Wap to print FIBBONACCI series.

```c
#include<stdio.h>
#include<conio.h>
Void main()
{
Int a=1 ,b=0, c=0, n, i;
Clrscr();
Printf("Enter how many terms u want to print series");
Scanf("%d",&n);
For (i=1 ; i<=n ; i++)
{
Printf("%d",c);
c=a+b;
a=b;
b=c;
}
getch();          }
```

### 40. Wap to print sequence 1,3,5,7,9.....n

```
#include<stdio.h>
#include<conio.h>
Void main()
{
Int    s=1,n, i;
Clrscr();
Printf("Enter how many terms u want to print ");
Scanf("%d",&n);
For (i=1 ; i<=n ; i++;s+2)
Printf("%d",s);
getch();
}
```

### 41. Wap to print 2,4,6,8,10.........n

```
#include<stdio.h>
#include<conio.h>
Void main()
{
Int    s=2, n, i;
Clrscr();
Printf("Enter how many terms u want to print series");
Scanf("%d",&n);
For (i=1 ; i<=n ; i++,s+=2)
Printf("%d",s);
getch();
}
```

### 42. Wap to print sequence 1,4,9,16,25,..............n

```
#include<stdio.h>
#include<conio.h>
Void main()
{
Int  n, i;
Clrscr();
Printf("Enter how many terms u want to print ");
Scanf("%d",&n);
For (i=1 ; i<=n ; i++)
Printf("%d", i*i);
getch();
}
```

## 43. Wap to print  $1/1! + 2/2! + 3/3! + \ldots\ldots\ldots\ldots n$

```c
#include<stdio.h>
#include<conio.h>
Void main()
{
Int    n, i, s=1;
Float    fact=1;
Clrscr();
Printf("Enter how many terms u want to print series");
Scanf("%d",&n);
For (i=1 ; i<=n ; i++)
{
Fact = fact* i;
Printf("%f +", i / fact);
}
getch();
}
```

## 44. Wap to print  $1 + x2/y2 + x4/y4 + \ldots\ldots\ldots\ldots n$

```c
#include<stdio.h>
#include<conio.h>
#include<math.h>
Void main()
{
Int    n, i,p=2,x,y;
Float   s,N,D;
Clrscr();
Printf("Enter how many terms u want to print series");
Scanf("%d",&n);
Printf("Enter the value of x and y");
Scanf("%d%d",&x,&y);
Printf("1+")
For (i=1 ; i<=n ; i++)
{
N=pow(x,p);
D=pow(y,p);
S=N/D;
Printf("%F +",S);
P=P+2;
}
getch();
}
```

## 45. Wap to print 1+X2 /Y + X4/Y3 +.....N.

```
#include<stdio.h>
#include<conio.h>
#include<math.h>
Void main()
{
Int    n, i,p=2,q=1,x,y;
Float   s,N,D;
Clrscr();
Printf("Enter how many terms u want to print series");
Scanf("%d",&n);
Printf("Enter the value of x and y");
Scanf("%d%d",&x,&y);
Printf("1+")
For (i=1 ; i<=n ; i++)
{
N=pow(x,p);
D=pow(y,q);
S=N/D;
Printf("%F +",S);
P=P+2;
Q=q+2;
}
getch();
}
```

## 46. Wap to print 1-X2 /Y + X4/Y3 -.....N.

```
#include<stdio.h>
#include<conio.h>
#include<math.h>
Void main()
{
Int    n, i,p=2,q=1,x,y;
Float   s,N,D;
Clrscr();
Printf("Enter how many terms u want to print series");
Scanf("%d",&n);
Printf("Enter the value of x and y");
Scanf("%d%d",&x,&y);
Printf("1-")
For (i=1 ; i<=n ; i++)
{
N=pow(x,p);          D=pow(y,q);
S=N/D;
If(i%2==0)
Printf("%f -",s);
else
Printf("%f +",S);
P=P+2;
}
getch();            }
```

## 47. Wap to print following shape with the help of loops.

```
*
* *
* * *
* * * *
* * * * *
```

```
#include<stdio.h>
#include<conio.h>
Void main()
{
Int   n, i, j;
Clrscr();
Printf("Enter how many rows u want to print series");
Scanf("%d",&n);
For (i=1 ; i<=n ; i++)
{
For (j=1 ; i<=i; j++)
Printf("*");
Printf("\n");
}
getch();
}
```

## 48. Wap print this shape.

```
* * * * *
* * * *
* * *
* *
*
```

```
#include<stdio.h>
#include<conio.h>
Void main()
{
Int   n, i, j;
Clrscr();
Printf("Enter how many rows u want to print series");
Scanf("%d",&n);
For (i=n ; i>=1 ; i++)
{
For (j=5 ; j>=i; j--)
Printf("*");
Printf("\n");
}
getch();
}
```

## 49. print this shape.

```
1
1 2
1 2 3
1 2 3 4
1 2 3 4 5
```

```
#include<stdio.h>
#include<conio.h>
Void main()
{
Int    n, i, j;
Clrscr();
Printf("Enter how many rows u want to print series");
Scanf("%d",&n);
For (i=1 ; i<=n ; i++)
{
For (j=1 ; j<=i; j++)
Printf("%d", j);
Printf("\n");
}
getch();
}
```

## 50. Wap to print this shape.

```
1
2 2
3 3 3
4 4 4 4
5 5 5 5 5
```

```
#include<stdio.h>
#include<conio.h>
Void main()
{
Int    n, i, j;
Clrscr();
Printf("Enter how many rows u want to print series");
Scanf("%d",&n);
For (i=1 ; i<=n ; i++)
{
For (j=1 ; j<=i; j++)
Printf("%d", i);
Printf("\n");
getch();
}
```

## 51. Wap to print this shape.

```
1
2 3
4 5 6
7 8 9 10
11 12 13 14 15
```

```c
#include<stdio.h>
#include<conio.h>
Void main( )
{
Int n, i, j,k=1;
Clrscr( );
Printf("Enter how many rows u want to print series");
Scanf("%d",&n);
For (i=1 ; i<=n ; i++)
{
For (j=1 ; j<=i; j++)
Printf("%d", k++);
Printf("\n");
}
getch( );
}
```

## 52. Wap to print this shape.

```
A
AB
ABC
ABCD
ABCDE
```

```c
#include<stdio.h>
#include<conio.h>
Void main( )
{
Int    n, i, j;
char ch;
ch='A' ;
Clrscr( );
Printf("Enter how many rows u want to  print series");
Scanf("%d",&n);
For (i=1 ; i<=n ; i++)
{
For ( j=1 ; j<=i; j++)
Printf("%c", ch++);
Printf("\n");
}
getch( );     }
```

## 53. Wap to print this shape.

```
                    A
                    BB
                    CCC
                    DDDD
                    EEEEE
```

```
#include<stdio.h>
#include<conio.h>
Void main()
{
Int n, i, j;
char ch;
ch='A' ;
Clrscr();
Printf("Enter how many rows u want to print series");
Scanf("%d",&n);
For (i=1 ; i<=n ; i++)
{
For ( j=1 ; j<=i; j++)
Printf("%c",ch);
ch++;
Printf("\n");
}
getch();
}
```

## 54. Wap to print this shape.

```
                    A
                    BC
                    DEF
                    GHIJ
                    KLMNO
```

```
#include<stdio.h>
#include<conio.h>
Void main()
{
Int n, i, j;
char ch;
ch='A' ;
Clrscr();
Printf("Enter how many rows u want to print series");
Scanf("%d",&n);
For (i=1 ; i<=n ; i++)
{
For ( j=1 ; j<=i; j++)
Printf("%c",ch++);
Printf("\n");
}
getch();}
```

## 55.WAP TO PRINT THIS STARS SHAPE.

```
        *
       ***
      *****
     *******
    *********
```

```
#include<stdio.h>
#include<conio.h>
Void main()
{
Int n,i,j,K;
Clrscr();
Printf("Enter how many rows u want to print series");
Scanf("%d",&n);
For (i=1;i<=n;i++)
{
For (j=1;j<=n-i;j++)
Printf(" ");
for(k=1;k<=2*i-1;k++)
printf("*");
Printf("\n");
}
getch();
}
```

## 56. Wap to print this shape.

```
    *********
     *******
      *****
       ***
        *
```

```
#include<stdio.h>
#include<conio.h>
Void main()
{
Int n,i,j,K;
Clrscr();
Printf("Enter how many rows u want to print series");
Scanf("%d",&n);
For (i=n;i>=1;i--)
{
For (j=1;j<=n-i;j++)
Printf(" ");
```

```
for(k=1;k<=2*i-1;k++)
printf("*");
Printf("\n");
}
getch();
}
```

## 57. Wap to print this star shape in this form.

```
    *
   ***
  *****
 *******
********
 *******
  *****
   ***
    *
```

```
#include<stdio.h>
#include<conio.h>
Void main()
{
Int n,i,j,K;
Clrscr();
Printf("Enter how many rows u want to print series");
Scanf("%d",&n);
For (i=1;i<=n;i++)
{
For (j=1;j<=n-i;j++)
Printf(" ");
for(k=1;k<=2*i-1;k++)
printf("*");
Printf("\n");
}
for (i=n-1;i>=1;i--)
{
For (j=1;j<=n-i;j++)
Printf(" ");
for(k=1;k<=2*i-1;k++)
printf("*");
Printf("\n");
}
getch();
}
```

298

## 58. Wap to print this star shape in this form.

```
********
 *******
  *****
   ***
    *
   ***
  *****
 *******
********
```
```c
#include<stdio.h>
#include<conio.h>
Void main()
{
Int n,i,j,K;
Clrscr();
Printf("Enter how many rows u want to print series");
Scanf("%d",&n);
For (i=n;i>=1;i--)
{
For (j=1;j<=n-i;j++)
Printf(" ");
for(k=1;k<=2*i-1;k++)
printf("*");
Printf("\n");
}
for (i=2;i<=n;i++)
{
For (j=1;j<=n-i;j++)
Printf(" ");
for(k=1;k<=2*i-1;k++)
printf("*");
Printf("\n");
}
getch();
}
```

**59. Wap to print this binary shape.**

```
10000
01000
00100
00010
00001
```

```
#include<stdio.h>
#include<conio.h>
Void main()
{
Int n,i,j,K;
Clrscr();
Printf("Enter how many rows u want to print series");
Scanf("%d",&n);
For (i=1;i<=n;i++)
{
For (j=1;j<=n;j++)

if (i==j)
printf("1");
else
printf("0");
printf("\n");
}
getch();
}
```

**60. Wap to print this binary shape.**

```
   A
  ABA
 ABCBA
ABCDCBA
```

```
#include<stdio.h>
#include<conio.h>
Void main()
{
Int n,i,j,K,l;
```

```
char ch;
Clrscr();
Printf("Enter how many rows u want to print series");
Scanf("%d",&n);
For (i=1;i<=n;i++)
{
ch='A';
For (j=1;j<=n-i;j++)
print(" ");
for(k=1;k<=i;k++);
printf("%c",ch++);
ch=ch-2;
for(l=1;l<i;l++)
printf("%c",ch--);
printf("\n");
}
getch();
}
```

## 61. Wap to print this binary shape.

```
       1
      121
     12321
    1234321
```

```
#include<stdio.h>
#include<conio.h>
Void main()
{
Int n,i,j,K,l,m;
Clrscr();
Printf("Enter how many rows u want to print series");
Scanf("%d",&n);
For (i=1;i<=n;i++)
{
m=1;
For (j=1;j<=n-i;j++)
print(" ");
for(k=1;k<=i;k++);
printf("%d",m++);
m=m-2;
for(l=1;l<i;l++)
printf("%d",m--);
printf("\n");
}
getch();
}
```

## 62. Wap to print this shape.

```
        1
       12
      123
     1234
```

```
#include<stdio.h>
#include<conio.h>
Void main()
{
Int n,i,j,K;
Clrscr();
Printf("Enter how many rows u want to print series");
Scanf("%d",&n);
For (i=1;i<=n;i++)
{
For (j=1;j<=n-i;j++)
printf(" ");
for(k=1;k<=i;k++);
printf("%d",k);
print("\n");
}
getch();
}
```

**\*\*\*\*\*\*\*\*\***
**\*ARRAYS\***
**\*\*\*\*\*\*\*\*\***

## 63. Wap to read an array of 20 integers and print sum of all Entered no.'s.

```
#include<stdio.h>
#include<conio.h>
Void main()
{
Int a[20],i,sum=0;
Clrscr();
Printf("Enter how many elements of this array series u
want to Enter");

For (i=0;i<=19;i++)
{
Scanf("%d",&a[i] );
sum=sum+a[i];
}
printf("\n sum=%d",sum);
getch();
}
```

**64. Wap to read an array of 20 integers and count total no's of even and odd elements.**

```
#include<stdio.h>
#include<conio.h>
Void main()
{
Int a[20],i,odd=0,even=0;
Clrscr();
Printf("Enter how many elements of this array series u
want to Enter");
For (i=0;i<=19;i++)
{
Scanf("%d",&a[i] );
if  (a[i] % 2==0)
      even++;
else
      odd++;
}
printf("\n  even=%d,    odd=%d",even,odd );
getch();
}
```

**65. Wap to read an array of 20 integers and count total no's of pos. and neg. & zero elements.**

```
#include<stdio.h>
#include<conio.h>
Void main()
{
Int a[20],i,pos=0,neg=0,zero=0;
Clrscr();
Printf("Enter how many elements of this array series u
want to Enter");
For (i=0;i<=19;i++)
{
Scanf("%d",&a[i] );
if (a[i]>0)
              pos++;
else if( a[i]<0)
              neg++;
else
              zero++;
}
printf("\n pos=%d, neg=%d, zero=%d",pos,neg,zero);
getch();
}
```

## 66. Wap to read an array of 20 integers and store Addition of those arrays in to third array.

```
#include<stdio.h>
#include<conio.h>
Void main()
{
Int a[20],b[20],c[20],i;
Clrscr();
Printf("Enter how many elements of the first array");
For (i=0;i<=19;i++)
{
Scanf("%d",&a[i] );
}
Printf("Enter how many elements of the second array");
For (i=0;i<=19;i++)
{
Scanf("%d",&b[i] );
}
For (i=0;i<=19;i++)
{
c[i]=a[i]+b[i];
}
printf("\n Addition after first and second array \n");
for(i=0;i<=10;i++)
{
printf("%d",c[i]);
}
getch();
}
```

## 67. Wap to read two arrays of 10 integers and swap their values using third variable.

```
#include<stdio.h>
#include<conio.h>
Void main()
{
Int a[20],b[20],c,i;
Clrscr();
Printf("Enter how many elements of the first array");
For (i=0;i<=19;i++)
{
Scanf("%d",&a[i] );
}
Printf("Enter how many elements of the second array");
```

```
For (i=0;i<=19;i++)
{
Scanf("%d",&b[i] );
}
/*swapping of arrays*/
for (i=0; i<19;i++)
{
c=a[i];
a[i]=b[i];
b[i]=c;
}
printf("\n after swapping first array \n")
for (i=0; i<19;i++)
{
printf("%d",a[i]);
}
printf("\n after swapping second array \n")
for (i=0; i<19;i++)
{
printf("%d",b[i]);
}
getch();
}
```

## 68. Wap to Reverse an Array.

```
#include<stdio.h>
#include<conio.h>
Void main()
{
Int a[20],i,j;
Clrscr();
Printf("\n Enter how many elements of the first array");
For (i=0;i<=19;i++)
{
Scanf("%d",&a[i] );
}
for (i=0;j=10-1;i<10/2;i++;j--)
{
c=a[i];
a[i]=a[j];
a[j]=c;
}
printf("\n Reverse of  array \n")
for (i=0; i<19;i++)
printf("%d",a[i]);
getch();
}
```

### 69. Wap to read a 3*3 matrix and find out max and min elements.

```c
#include<stdio.h>
#include<conio.h>
Void main()
{
Int a[5][5],i,j,min=-32767,max=-32768;
Clrscr();
Printf("\n Enter elements of the matrix");
For (i=0;i<=4;i++)
{
for (j=0; j<=4;j++)
{
scanf("%d",&a[i][j]);
if (max<a[i][j])
    max=a[i][j];
else if(min>a[i][j]
    min=a[i][j];
  }
}
printf("\n max=%d, min=%d", max,min);
getch();
}
```

### 70. Wap to read a 3*3 matrix and print sum of all rows.

```c
#include<stdio.h>
#include<conio.h>
Void main()
{
Int a[5][5],i,j,sum=0;
Clrscr();
Printf("\n Enter elements of the matrix");
For (i=0;i<=4;i++)
{
for (j=0; j<=4;j++)
    {
      scanf("%d",&a[i][j]);
    }
}
for (i=0;i<=4;i++)
{
sum=0;
for (j=0;j<=4;j++)
{
sum=sum+a[i][j];
}
printf("\n sum of %d row is =%d",i+1,sum);
}
getch();}
```

## 71. Wap to print 3*3 matrix and print its transpose.

```
#include<stdio.h>
#include<conio.h>
Void main()
{
Int a[3][3],i,j;
Clrscr();
Printf("\n Enter elements of the matrix");
For (i=0;i<3;i++)
{
for (j=0; j<3;j++)
     {
        scanf("%d",&a[i][j]);
     }
}
printf("\n Transpose \n");
for (i=0;i<3;i++)
{
for(j=0;j<3;j++)
printf("%d",a[j][i]);
printf("\n");
}
getch();
}
```

## 72. Wap to read two 3*3 matrix and add their values in to third matrix.

```
#include<stdio.h>
#include<conio.h>
Void main()
{
Int a[3][3],b[3][3],c[3][3]i,j;
Clrscr();
Printf("\n Enter elements of first matrix");
For (i=0;i<3;i++)
{
for (j=0; j<3;j++)
     {
        scanf("%d",&a[i][j]);
     }
}
Printf("\n Enter elements of second matrix");
For (i=0;i<3;i++)
{
for (j=0; j<3;j++)
     {
```

```
        scanf("%d",&b[i][j]);
        }
}
/* Addition of matrix*/
for (i=0;i<3;i++)
for(j=0;j<3;j++)
c[i][j]=a[i][j]+b[i][j];
printf("\n Addition of first and second matrix \n");
For (i=0;i<3;i++)
{
for (j=0;  j<3;j++)
        {
        printf("%d",c[i][j]);
        }
printf("\n");
}
getch();
}
```

## 73. Wap to read two 3*3 matrix and subtract their values and store them in to third.

```
#include<stdio.h>
#include<conio.h>
Void main()
{
Int a[3][3],b[3][3],c[3][3]i,j;
Clrscr();
Printf("\n Enter elements of first matrix");
For (i=0;i<3;i++)
{
for (j=0;  j<3;j++)
        {
        scanf("%d",&a[i][j]);
        }
}
Printf("\n Enter elements of second matrix");
For (i=0;i<3;i++)
{
for (j=0;  j<3;j++)
        {
        scanf("%d",&b[i][j]);
        }
}
/* Subtraction of matrix*/
for (i=0;i<3;i++)
        for(j=0;j<3;j++)
```

```
c[i][j]=a[i][j]-b[i][j];
printf("\n Subtraction of first and second matrix \n");
For (i=0;i<3;i++)
{
for (j=0;  j<3;j++)
        {
          printf("%d",c[i][j]);
        }
printf("\n");
}
getch();
}
```

## 74. Wap to read two 3*3 matrix and multiply there values and store them in third matrix.

```
#include<stdio.h>
#include<conio.h>
Void main()
{
Int a[3][3],b[3][3],c[3][3]i,j,k;
Clrscr();
Printf("\n Enter elements of first matrix");
For (i=0;i<3;i++)
{
for (j=0;  j<3;j++)
        {
          scanf("%d",&a[i][j]);
        }
}
Printf("\n Enter elements of second matrix");
For (i=0;i<3;i++)
{
for (j=0;  j<3;j++)
        {
          scanf("%d",&b[i][j]);
        }
}
/* Multiply of matrix*/
For (i=0;i<3;i++)
{
for (j=0;  j<3;j++)
        {
            c[i][j]=0
for(k=0;k<3;k++)
        c[i][j]=c[i][j]+a[i][k]*b[k][j];
        }
```

```
}
printf("\n MULTIPLY OF BOTH MATRIX \n");
For (i=0;i<3;i++)
{
for (j=0;  j<3;j++)
        {
        printf("%d",c[i][j]);
        }
        printf("\n");
}
getch();
}
```

## 75. Wap to read an array and print the occurrence of any particular element.

```
#include<stdio.h>
#include<conio.h>
Void main()
{
Int a[10],i,j,item,count=0;
Clrscr();
Printf("\n Enter elements of  array");
For (i=0;i<10;i++)
        {
          scanf("%d",&a[i] );
        }
printf("\n Enter the element you want to count
occurrence \n");
scanf("%d",item);
for (i=0;i<10;i++)
{
      if(a[i]==item)
      {
        count++;
      }
}
printf("\n No. Occurrence %d times",count);
getch();
}
```

## 76. Wap to read 2*2 matrix and convert it into third matrix.

```c
#include<stdio.h>
#include<conio.h>
Void main()
{
Int a[3][3],i,j,r=0,c=0;
Clrscr();
Printf("\n Enter elements of first matrix");
For (i=0;i<3;i++)
{
for (j=0; j<3;j++)
    {
      scanf("%d",&a[i][j]);
    }
}
for(i=0;i<3;i++)
{
  r=c=0;
  for(j=0;j<3;j++)
  {
    r=r+a[i][j];
    c=c+a[j][i];
  }
a[2][2]=a[0][2]+a[1][2];
getch();
}
```

## **STRINGS **
************

### 77. Wap to calculate length of a string.

```
#include<stdio.h>
#include<conio.h>
#include<string.h>
Void main()
{
char str[10];
int i,count=0;
clrscr();
printf("\n Enter a string \n");
gets(str);
for(i=0;str[i]!='\o';i++)
    count++;
printf("\n Length of the string is= %d",count);
getch();
}
```

### 78. Wap to copy a string into another string.

```
#include<stdio.h>
#include<conio.h>
#include<string.h>
Void main()
{
char s1[10],s2[10];
int i;
clrscr();

printf("\n Enter a string \n");
gets(s1);

for(i=0;s1[i]!='\o';i++)
    s2[i]=s1[i];
    s2[i]='\0';

puts(s1);
puts(s2);
getch();
}
```

### 79. Wap to concatenate two strings.

```
#include<stdio.h>
#include<conio.h>
#include<string.h>
Void main()
{
char s1[10],s2[10];
int i,j;
clrscr();
printf("\n Enter first string \n");
gets(s1);
printf("\n Enter second string \n");
gets(s2);
for(i=0;s1[i]!='\o';i++)
for(j=0;s2[j]!='\o';j++)
s1[i]=s2[j];
s1[i]='\0';
puts(s1);
getch();
}
```

### 80. Wap to compare two strings.

```
#include<stdio.h>
#include<conio.h>
#include<string.h>
Void main()
{
char s1[10],s2[10];
int i,f=0;
clrscr();
printf("\n Enter first string \n");
gets(s1);
printf("\n Enter second string \n");
gets(s2);
for(i=0;s1[i]!='\o' || s2[i]!='\0';i++)
{
if(s1[i]==s2[i])
continue;
else
{
f=s1[i]-s2[i];
break;
    }
}
if(f==0)
printf(" \n string are equal \n");
            else
printf("\n strings are not equal");
getch();    }
```

## 81. Wap to reverse a string.

```c
#include<stdio.h>
#include<conio.h>
#include<string.h>
Void main()
{
char c, str[10];
int i,n;
clrscr();
printf("\n Enter a string \n");
gets(str);
n=strlen(str);
for(i=0,j=n-i;i<n/2;i++,j--)
{
                c=str[i];
                str[i]=str[j];
                str[j]=c;
}
printf("\n REVERSE IS \n");
puts(str);
getch();
}
```

## 82.wap to find occurrence of any particular character in a string.

```c
#include<stdio.h>
#include<conio.h>
#include<string.h>
Void main()
{
char c, str[10];
int i,count=0;
clrscr();

printf("\n Enter a string \n");
gets(str);
printf("\n Enter a character \n");
scanf("%c"&c);
for(i=0;str[i]!='\o' ;i++)
{
   if (str[i]==c)
   count++;
}
printf("\n character comes in string %d times",count );
getch();
}
```

314

### 83. Wap to check whether a character is present in string or not.

```c
#include<stdio.h>
#include<conio.h>
#include<string.h>
Void main()
{
char c, str[10];
int i,f=0;
clrscr();
printf("\n Enter a string \n");
gets(str);
printf("\n Enter a character u want to search \n");
scanf("%c"&c);
for(i=0;str[i]!='\o' ;i++)
{
    if (str[i]==c)
    {
      f=1;
      break;
    }
}
if(f==1)
printf("\n The character is present in string" );
else
printf("\n The character is not present in string" );
getch();
}
```

### 84. Wap to count total no. of vowels in a string.

```c
#include<stdio.h>
#include<conio.h>
#include<string.h>
Void main()
{
char  str[10];
int i,vowel=0;
clrscr();
printf("\n Enter a string \n");
gets(str);
for(i=0;str[i]!='\o' ;i++)
{
    if(str[i]=='a' || str[i]=='e' || str[i]=='i' ||
str[i]=='o' || str[i]=='u')
        vowel++;
}
printf("\n total vowels in this string is=%d",vowel);
getch();
}
```

## 85. program to convert lower case to upper case.

```
#include<stdio.h>
#include<conio.h>
#include<string.h>
Void main()
{
char  str[10];
int i;
clrscr();
printf("\n Enter a string in lower case \n");
gets(str);
for(i=0;str[i]!='\o' ;i++)
{
    if(str[i]>=65 && str[i]<=90)
        continue;
    else
        str[i]=str[i]-32;
}
puts(str);
getch();
}
```

## 86. Wap to count lower case,upper case,digits,special symbols in given line of text.

```
#include<stdio.h>
#include<conio.h>
#include<string.h>
Void main()
{
char  str[10];
int i,lwr=0,upr=0,dig=0,ss=0;
clrscr();
printf("\n Enter a string  \n");
gets(str);
for(i=0;str[i]!='\o' ;i++)
{
    if(str[i]>=65 && str[i]<=90)
        upr++;
else
        if(str[i]>=97 && str[i]<=122)
        lwr++;
else
        if(str[i]>=48 && str[i]<=57)
        dig++;
```

```
else
        ss++;
}
printf("\n Total upper    case is=%d",upr);
printf("\n Total lower    case is=%d",lwr);
printf("\n Total digit     case is=%d",dig);
printf("\n Total sp.sym. case is=%d",ss);
getch();
}
```

## 87. Wap to count total char and words in a string.

```
#include<stdio.h>
#include<conio.h>
#include<string.h>
Void main()
{
char  str[10];
int i,chr=0,word=1;
clrscr();
printf("\n Enter a string  \n");
gets(str);
for(i=0;str[i]!='\o' ;i++)
{
   chr++;
   if(str[i]=='    ')
   words++;
}
printf("\n Total characters=%d",chr);
printf("\n Total words =%d",word);
getch();
}
```

## 88.wap to print ASCII values of Entered string or name.

```
#include<stdio.h>
#include<conio.h>
#include<string.h>
Void main()
{
char  str[10];
int i;
clrscr();
printf("\n Enter a string  \n");
gets(str);
printf("\n ASCII values is  \n");
for(i=0;str[i]!='\o' ;i++)
{
    printf("%d",str[i]);
}
getch();}
```

**89.wap to replace char of string with another char.**

```c
#include<stdio.h>
#include<conio.h>
#include<string.h>
Void main()
{
char   str[10],ch,chr;
int i,f=0;
clrscr();
printf("\n Enter a string  \n");
gets(str);
printf("\n Enter the char which u want to replace \n");
scanf("%c"&ch);
printf("\n Enter the char by which u want to replace
\n");
scanf("%c"&chr);
for(i=0;str[i]!='\o' ;i++)
{
     if(str[i]==ch)
     {
     str[i]=chr;
     f=1;
     }
}
if(f==0)
  printf("\n This Character is not present in this
string");
getch();
}
```

**90. Wap to convert first letter of each word in capital letter case.**

```c
#include<stdio.h>
#include<conio.h>
#include<string.h>
Void main()
{
char   str[10];
int i;
clrscr();
printf("\n Enter a string  \n");
gets(str);
if (str[0]>=97 && str[0]<=122)
    str[0]=str[0]-32;
for(i=0;str[i]!='\o' ;i++)
{
```

318

```
    if(str[i]=='    ')
            if(str[i+1]>=97 && str[i+1]<=122)
                str[i+1]=str[i+1]-32;
}
puts(str);
getch();
}
```

## 91. Wap to find Length,Copy,concatinate,Compare,reverse-using pre-Define string functions.

```
#include<stdio.h>
#include<conio.h>
#include<string.h>
Void main()
{
char   s1[30],S2[30];
int n;
clrscr();
printf("\n Enter first  string  \n");
gets(s1);
printf("\n Enter second  string  \n");
gets(s2);

/*To Find length of s1*/
n=strlen(s1);
printf("\n Length of first string is =%d",n);

/*To copy s1 into s2*/
strcpy(s2,s1);
puts(s2);

/*To concatenate s1 and s2*/
strcat(s1,s2);
puts(s1);

/*To compare s1 and  s2*/
n=strcmp(s1,s2);
if(n==0)
        printf("\n strings are Equal")
else
        printf("\n string are Unequal");

/*To Reverse S1*/
strrev(s1);
puts(s1);
getch();
}
```

## 92. Wap to read Two variables and swap them by pointers.

```
#include<stdio.h>
#include<conio.h>
Void main()
{
int   a,b,c,*p1,*p2;
clrscr();
printf("\n Enter Two Numbers  \n");
scanf("%d%d",&a,&b);
/* Giving Variables References to Pointers */
p1=&a;
p2=&b;

/* swapping */
c=*p1;
*p1=*p2;
*p2=c;

printf("\n  After swapping a=%d, b=%d",a,b);
getch();
}
```

## 93. Wap to read two no's and add them by pointers.

```
#include<stdio.h>
#include<conio.h>
Void main()
{
int   a,b,sum=0,*p1,*p2;
clrscr();
printf("\n Enter Two Numbers  \n");
scanf("%d%d",&a,&b);
/* Giving Variables References to Pointers */
p1=&a;
p2=&b;

/* sum */
sum=(*p1)+(*p2);
printf("\n  Sum=%d ",sum);
getch();
}
```

## 94. Wap to read 'n' numbers and add them using pointers.

```
#include<stdio.h>
#include<conio.h>
Void main()
{
int   a,n,i,sum=0,*p;
clrscr();
printf("\n Enter How Many no.'s u want to add?   \n");
scanf("%d",&n);
/* Giving Variables References to Pointers */
*p=&sum;
for(i=0;i<=n;i++);
{
      printf("\n Enter a no.");
      scanf("%d",&a);
      *p=*p+a;
}
printf("\n  Sum=%d ",sum);
getch();
}
```

```
**********************************
```
**Pointers operations with Arrays**
```
**********************************
```

## 95. Wap to read 10 elements in an array and add them using pointer.

```c
#include<stdio.h>
#include<conio.h>
Void main()
{
int   a[10],i,sum=0,*p;
clrscr();
printf("\n Enter ten numbers.   \n");
for(i=0;i<10;i++);
scanf("%d",&a[i]);
/* Giving Variables References to Pointers */
*p=&a;
for(i=0;i<10;i++);
{
     sum=sum+(*p);
     p++;
}
printf("\n  Sum of all arrays is =%d ",sum);
getch();
}
```

## 96. Wap to read two arrays of 10 elements and add-their values using pointer in third Array.

```c
#include<stdio.h>
#include<conio.h>
Void main()
{
int   a[10],b[10],c[10],i,*p1,*p2;
clrscr();
printf("\n Enter ten elements for first array.   \n");
for(i=0;i<10;i++);
scanf("%d",&a[i]);
printf("\n Enter ten elements for second array.   \n");
for(i=0;i<10;i++);
scanf("%d",&b[i]);
p1=a;
p2=b;
for(i=0;i<10;i++)
{
c[i]=(*p1)+(*p2);
```

322

```
p1++;
p2++;
}
printf("\n After addition third array");
for(i=0;i<10;i++)
printf("\n "%d",c[i]   \n");
getch();
}
```

## 97. Wap to calculate Factorial using Pointer.

```
#include<stdio.h>
#include<conio.h>
Void main()
{
int   n,*p,i,f=1;
clrscr();
printf("\n Enter Any number for Factorial.\n");
scanf("%d",&n);
p=&f;
for(i=0;i<=n;i++)
*p=*p*i;
printf("\n Factorial using pointer is =%d", f);
getch();
}
```

## 98. Wap to calculate length of a string using pointer.

```
#include<stdio.h>
#include<conio.h>
Void main()
{
char str[10],*p;
int count=0;
clrscr();
printf("\n Enter a string");
gets(str);
p=str;
while(*p!='\0')
{
    count++;
    p++;
}
printf("\n Length of string is =%d",count);
getch();
}
```

### 99. Wap to copy a string into another using pointers.

```
#include<stdio.h>
#include<conio.h>
Void main()
{
char s1[10],s2[10],*p1,*p2;
clrscr();
printf("\n Enter a string");
gets(s1);
p1=s1;
p2=s2;
while(*p1!='\0')
{
*p2=*p1;
p1++;
p2++;
}
*p2='\0';
puts(s1);
puts(s2);
getch();
}
```

### 100. Wap to concatenate two strings using pointers.

```
#include<stdio.h>
#include<conio.h>
Void main()
{
char s1[10],s2[10],*p1,*p2;
int i,j;
clrscr();
printf("\n Enter first string");
gets(s1);
printf("\n Enter second string");
gets(s2);
p1=s1;
p2=s2;
while(*p1!='\0')
{
p1++;
}
while(*p2!='\0')
{
*p1=*p2;
p1++;
```

```
p2++;
}
*p1='\0'
puts(s1);
getch();
}
```

## 101. Wap to compare two strings using pointers.

```
#include<stdio.h>
#include<conio.h>
Void main()
{
char s1[10],s2[10],*p1,*p2;
int i,f=0;
clrscr();

printf("\n Enter first string");
gets(s1);

printf("\n Enter second string");
gets(s2);

p1=s1;
p2=s2;

while(*p1!='\0' ||*p2!='\0' )
{
if(*p1==*p2)
{
p1++;
p2++;
continue;
}
else
   {
   f=*p1-*p2;
   break;
   }
}
  if (f==0)
   printf("\n string are equal");
   else
   printf("\n string are not equal");
getch();
}
```

## 102. WAP TO CREATE A STRUCTURE BOOK, READ AND DISPLAY INFORMATION OF A BOOK.

```
#include<stdio.h>
#include<conio.h>
Struct book
{
char name[10];
int pages;
float price;
};
void main()
{
  struct book b;

  printf("\n Enter information about book");

  printf("\n Enter Name  of the book");
    gets(b.name);

  printf("\n Enter total pages and price of the book");
    scanf("%d%f",&b.pages,&b.price);

    printf("\n Displaying information about book");
    printf("\n name =%s",b.name);
    printf("\n pages=%d",b.pages);
    printf("\n price=%d",b.price);
getch();
}
```

## 103. Wap to create a structure of student, read info. of ten students and print name of those students whose marks is grater then 90.

```
#include<stdio.h>
#include<conio.h>
Struct student
{
char name[10];
int r_no;
float marks;
};
void main()
```

```
{
 struct student s[10];
 int i;
 printf("\n Enter info. about students");
 for(i=0;i<10;i++)
 {
    printf("\n Plz Enter the name of the student");
    gets(s[i].name);
    printf("\n Enter r_no and marks");
    scanf("%d %f",&s[i].r_no,&s[i].marks);
 }
printf("\n name of those whose have >90"):
for (i=0;i<10;i++)
{
  if (s[i].marks>90)
      puts(s[i].name);
getch();
}
```

## 104. Wap to read personal info. of 10 peoples and print-details of those people living in particular city.

```
#include<stdio.h>
#include<conio.h>
#include<string.h>
struct personalinfo
{
 char name[10];
 char city[20];
 char add [20];
};
void main()
{
 struct personalinfo s[10];
 int i,n;
 char ct;
printf("Enter info of ten peoples");
for (i=0;i<10;i++)
{
    printf("\n Plz Enter the name of the Person");
    gets(s[i].name);
    printf("\n Plz Enter the name of the city");
    gets(s[i].city);
    printf("\n Plz Enter the address of the person");
    gets(s[i].add);
}
```

```c
    printf("\n Enter the city whose persons detail u
want display");
    gets(ct);
    for (i=0;i<10;i++)
{
    n=strcmp(s[i].city,ct);
    if(n==0)
  {
    puts(s[i].name);
    puts(s[i].city);
    puts(s[i].add);
  }
}
getch();
}
```

## 105. Wap to create a structure complex to model complex no. read two complex no. and add them.

```c
#include<stdio.h>
#include<conio.h>
struct complex
{
float real,image;
};
void main()
{
    struct complex c1,c2,c3;
    printf("\n Plz Enter first complex no.");
    printf("\n Plz Enter the real part");
    scanf("%f",&c1.real);
    printf("\n Plz Enter the imagenary part");
    scanf("%f",&c1.image);
    printf("\n Plz Enter the second complex no.");
    printf("\n Plz Enter the real part");
    scanf("%f",&c2.real);
    printf("\n Plz Enter the imagenary part");
    scanf("%f",&c2.image);
c3.real=c1.real+c2.real;
c3.image=c1.image+c2.image;
    printf("\n sir After Adition both parts");
    printf("\n real = %f,image=%f",c3.real,c3.image);
getch();
}
```

## 106. Wap to create a structure Distance And read two distances in-feet and inches and print there Additions. okay !!

```c
#include<stdio.h>
#include<conio.h>
struct distance
{
 float feet,inch;
};
void main()
{
    struct distance d1,d2,d3;

    printf("\n Plz Enter first distance.");
    printf("\n Plz Enter the feets");
    scanf("%f",&d1.feet);
    printf("\n Plz Enter the inches");
    scanf("%f",&d1.inch);

    printf("\n Plz Enter second distance.");
    printf("\n Plz Enter the feets");
    scanf("%f",&d2.feet);
    printf("\n Plz Enter the inches");
    scanf("%f",&d2.inch);

    d3.feet=d1.feet+d2.feet;
    d3.inch=d1.inch+d2.inch;

while(d3.inch>=12)
{
    d3.feet++
    d3.inch=d3.inch-12;
}   printf("\n sir After Adition both parts");
    printf("\n feet = %f,inches=%f",d3.feet,d3.inch);
getch();
}
```

**107. Wap to create a Date structure and increase date by Addition No. of days and date should be valid.**

```c
#include<stdio.h>
#include<conio.h>
struct date
{
    int dd,mm,yy;
};
void main()
{
    struct date d;
    int date
    printf("\n Plz Enter days,month,year.");
    scanf("\n %d%d%d",&d.dd,&d.mm,&d.yy);

    printf("\n Plz Enter no. of days you want to add");
    scanf("%d",&day);

    d.dd=d.dd+day
while(d.dd>=30)
{
  d.mm++;
  d.dd=d.dd-30;
}
while(d.mm>12)
{
  d.yy++;
  d.mm=d.mm-12;
}

    printf("\n sir DateAfter Aditions");
    printf("\n %d%d%d",d.dd,d.mm,d.yy);

getch();
}
```

**108. Wap to read info of 20 books and print names and author names of those books whose price is more than 1000 Rs.**

```c
#include<stdio.h>
#include<conio.h>

struct book
{
   char name[10];
   char aname[10];
   int  pages;
   float prices;
};
void main()
{
    struct book b[20];
    int i;
    printf("\n Plz Enter info. of 20 books.");
    for(i=0;i<20;i++)
{

   printf("\n Plz Enter name of books.");
   gets(b[i].name);
   printf("\n Plz Enter name of author.");
   gets(b[i].aname);
   printf("\n Plz Enter total pages and price of book");
    scanf("%d%f",&b[i].pages,&b[i].price);
}

for(i=0;i<20;i++)
{
   if(b[i].price>1000)
  {
     printf("\n name =%s",b[i].name);
     printf("\n Author Name =%s",b[i].aname);
    }
   }
getch();
 }
```

## 109. Wap to read a line of text from screen and store in to File.

```c
#include<stdio.h>
#include<conio.h>
#include<stdlib>
#include<string.h>
void main()
{
    FILE *fp;
    char str[20];
    fp=fopen("sample.txt","w");
    printf("\n Enter a line of text");
    gets(str);
    fprintf(fp,"%s",str);
    fclose(fp);
getch();
}
```

## 110. Wap to read a line of text from a file and Display it.

```c
#include<stdio.h>
#include<conio.h>
#include<stdlib>
#include<string.h>
void main()
{
    FILE *fp;
    char str[20];
    fp=fopen("sample.txt","r");
if(fp==null)
{
    printf("\n File doesn't exixt");
    exit(1);
}
    fscanf(fp,"%s",str);
    printf("\n file contains...");
    puts(str);
    fclose(fp);
    getch();
}
```

## 111. Wap to read 'n' names from user and store them into a file also create a copy of it into another file.

```c
#include<stdio.h>
#include<conio.h>
#include<stdlib>
#include<string.h>
void main()
{
    FILE *fp1,*fp2;
    char str[20];
    int i,n;

fp1=fopen("file1.txt","w+");
printf("\n How many names u want to Enter");
scanf("%d",&n);

for(i=0;i<n;i++)
{
  printf("\n Enter the name");
  gets(str);
  fprintf(fp1,"\n %s",str);
}

rewind(fp1);
fp2=fopen("file2.txt","w");
while(!feof(fp1))
{
  fscanf(fp1,"\n %s",str);    /*read from first file     */
  fprintf(fp2,"\n%s",str);  /*storing in to second file*/
  puts(str);                      /*Displaying on the screen */
}
getch();
}
```

## 112. Wap to count total no. of characters and words in a file.

```c
#include<stdio.h>
#include<conio.h>
#include<stdlib>
void main()
{
    FILE *fp1;
    char c;
    int ch=0,word=1;

fp1=fopen("file1.txt","r");
```

```c
if(fp1==null)
{
   printf("\n Sir File Doesn't Exixt");
   exit(1);
}
while(! feof(fp1) )
{
   c=getc(fp1);
   ch++;
   if(ch=='   ')
   word++
}
printf("\n Total Characters=%d",ch);
printf("\n Total words =%d",word);
getch();
}
```

***************
**\*\*Functions\*\***
***************

## 113.wap which shows sending & receiving values between functions.

```c
#include<stdio.h>
#include<conio.h>
int calsum(int x,int y,int z);/* function prototype*/
void main()
{
 int a,b,c,sum;
 printf("\n Enter any three numbers");
 scanf("\n %d%d%d",&a,&b,&c);
 sum=calsum(a,b,c);                /*function calling*/
 printf("\n Sum=%d",sum);
getch();
}
                  /*function defination or body*/
int calsum(int x,int y,int z)
{
 int d;
 d= x+y+z;
 return(d);
}
```

334

## 114.wap to calculate square of no. with return type.

```c
#include<stdio.h>
#include<conio.h>
float square(float);/* function prototype*/
void main()
{
 float a,b;
 printf("\n Enter any number");
 scanf("\n %f",&a);
 b=square(a);
 printf("\n square of %f is %f",a,b);
getch();
}
float square(float x)
{
    float y;
    y=x*x;
    return(y);
}
```

## 115. Wap to swap two values using functions call by value.

```c
#include<stdio.h>
#include<conio.h>
void myswap(int x,int y);/* function prototype*/
void main()
{
   int a=10,b=20;
   myswap(a,b);
   printf("\n a=%d,b=%d",a,b);
getch();
}
void myswap(int x, int y)
{
 int t;
 t=x;
 x=y;
 y=t;
 printf(\n x=%d,y=%d",x,y);
}
```

### 116. Wap to swap two values using functions call by reference.

```c
#include<stdio.h>
#include<conio.h>
void myswap(int*,int*);/* function prototype*/
void main()
{
  int a=10,b=20;
  myswap(&a,&b);
  printf("\n a=%d,b=%d",a,b);
getch();
}
void myswap(int *x,int *y)
{
 int t;
 t=*x;
 *x=*y;
 *y=t;
}
```

### 117. Wap to calculate area & perimeter using call by reference.

```c
#include<stdio.h>
#include<conio.h>
void areaperi(int,float*,float*);/* function prototype*/
void main()
{
  int radius;
  float area,perimeter;
  printf("\n Enter radius of a circle");
  scanf("%d",&radius);
  areaperi(radius,&area,&perimeter);

  printf("\n Area =%f",area);
  printf("\n Perimeter=%f",perimeter);
getch();
}
void areaperi(int r,float *a,float *p)
{
*a=3.14*r*r;
*p=2*3.14*r;
}
```

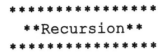

**Drill Note-** when functions calls themselves known as recursion.

**Drill Note-** when any function calls himself known as recursive function.

### 118. Wap to calculate factorial without Recursive Function.

```c
#include<stdio.h>
#include<conio.h>
int factorial(int);               /* function prototype*/
void main()
{
   int a,fact;
   printf("\n Enter any number");
   scanf("%d",&a);

   fact=factorial(a);
   printf("Factorial value=%d",fact);
getch();
}
int factorial(int x)
{
    int f=1;
    int i;
  for(i=x;i>=1;i--)
  f=f*i;
  return(f);
}
```

### 119.wap to calculate factorial using Recursive Function.

```c
#include<stdio.h>
#include<conio.h>
int rec(int);    /* function prototype*/
void main()
{
   int a,fact;
   printf("\n Enter any number");
   scanf("%d",&a);

   fact=rec(a);
   printf("Factorial value=%d",fact);
getch();
}
```

```
int rec(int x)
{
    int f;
    if(x==1)
    return(1);
else
    f=x*rec(x-1);
    return(f);
}
```

## 120. Wap to built mini calculator using function.

```
#include<stdio.h>
#include<conio.h>
int addi(int,int);        /* function prototype*/
int subt(int,int);       /* function prototype*/
int multi(int,int);     /* function prototype*/
float div(int,int);    /* function prototype*/
void main()
{
   int a,b,result,option;

   printf("\n\t\t\t Wel come to EvC iNSTITUTE JAIPUR");
   printf("\n\t\t\t plz Enter the values of a and b");
   scanf("%d%d",&a,&b);

   printf("\n\t\t\t Menu::-");
   printf("\n\t\t\t Enter 1 for Addition");
   printf("\n\t\t\t Enter 2 for subtraction");
   printf("\n\t\t\t Enter 3 for multiply");
   printf("\n\t\t\t Enter 4 for Division");
   printf("\n\t\t\t so, Select Your Option(1-4)");
   scanf("%d",&option);

switch(option)
{
case 1:
{
        result=addi(a,b);     /* function calling*/
        printf("%d",result);
        break;
```

338

```c
      }
case 2:
{
        result=subt(a,b);      /* function calling*/
        printf("%d",result);
        break;
}
case 3:
{
        result=multi(a,b);    /* function calling*/
        printf("%d",result);
        break;
}
case 4:
{
        result=div(a,b);      /* function calling*/
        printf("%f",result);
        break;
}
default:
{
   printf("\n\t\t u have Entered out of option okay!!");
  }
 }
getch();
}

int addi(int a, int b)    /* function body & definition*/
{
  return(a+b);
}
int subt(int a, int b)    /* function body & definition*/
{
  return(a-b);
}
int multi(int a, int b)  /* function body & definition*/
{
  return(a*b);
}
float div(int a,int b)    /* function body & definition*/
{
  float z;
  z=(float) (a/b);
  return(z);                  /* function return type      */
}
```

C - Programmer
Harry.

# CHAPTER
# ∞ 18- Part –II ∞

## (Creating & inserting own functions in to c library.)

**Creating & inserting own functions in to c library.**

As You all know very well most of time we use standard "c" library functions-or sometimes user define functions. But the most things that I want to show u here. how we can add our own made "c" functions to the pretty-"c"-Standard library??

Yes its possible it's a Experts approach in "c" -programming. After addition of our user define functions in to standard C library-we can easy access them any time read steps.

**Step 1 -**

Most of "c" compiler provide a special option menu in compiler utility by the use of this utility we easily can perform this task. i think in Turbo c/c++ compiler that provides a utility called "tlib.exe", Turbo Librarian. let-us use this utility and add function to "c" library.

**Step 2 –**

Here I'm adding my factorial function to "c" library -

**(a)** Write a function definition of factorial() in some file, may be **fact.c**

```
int factorial(int num)
{
int i,f=1;
 for(i=1;i<=num;i++)
f=f*i;
 return(f);
}
```

**(b)** compile this "fact.c" file using Alt+f9, now automatically a new file called "fact.obj" will get created containing the compiled code in machine language.

**(c)** add the function to the library "maths.lib" by issuing the following command- c:\>tlib maths.lib+c:\fact.obj

**Here,**"maths.lib" is library file name,+ is a switch, and c:\fact.obj is a path of our file to be adding in maths.lib

**(d)** declare the prototype of factorial() function in the header file, say "fact.h", **This file should be include while calling the function don't forget it .**

**(e)** For example look here how we use or call our added function in any program-

```
#include "c:\fact.h"
#include<stdio.h>
#include<conio.h>
void main()
{
int f;
f=factorial(5);
printf("%d",f);
getch();
}
```

**Deleting own functions in c library.**

**Step -** just use minus sign in between this

**(c)** add the function to the library "maths.lib" by issuing the following command- c:\>tlib maths.lib-c:\fact.obj

## Creating Own C Libraries-

Suppose u want to create own library in which have three or more wish own functions like:

1. factorial()
2. prime()
3. Fibonacci()

**Note :**

I think this will work in Turbo c/c++ compilers only. follow my following—

**Step 1 -**

Define the functions factorial( ), prime( ), fibonacci( ) in a file say, 'myfuncs.c'. Do not define main() in this file.

```
int factorial(int);
int prime(int);
void fibonacci(int);
```

**Step 2:-**

From the option menu of compiler select the option 'Application' now from the dialog box pops up menu select the option 'library' then

**Step 3:-**

Compile the program using Alt+f9. this would create the library file called 'myfuncs.lib'.

**Step: 4:-**

That's complete wow!! your library now stand created. now u can easily use these functions i will show u how use earlier created function lib.

```
#include<stdio.h>
#include<conio.h>
#include"myfuncs.h"
void main()
{
int f,result;
f=factorial(5);
result=prime(13);
fibonacci(6);
printf("\n %d %d",f,result);
getch();        }
```

**Note:-**

The file 'myfuncs.h' should be in the same dir as the file 'sample.c'. if not, then while including 'myfuncs.h' mention the appropriate path.

**Step:-**

Go to compiler menu 'project' and select 'open project' option. then pop up come give the name of project, say 'sample.prj' then ok.

**Step:-**

From project menu select 'Add item', on doing so a file dialog would appear. select the file 'sample.c' and then select 'Add', Also add the file 'myfuncs.h.lib' in the same previous manner select Done!

**step:-**

Compile and execute the project using ctrl+f9.

# CHAPTER
## ∞ 19- Part –II ∞
## (Graphics programming)

*****Graphics programming*****
\* \* \* \* \* \* \* \* \* \* \* \* \* \* \* \* \* \* \* \* \* \* \* \* \* \* \* \* \* \* \*

**Introduction-**

     **To** run graphics codes, make sure, you have installed graphics driver Software in your operating system. Some graphics codes require more than – 250 MB memory Graphics card.

**130. Wap to draw ellipse or circle in "c".**

```
#include<stdio.h>
#include<conio.h>
#include<graphics.h>'
void main()
{
int gd=DETECT,gm;          /*initiate graphics mode*/
intgraph(&gd,&gm,"");   /*initiate graphics driver & mode*/

circle(200,200,100);   /*To draw a circle*/
ellipse(450,200,0,360,150,100);
outtextxy(175,200,"circle");
outtextxy(425,200,"ellipse");
getch();
}
```

## 131. Wap to draw a rectangle using line functions(All three).

```c
#include<stdio.h>
#include<conio.h>
#include<graphics.h>'
void main()
{
int gd=DETECT,gm;          /*initiate graphics mode*/
intgraph(&gd,&gm,"");      /*initiate graphics driver & mode*/
line(75,50,200,50);
line(200,50,200,100);
line(200,100,75,100);
line(75,100,75,50);
outtextxy(10,50,"(50,50)");
outtextxy(200,50,"(200,50)");
outtextxy(200,100,"(200,100)");
outtextxy(10,100,"(50,100)");
outtextxy(75,115,"(50,100)");
moveto(75,150);            /*it moves starting position*/
lineto(200,150);
lineto(200,200);
lineto(75,200);
lineto(75,150);
outtextxy(75,215,"using function lineto()");
moveto(75,250);
linerel(125,0);
linerel(0,50);
linerel(-125,0);
linerel(0,-50);
outtextxy(75,315,"using function linerel()");
getch();
}
```

## 132. Wap to draw rectangle with different line styles.

```c
#include<stdio.h>
#include<conio.h>
#include<graphics.h>'
void main()
{
int gd=DETECT,gm;          /*initiate graphics mode*/
intgraph(&gd,&gm,"");/*initiate graphics driver & mode*/
setlinestyle(1,0,3);
line(75,50,200,50);
line(200,50,200,100);
line(200,100,75,100);
line(75,100,75,50);
outtextxy(10,50,"(50,50)");
outtextxy(200,50,"(200,50)");
outtextxy(200,100,"(200,100)");
outtextxy(10,100,"(50,100)");
```

```
outtextxy(75,115,"(50,100)");
setlinestyle(2,0,1);
moveto(75,150);        /*it moves starting position*/
lineto(200,150);
lineto(200,200);
lineto(75,200);
lineto(75,150);
outtextxy(75,215,"using function centreline()");
setlinestyle(0,0,3);
movrto(75,250);
linerel(125,0);
linerel(0,50);
linerel(-125,0);
linerel(0,-50);
outtextxy(75,315,"using function solidline()");
getch();
}
```

## Other Graphics commands or functions you can use any function like-

**1,** bar() -used for draw a bar.
   **syntax:-** bar(int left,int top,int right,int bottom);

**2,** bar3d() -used to draw a 3d bar.
   **syntax:-** bar3d(int left,int top,int right,int bottom,int depth,int top flor);

**3,** cleardevice() - used to clear graphics screen.
   **syntax:-** cleardevice();

**4,** closegraph() - its danger it shutdown the graphics system.
   **syntax:-** closegraph();

**5,** drawpoly() - it draw the outline of polygon
   **syntax:-** drawpoly(int numpoints,int farpolypoints)

**6,** getbkcolor - it return the back color.
   **syntax:-** int A= getbkcolor();

**7,** getcolor() -it return the current drawing color.
   **syntax:-** int A= getcolor();

**8,** getmaxx() - return the maximum value of x screen.
   **syntax:-** int A= getmaxx();

**9,** getmaxy() - returns maximum value of y screen.
   **syntax:-** int A= getmaxy();

**10,** getpixel() - it get color of a specified pixel.
   **syntax:-** unsigned A= getpixel(int x,int y);

**11,** getx() - it return the current position of x.
   **syntax:-** int A= getx();

**12,** gety() - it return the current position of y.
   **syntax:-** int A= gety();

**13,** outtext() - it display a string in current position of x and y in graphics mode.
   **syntax:-** outtext("string");

**14,** outtextxy() - it display a string in specify location in graphics mode.
   **syntax:-** outtextxy(int x,int y,"string");

**15,** setbkcolor() - if set the back ground color.
   **syntax:-** setbkcolor(int color);

**16,** setcolor() - set drawing color.
**syntax:-** setcolor(int color);

### Drawing and filling Images functions-

1, EMPTY-FILL        0 -TO FILL BACKGROUND COLOR.
2, SOLID-FILL        1 -FILL AREA BY BG COLOR.
3, LINE-FILL         2 -FILL AREA BY SMACK BG COLOR.
4, BKSLASH-FILL      3 -FILL WITH THICK LINE.
5, HATCH-FILL        7 -FILL WITH LIGHT HATCH LINE.
6, XHATCH-FILL       8 -HEAVY CROSS HATCH FILL.
7, INTERLEAVE-FILL 9 -INTERLEAVING LINE FILL.
8, WIDE-DOT-FILL    10-WIDELY SPACES DOT FILL.
9, CLOSE-DOT-FILL  11-CLOSE SPACES DOT FILL.
10,USER-FILL         12-USER DEFINE FILL.

# CHAPTER
# ∞ 20- Part –II ∞
## (Operating System Development)

**Introduction of Operating System Development-**

**(1)** powerful API functions.
**(2)** sharing of functions.
**(3)** look and feel for application.
**(4)** Hardware-independent programming.
**(5)** Event-Driven programming model
**(6)** Dos model.

**1. Powerful API Functions.**

windows provide functions within itself which can be called by other user define or library functions.thease windows functions called API. Application Programming Functions. there are literally hundreds of very rich functions available.

They help an application perform not only the simple task like creating window, drawing a line, performing file i/o but also complicated tasks like connecting to ports, interfacing to the networks, modifying the bitmap, playing a mp3 file. etc.the key to windows-programming is to udrstd these API functions and use them effectively to create rich applications with effortless ease.

## 2. Sharing of functions.

During the Execution windows program calls several API functions. Imagine how much disk space would have been watage had each of these functions became part of the .Exe file of the each program. to avoid this, the API, Functions are defined in special files that have a special extension .DLL,the .DLL stand for Dynamic Link Liberary.

Thaese are binary files.the functions presented in .dll files can be linked during the Execution or installing time.these all functions can share for calling each other when several programs running under windows.

These functions linking with each other is done dynamically.(during execution) the functions do not became part of the executable file.as a result the size of the Exe files doesn't go out of the hand. it is also possible to create your own DLLs. because of the two reasons u need to do this.

**(a)**sharing common code between different executable files.

**(b)**Breaking the Applications in to components parts known as segments.

*Provide the way to easily upgrade Application's Components.*

## 3.Look and feel Consistent:

This means that each program offers a consistent and semi liar user interface. As a result, user doesn't have to spend long periods of times mastering a new program.Every program occupies a window-a rectangle area on the computer screen, a window is Identified by its personal title bar.

Most programs functions are initiated throughThe program's menu. If info. Is large then use of scroll bars, dialog boxes for Entering Some user info. Once u know how to use one window program, then u can easily understand Another. Keyboard and mouse interfacing.

## 4.Hardware Independent Programming:

As I tell u that a window program can easily call windows API Function. thus an application can easily communicate with operating system, how windows easily communicate with hardware ?

suppose we have a written program that contains a menu item, which on selection is suppose to display a string "wel come to eve reserch labs India" in the window. the menu item can be selected by keyboard or using the mouse. on executing this program it will perform initialization and then wait for the user input.

After input by user any key or click the mouse to select the menu item. the key-press or mouse-click is known as an 'event' as u know Visual Basic programming.the occurrence of this event is sensed by the keyboard or mouse driver. the device driver would now informed windows about it.

Windows would in turn notify the application about the occurrence of this event of this particular event. this notification known as "message". thus the o.s has communicated with application.

When than application receive the message, it communicated back with the o.s by the calling a windows API function to display the string "wel come to EVC reserch labs India" in this API function in turn communicates with the **device driver of the graphics card** that drives the screen, to display the string. thus there is a two-way communication between the o.s and the application.

## 5.Event Driven Programming model.

When a user intract with windows program a lot of events occur.for each event a message is sent to the program and the program reacts to it.since the order in which the user would interact with the user-interface elements of the program can not be predicted the order of occurrence of events.

And hence the order of the messages,also became unpredictable.as the result,the order of calling the functions in the program (that react to different messages) is dicatated by the order of occurrence of events. Hence this programming model is called "Event Driven Programming Model".

There can be hundreds of the ways in which the user may interact with an application. In addition to this , some events may occur without any user user interaction. For example, events occur when we create a window, when the window contant are to be drawn,etc.

Thus ,literally hundereds of the messages may be sent to an application thereby creating a chaos. Naturally a question comes- in which order would thease messages get processed by the application. Order is brought to this chaos by putting all the messages that reach the application into a "Queue". The messages in the queue are processed in first in first out (FIFO) Algorithm order.

In fact the o.s maintains several such queues. There is one queue, which is common for all application. This queue is known as "system Message Queue". In addition, there is one queue per application. Such queues are called "Application Message Queue". Let understand the need for maintaining so many queues.

When we click a mouse and an event occurs the device driver posts a message into the system message queue. The OS retrives this message finds out with regard to which application the message has been sent. Next it posts a message into the Application Message Queue of the application in which the mouse was clicked.

Thus really all that is there to event-driven programming. Your job is to anticipate what user are likely to do with ur Application's user interface objects and have a function waiting,Ready to execute at the appropriate time.just when that time is, no one except the user really wanna to say.

You need to understand this first that the difference of simple software programming and window o.s development programming, the window programming model is in the "MACRO" level, let us dig futher and see some obvious issues that will need while u developing programming for the window o.s enviornment.

**There are following issues:-**

**(A)**    SIZE OF POINTERS.
**(B)**    SIZE OF INTEGERS.
**(C)**    HEAVY USE OF typedef.

**1.    SIZE OF POINTERS:**

You must know that window permits multiple programs to co-exixt in memory at that time it needs powerful 32-bit microprocessor to execute thease programs and simple memory to house them. Whenever we store a value at a memory location the address of this memory location has to be stored first in the c.p.u register at the same point in time.

And one most thing the Amount of memory that a microprocessor can access depends on the size of the cpu registers. This means we can store 232 unique addresses in the cpu registers at different times, as a result, we can access 4 GB memory locations using 32-bit registers. In our programs the 32 bit address have to be stored in pointers,do not forget that every pointer under 32-bit environment is a 4 byte entity.

**2.    SIZE OF INTEGERS:**

I wanna to tell u that in 16 bit environment the size of integer is of 2 bytes, in the other hand in 32 bit environment the size of the interger is of 4 bytes. After 32 bit the range of interger is going to be -2147483648   to +2147483647. By this u think there is know difference between int and long int, but what if we wish to store age of person? And we know that age is going to be hardly 100,in such case its best to use short int. 3

352

## 3. HEAVY USE OF typedef:

### If I write the following declairations--

HANDLE h;
WAPRAM w;
LPARAM I;

Is theae are the data types?
No, they are typedef's okay.
Why c program under windows used heavily typedef?
Its have a 2 reasons!!

### (A)
A typical window program is required to perform several complex tasks for ex:- print documents, send mails, performing i/o , managing multiple threads , data processing tasks etc. all of thease used to need integers. But if we use normal interger datatype to represent normal variables that holds different entities, then we will soon lose the track of what the integer values actually represents, this is handle by use of typedef's okey!!

### (B)
In window programming at several places we are requre to gather and work with disimiliar but inter-related data's. this can be done using a structure.

### Most notes-

- Use a 32 bit compiler for window programming like visual c++.

- Use the header file windows.h

### Oue first "c" under windows programming.

### 150. wawpuc that print hello! With the help of 32 bit ex: ms visual c++ compiler.

```
#include<windows.h>
Int_stdcall WinMain(HINSTANCE hlnstance, HINSTANCE
hprevlnstance, LPSTR
pszCmdline, int nCMDShow)
{
 MessageBox(0,"Hello!","Title",0);
 Return(0);
}
```

**Heavey Mind Wash Drill Note -**

**1,**

Always use a 32 bit compiler for 32 bit operatong system development like microsoft visual c++,Or for 64 bit operating system development use 64 bit compiler okey!!

**2,**

I want to tell you that every dos programs execution begains with main() function in the other hand every window program begains its execution with WinMain() function as u see before.

**3,**

 **_stdcall** is used before WinMain()- its show the calling conventions used by WinMain() function,calling conventions indicate two thing:

**(a)**

The order (left to right or right to left) in which the arguments are pushed onto the stack when a function call is made.!

**(b)**

The caller function or called function removes the arguments from the stack at the end of the call. There are many calling conventions avilable like _cdecl and _stdcall both of these calling conventions pass arguments from right to left. All API functions use _stdcall if not mentioned then compiler assumed _cdecl conventions okey!!

**4,**

**HINSTANCE and LPSTR** are nothing but typedef's. The first is an unsigned int and second is a pointer to a char. These typedefs are defined in 'windows.h'. this header file always cointain these typedef's while writing any "c" under windows program.

**5,**

**hInstance, hpPrevInstance,** lpszCmdLine and nCmdShow are variable namesu can also used variable names like i,j,k any in replace of them.

354

**Explanation of whole program:-**

**WinMain()** recive four parameters which are as under:

**hInstance:**

This is a "instance handle" for the running Application. Windows create this id number when the Application start. We will use this value in many windows functions to identify an application Data. And the most thing, handle is simply a 32 bit number that refers to an entity, entity may be a curser or the brush,icon a file,device anything okey!!

**hPrevInstance :**

This parameter is a remnant of earlier version of windows now this is no longer use hence its value cointains 0. This show only the backward compatibility.

**lpszCmdLine:-**

This is a pointer to a character string containing the command line arguments passed to the program. This is semilior to the argv, argc parameters passed to main() just like in a Dos Program.

**nCmdShow:-**

This is an interger value that is passed to the function. This interger tells the program how the window should appear when it is displayed for the first time.

**MessageBox()**

Function this function pops up a message box whose title is 'Title' and which cointain a message 'Hello!'

*Returning 0 from WinMain() indicate success, or non zero value show failure.*

# CHAPTER
# ∞ 21- Part –II ∞

## (Programming Guidelines)

**Introduction-**

This Chapter explains how to write computer programs that *work* and that are understandable to other intelligent beings! This two attributes are *not* independent! In general, programs that other programmers cannot understand do not work very well. (Not to mention the fact that they are maintenance nightmares!)

Writing structured programs (structured code *and* data!) helps greatly in debugging the code. Here is a quick review of some of the features of a structured program.

1. *Lots* of well-defined functions!
2. Using structured loop constructs (*i.e.*, while and for) instead of goto.
3. Using variables that have *one* purpose and *meaningful names*.
4. Using structured data types to represent complex data.
5. Using the ADT (*Abstract Data Type*) or OOP (*Object-Oriented Programming*) paradigm of programming.

# 1. How to Start

The most common types of mistakes when programming are:

1. Programming without *thinking.*
2. Writing code in an unstructured manner.
   Let's take these in order

## 1.1 Thinking about Programming.-

When a real programmer (or programming team) is given a problem to solve, they do *not* immediately sit down at a terminal and start typing in code! They first design the program by thinking about the numerous ways the problem's solution may be found.

One of the biggest myths of programming is that: *The sooner I start coding the sooner a working program will be produced.* **This is NOT true!!** A program that is planned before coding will become a working program before an unplanned program.

Yes, an unplanned program will be typed in and maybe compiled faster, but these are just the *first* steps of creating a *working* program! Next comes the debugging stage.

This is where the benefits of a planned program will appear. In the vast majority of the time, a planned program will have fewer bugs than an unplanned program. In addition, planned programs are generally more structured than unplanned programs. Thus, finding the bugs will be easier in the planned program.

So how does one *design* a program before coding? There are several different techniques. One of the most common is called *top-down design.* Here an outline of the program is first created. (Essentially, one first looks at the general form of the main() function and then recursively works down to the lowest level functions.) There are many references on how to write programs in this manner.

Top-down design divides the program into sub-tasks. Each sub-task is a smaller problem that must be solved. Problems are solved by using an algorithm.

Functions (and data) in the program implement the algorithm. Before writing the actual code, take a very small problem and trace by hand how the chosen algorithm would solve it.

**This serves several purposes:**

1.  It checks out the algorithm to see if will actually work on the given problem. (If it does not work, you can immediately start looking for another algorithm. Note that if you had immediately starting coding you would probably not discover the algorithm would not work until many lines of code had been entered!)

2.  Makes sure that *you* understand how the algorithm actually works! (If you cannot trace the algorithm by hand, you will *not* be able to write a program to do it!)

3.  Gives you the detail workings of a short, simple run of the algorithm that can be used later when debugging the code.

Only when you are confident that you understand how the entire program will look should you start typing in code.

**1.2 Structured Programming.-**

When a program is structured, it is divided into sub-units that may be tested separately. This is a *great* advantage when debugging! Code in a sub-unit may be debugged separately from the rest of the program code. I find it useful to debug each sub-unit as it is written. If no debugging is performed until the entire program is written, debugging is much harder.

The entire source of the program must be searched for bugs. If sub-units are debugged separately, the source code that must be searched for bugs is much smaller! Storing the sub-units of a program into separate source files can make it easier to debug them separately.

The ADT and OOP paradigms also divide programs into sub-units. Often with these methods, the sub-units are even more independent than with normal structured code. This has two main advantages:

1.  Sub-units are even easier to debug separately.
2.  Sub-units can often be *reused* in other programs. (Thus, a new program can use a previously debugged sub-unit from an earlier program!)

Sub-units are generally debugged separately by writing a small *driver program*. Driver programs set up data for the sub-task that the sub-unit is supposed to solve, calls the sub-unit to perform his sub-task, and then displays the results so that they can be checked.

*Of course,* all the following debugging methods can be used to debug a sub-unit, just as they can be used to debug the entire program. Again, the advantages of sub-units are that they are only part of the program and so are *easier* to debug than the entire program at once!

## 2. Compiling Programs-

The first step after typing in a program (or just a sub-unit of a program) is to compile the program. The compiling process converts the source code file you typed in into machine language and is stored in an *object file*. This is known as *compiling*.

With most systems, the object file is automatically *linked* with the system libraries. These libraries contain the code for the functions that are part of the languages library. (For example, the C libraries contain the code for the **printf()** function.)

## 2.1 Compiler Errors-

Every language has syntax rules. These rules determine which statements are legal in the language and which are not. Compiler programs are designed to enforce these rules. When a rule is broken, the compiler prints an error message and an object file is not created.

Most compilers will continue scanning the source file after an error and report other errors it finds. However, once an error has been found, the compiler made be confused by later perfectly legal statements and report them as errors. This brings us to the first rule of compiler errors:

## First Rule of Compiler Errors-

*The first listed compiler error is always a true error; however, later errors may not be true errors.*

Succeeding errors may disappear when the first error is removed. So, if later error messages are puzzling, ignore them. Fix the errors that you are sure are errors and re-compile. The puzzling errors may magically disappear when the other true errors are removed.

If you have many errors, the first error may scroll off the screen. One solution to this problem is to save the errors into a file using redirection. One problem is that errors are written to stderr not stdout which the > redirection operator uses.

To redirect output to stderr use the 2> operator.

**Here's an example:**

```
$cc x.c 2>errors
$more errors
```

The compiler is just a program that other humans created. Often the error messages it displays are confusing (or just plain *wrong!*). Do not assume that the line that an error message refers to is always the line where the true error actually resides.

The compiler scans source files from the top sequentially to the bottom. Sometimes an error is not detected by the compiler until many lines below where the actual error is. Often the compiler is too stupid to realize this and refers to the line in the source file where it realized something is wrong. The true error is earlier in the code. This brings us to the second rule of compiler errors:

**Second Rule of Compiler Errors-**

*A compiler error may be caused by any source code line above the line referred to by the compiler; however, it can not be caused by a line below.*

In C (and C++), do not forget that the **#include** preprocessor statement inserts the code of a header file into the source file. An error in the header file, may cause a compiler error referencing a line in the main source file.

Most systems allow the preprocessed code (that the C compiler actually compiles!) to be stored in a file. This allows you to see exactly what is being compiled. This file will also show how each C macro was expanded. This can be *very* helpful to discover the cause of normally very hard to find errors.

A useful technique for finding the cause of puzzling compiler errors is to delete (or comment out) preceding sections of code until the error disappears. When the error disappears, the last section removed must have caused the error.

The compiler can also display *warnings*. A warning is not a syntax error; however, it *may* be a logical error in the program. It marks a statement in your program that is legal, but is suspicious.

You should treat warnings as errors unless you understand why the warning was generated. Often compilers can be set to different warning levels. It is to your advantage to set this level as high as possible, to have the compiler give as many warnings as possible. Look at these warnings *very* carefully!.

**Brain Wash Drill-**

**Remember** that just because a program compiles with no errors or warnings does *not* mean that the program is correct! It only means that every line of the program is syntactically correct. That is, the compiler understands what each statement says to do. The program may still have many *logical errors*! An English paper may be grammatically correct (*i.e.*, have nouns, verbs, *etc.* in the correct places), but be gibberish.

## 2.2 Linker Errors-

The *linker* is a program that links object files (which contain the compiled machine code from a single source file) and libraries (which are files that are collections of object files) together to create an executable program.

The linker matches up functions and global variables used in object files to their definitions in other object files. The linker uses the *name* (often the term *symbol* is used) of the function or global variable to perform the match.

The most common type of linker error is an unresolved symbol or name. This error occurs when a function or global variable is used, but the linker cannot find a match for the name. For example, on an IBM AIX system, the error message looks like this:

0706-317 ERROR: Unresolved or undefined symbols detected:

Symbols in error (followed by references) are dumped to the load map.
The -bloadmap:<filename> option will create a load map..fun

This message means that a function (or global variable) named fun (ignore the period) was referenced in the program, but never defined. There are two common causes of these errors:

### Misspelling the name of the function-

In the example, above there was a function named func. This is *not* a compiler error. Code in one source file can use functions defined in another. The compiler assumes that any function referenced, but not defined in the file that references it, will be defined in another file and linked.

It is only at the link stage that this assumption can be checked. (Note that C++ compilers will usually generate compiler errors for this, since C++ requires prototypes for *all* referenced functions!)

The linker must know what libraries and object files are needed to form the executable program. The standard C libraries are automatically linked. UNIX systems, like the AIX system, do *not* automatically link in the standard C math library! To link in the math library on the AIX system, use the -lm flag on the compile command. For example, to compile a C program that uses sqrt,type:cc prog.c –lm

**Remember** that the #include statement only inserts text into source files. It is a common *myth* that it also links in the appropriate library! The linker *never* sees this statement!

There are also bugs related to the linker. One difficult bug to uncover occurs when there are two definitions of a function or global variable. The linker will pick the first definition it finds and ignores the other. Some linkers will display a warning message when this occurs (The AIX linker does not!)

Another bug related to linking occurs when a function is called with the wrong arguments. The linker only looks at the name of the function when matching. It does no argument checking. **Here's an example:**

*File: x.c*
```
int f( int x, int y)
{
  return x + y;
}
```
*File: y.c*
```
int main()
{
  int s = f(3);
  return 0;
}
```

These types of bugs can be prevented by using prototypes. For example, if the prototype:          int f( int, int);

Is added to *y.c* the compiler will catch this error. Actually, the best idea is to put the prototype in a header file and include it in both *x.c* and *y.c*. Why use a header file?

So that there is only one instance of the prototype that all files use. If a separate instance is typed into each source file, there is no guarantee that each instance is the same.

If there is only one instance, it can not be inconsistent with itself! Why include it in *x.c* (the file the function is defined in)? So that the compiler can check the prototype and ensure that it is consistent with the function's definition. (Additional note: C++ uses a technique called *name mangling* to catch these type of errors.)

## 3. Runtime Errors-

A runtime error occurs when the program is running and usually results in the program aborting. On a UNIX/Linux system, an aborting program creates a *coredump*.

A coredump is a binary file named core that contains information about the state of program when it aborted. Debuggers like *gdb* and *dbx* can read this file and tell you useful information about what the program was doing when it aborted. There are several types of runtime errors:

### Illegal memory access-

This is probably the most common type of error. Under UNIX/Linux, the program will coredump with the messageSegmentation fault(coredump).

Using Win95 or NT, programs will also abort. However, traditional DOS does not check for illegal memory accesses; the program continues running, but the results are unpredictable.

The DOS Borland/Turbo C/C++ compilers will check for data written to the NULL address. However, the error message NULL pointer assignment is not displayed until the program terminates. Division by zero All operating systems detect this error and abort the program.

## 4. Debugging Tools-

Many methods of debugging a program compare the program's behavior with the correct behavior in great detail. Usually the normal output of the program does not show the detail needed. Debugging tools allow you to examine the behavior of the in more detail.

### 4.1 The assert Macro-

The assert macro is a quick and easy way to put debugging tests into a C/C++ program. To use this macro, you must include the assert.h header file near the top of your source file. Using assert is simple. The format is:

assert(*boolean (or int) expression*);

If the *boolean expression* evaluates to true (*i.e.*, not zero), the assert does nothing. However, if it evaluates to false (zero), assert prints an error message and aborts the program. As an example, consider the following assert:

assert( x != 0 );

If $x$ is zero, the following will be displayed:

Assertion failed: x != 0, file err.c, line 6

*Abnormal program termination*

And the program will abort. Notice that the actual assertion, the name of the file and the line number in the file are displayed.

The assert macro is very useful for putting sanity checks into programs. These are conditions that should always be true if the program is working correctly. It should not be used for user error checking (such as when the file a user requested to read does not exist). Normal if statements should be used for these runtime errors.

Of course, in a commercial program, an assertion failure is not particular helpful to an end user. Also, checking assertions will make the program run at least a little slower than without them. Fortunately, it is easy to disable theassert macro without even removing it.

If the macro NDEBUG is defined (above the statement that includesassert.h!), the assert macro does absolutely nothing. If the assertions need to be enabled later, just remove the line that defines NDEBUG.

(If this technique is used, be sure that the assert statements do not execute code needed for the program to run correctly. If NDEBUG is defined, the code would *not* be run!)

## 4.2 Print Statements-

This time honored method of debugging involves inserting debugging print statements liberally in your program. The print statements should be designed to show both what code the program is executing and what values critical variables have.

### 4.3 Debuggers-

The previous method of debugging by adding print statements has two **disadvantages:**

1. When new print statements are added, program must be recompiled.

2. Information output is fixed and cannot be changed as program is running.

Source-level debuggers provide a much easier way to trace the execution of programs. **They allow one to:**

1. Look at the value of any variable as the program is running.

2. Pause execution when program reaches any desired statement. (This position in the program is called a *breakpoint*).

3. Single step statement by statement through a program.

I *strongly* recommend that you learn to use the debugger for whatever system you program on. Debuggers can save *lots* of time when debugging your program!

### 4.4 Lint -

The lint program checks C programs for a common list of bugs. It scans your C source code and prints out a list of possible problems. Be warned that lint is *very* picky! For example, the line:

    printf("Hello, World ");

Will produce a warning message because printf returns an integer value that is not stored. The return value of printf is often ignored, but lint still produces an warning. There are several ways to make lint happy with this statement, one is:

    (void) printf("Hello, World ");

This says to ignore the return value.

### 4.5 Walk through -

A *walk through* is a process of hand checking the logic of a program. The programmer sits down with someone else (best if another programmer, but anybody will do) and walks through the program for an

-example case. Often it is the programmer himself who finds the bug in the process of explaining how the program is supposed to work and carefully looking at his code.

However, it is easy for the programmer to *"know"* what the program *should be doing* and remain blind to what the program is *actually doing*.

Students need to be very careful using this approach with other students. Two students in the same class should not walk through a program together.

## 5. General Tips -

Here are some general tips for debugging programs.

### 5.1 Finding Bugs

Before bugs are removed they must be discovered!

- Aggressively test programs!
- Start with *small* problems that can be easily checked by hand. (You should already have one of these worked out from the planning stage!)
- Test every feature of the program at least once! And is once really enough? Test features in different ways if possible.
- Do not forget to test trivial problems.
- Do not make invalid assumptions about input data.

### 5.2 Determining the Causes of Bugs -

A bug can only be caused by the code in the program that has already executed. Be sure you do not waste time searching through code that has not run yet. A debugger or print statements can be used to determine which code has executed and which has not.

Do not fix bugs by mindlessly changing code until it seems to work. You need to figure out why one statement does work and another does not. You should have a good reason for every line of code. *"It doesn't work without this line"* is not a good reason!

# CHAPTER
# ∞ 22- Part –II ∞
## (Common C Programming Errors)

**Introduction-**

**Bug -**
　　A software bug is an error, flaw, failure, or fault in a computer program or system that causes it to produce an incorrect or unexpected result, or to behave in unintended ways. Most bugs arise from mistakes and errors made by people in either a program's source code or its design, or in frameworks and operating systems used by such programs, and a few are caused by compilers producing incorrect code.

　　A program that contains a large number of bugs, and/or bugs that seriously interfere with its functionality, is said to be **buggy**. Reports detailing bugs in a program are commonly known as bug reports, defect reports, fault reports, problem reports, trouble reports, change requests, and so forth.

**How bugs get into software-**

　　In software development projects, a "mistake" or "fault" can be introduced at any stage during development. Bugs are a consequence of the nature of human factors in the programming task. They arise from oversights or mutual misunderstandings made by a software team during specification, design, coding, data entry and documentation.

**For example,**

In creating a relatively simple program to sort a list of words into alphabetical order, one's design might fail to consider what should happen when a word contains a hyphen. Perhaps, when converting the abstract design into the chosen programming language,

**Prevention-**

The software industry has put much effort into finding methods for preventing programmers from inadvertently introducing bugs while writing software. **These include:**

**Programming style-**

While typos in the program code are often caught by the compiler, a bug usually appears when the programmer makes a logic error. Various innovations in programming style and defensive programming are designed to make these bugs less likely, or easier to spot.

In some programming languages, so-called typos, especially of symbols or logical/mathematical operators, actually represent logic errors, since the mistyped constructs are accepted by the compiler with a meaning other than that which the programmer intended.

**Programming techniques-**

Bugs often create inconsistencies in the internal data of a running program. Programs can be written to check the consistency of their own internal data while running. If an inconsistency is encountered, the program can immediately halt, so that the bug can be located and fixed. Alternatively, the program can simply inform the user, attempt to correct the inconsistency, and continue running.

**Development methodologies-**

There are several schemes for managing programmer activity, so that fewer bugs are produced. Many of these fall under the discipline of software engineering (which addresses software design issues as well). For example, formal program specifications are used to state the exact behavior of programs, so that design bugs can be eliminated.

Unfortunately, formal specifications are impractical or impossible[citation needed] for anything but the shortest programs, because of problems of combinatorial explosion and indeterminacy.

In modern times, popular approaches include automated unit testing and automated acceptance testing (sometimes going to the extreme of test-driven development), and agile software development (which is often combined with, or even in some cases mandates, automated testing).

All of these approaches are supposed to catch bugs and poorly-specified requirements soon after they are introduced, which should make them easier and cheaper to fix, and to catch at least some of them before they enter into production use.

**Programming language support-**

Programming languages often include features which help programmers prevent bugs, such as static type systems, restricted namespaces and modular programming, among others. For example, when a programmer writes (pseudocode) LET REAL_VALUE PI = "THREE AND A BIT", although this may be syntactically correct, the code fails a type check. Depending on the language and implementation, this may be caught by the compiler or at run-time.

In addition, many recently invented languages have deliberately excluded features which can easily lead to bugs, at the expense of making code slower than it need be: the general principle being that, because of Moore's law, computers get faster and software engineers get slower; it is almost always better to write simpler, slower code than "clever", inscrutable code, especially considering that maintenance cost is considerable. For example, the Java programming language does not support pointer arithmetic; implementations of some languages such as Pascal and scripting languages often have runtime bounds checking of arrays, at least in a debugging build.

**Code analysis-**

Tools for code analysis help developers by inspecting the program text beyond the compiler's capabilities to spot potential problems. Although in general the problem of finding all programming errors given a specification is not solvable (see halting problem), these tools exploit the fact that human programmers tend to make the same kinds of mistakes when writing software.

**Instrumentation-**

Tools to monitor the performance of the software as it is running, either specifically to find problems such as bottlenecks or to give assurance as to correct working, may be embedded in the code explicitly (perhaps as simple as a statement saying PRINT "I AM HERE"), or provided as tools. It is often a surprise to find where most of the time is taken by a piece of code, and this removal of assumptions might cause the code to be rewritten.

## Debugging-

Debugging is a methodical process of finding and reducing the number of bugs, or defects, (Errors) in a computer program, thus making it behave as expected. Finding and fixing bugs, or "debugging", has always been a major part of computer programming.

Maurice Wilkes, an early computing pioneer, described his realization in the late 1940s that much of the rest of his life would be spent finding mistakes in his own programs. As computer programs grow more complex, bugs become more common and difficult to fix.

Often programmers spend more time and effort finding and fixing bugs than writing new code. Software testers are professionals whose primary task is to find bugs, or write code to support testing. On some projects, more resources can be spent on testing than in developing the program.

Usually, the most difficult part of debugging is finding the bug in the source code. Once it is found, correcting it is usually relatively easy. Programs known as debuggers exist to help programmers locate bugs by executing code line by line, watching variable values, and other features to observe program behavior.

Without a debugger, code can be added so that messages or values can be written to a console (for example with printf in the C programming language) or to a window or log file to trace program execution or show values.

However, even with the aid of a debugger, locating bugs is something of an art. It is not uncommon for a bug in one section of a program to cause failures in a completely different section,[citation needed] thus making it especially difficult to track (for example, an error in a graphics rendering routine causing a file I/O routine to fail), in an apparently unrelated part of the system.

## Introduction-

This Chapter lists the common C programming errors that the author sees time and time again. Solutions to the errors are also presented.

## 2. Beginner Errors-

These are errors that beginning C students often make. However, the professionals still sometimes make them too!

## 2.1 Forgetting to put a break in a switch statement.

**Remember** that C does not break out of a switch statement if a case is encountered. **For example:**

```
int x = 2;
switch(x) {
case 2:
 printf("Two\n");
case 3:
 printf("Three\n");
}
```

**Output:**

```
Two
Three
```

**Put a break to break out of the switch:**

```
int x = 2;
switch(x) {
case 2:
 printf("Two\n");
 break;
case 3:
 printf("Three\n");
 break;  /* not necessary, but good if additional cases are added later */
}
```

## 2.2 Using = instead of ==

C's = operator is used exclusively for assignment and returns the value assigned. The == operator is used exclusively for comparison and returns an integer value (0 for *false*, not 0 for *true*). Because of these return values, the C compiler often does not flag an error when = is used when one really wanted an ==.

**For example:**

```
int x = 5;
if ( x = 6 )
printf("x equals 6\n");
```

This code prints out x equals 6! Why? The assignment inside the if sets x to 6 and returns the value 6 to the if. Since 6 is not 0, this is interpreted as *true*.

One way to have the compiler find this type of error is to put any constants (or any r-value expressions) on the left side. Then if an = is used, it will be an error:

if ( 6 = x)

## 2.3 scanf() errors -

There are two types of common scanf() errors:

### 2.3.1 Forgetting to put an ampersand (&) on arguments -

scanf() must have the address of the variable to store input into. This means that often the ampersand address operator is required to compute the addresses.

**Here's an example:**

```
int x;
char * st = malloc(31);

scanf("%d", &x);          /* & required to pass address to scanf()   */
scanf("%30s", st);        /* NO & here, st itself points to variable! */
```

As the last line above shows, sometimes no ampersand is correct!

### 2.3.2 Using the wrong format for operand -

C compilers do *not* check that the correct format is used for arguments of a scanf() call. The most common errors are using the %f format for doubles (which must use the %lf format) and mixing up %c and %s for characters and strings.

## 2.4 Size of arrays

Arrays in C always start at index 0. This means that an array of 10 integers defined as:

int a[10];

Has valid indices from 0 to 9 *not* 10! It is very common for students go one too far in an array. This can lead to unpredictable behavior of the program.

## 2.5 Integer division

Unlike Pascal, C uses the / operator for both real and integer division. It is important to understand how C determines which it will do. If both operands are of an integal type, integer division is used, else real division is used. **For example:**

    double half = 1/2;

This code sets half to 0 not 0.5! Why? Because 1 and 2 are integer constants. To fix this, change at least one of them to a real constant.

    double half = 1.0/2;

If both operands are integer variables and real division is desired, cast one of the variables to double (or float).

    int x = 5, y = 2;
    double d = ((double) x)/y;

## 2.6 Loop errors –

In C, a loop repeats the very next statement after the loop statement. The code:

            int x = 5;
            while( x > 0 );
            x--;

Is an infinite loop. Why? The semicolon after the while defines the statement to repeat as the null statement (which does nothing). Remove the semicolon and the loop works as expected.

Another common loop error is to iterate one too many times or one too few. Check loop conditions carefully!

## 2.7 Not using prototypes -

Prototypes tell the compiler important features of a function: the return type and the parameters of the function. If no prototype is given, the compiler *assumes* that the function returns an int and can take any number of parameters of any type.

One important reason to use prototypes is to let the compiler check for errors in the argument lists of function calls. However, a prototype *must* be used if the function does not return an int. For example, the sqrt() function returns a double, not an int.

**The following code:**

double x = sqrt(2);

will not work correctly if a prototype:

double sqrt(double);

Does not appear above it. **Why?** Without a prototype, the C compiler assumes that sqrt() returns an int. Since the returned value is stored in a double variable, the compiler inserts code to convert the value to a double. This conversion is not needed and will result in the wrong value.

The solution to this problem is to include the correct C header file that contains the sqrt() prototype, math.h. For functions you write, you must either place the prototype at the top of the source file or create a header file and include it.

## 2.8 Not initializing pointers-

Anytime you use a pointer, you should be able to answer the question: *What variable does this point to?* If you cannot answer this question, it is likely it doesn't point to *any* variable.

This type of error will often result in a Segmentation fault/coredump error on UNIX/Linux or a general protection fault under Windows. (Under good old DOS (ugh!), anything could happen!)

**Here's an example of this type of error.**

```
#include <string.h>
int main()
{
  char * st;          /* defines a pointer to a char or char array */
  strcpy(st, "abc");  /* what char array does st point to?? */
  return 0;
}
```

How to do this correctly? Either use an array or dynamically allocate an array.

```
#include <string.h>
int main()
{
  char st[20];                    /* defines an char array */
```

374

```
  strcpy(st, "abc");              /* st points to char array */
  return 0;
}
```

**Or**

```
#include <string.h>
#include <stdlib.h>
int main()
{
  char *st = malloc(20);      /* st points to allocated array*/
  strcpy(st, "abc");          /* st points to char array */
  free(st);                   /* don't forget to deallocate when done! */
  return 0;
}
```

**Actually**, the first solution is much preferred for what this code does. Why? Dynamical allocation should only be used when it is required. It is slower and more error prone than just defining a normal array.

## 3. String Errors -

### 3.1 Confusing character and string constants-

C considers character and string constants as very different things. Character constants are enclosed in *single quotes* and string constants are enclosed in *double quotes*. String constants act as a pointer to the actually string. Consider the following code:

```
char ch = 'A';    /* correct */
char ch = "A";    /* error  */
```

The second line assigns the character variable ch to the address of a string constant. This should generate a compiler error. The same should happen if a string pointer is assigned to a character constant:

```
const char * st = "A";    /* correct */
const char * st = 'A';    /* error  */
```

### 3.2 Comparing strings with ==
### 3.3
Never use the == operator to compare the value of strings! Strings are char arrays. The name of a char array acts like a pointer to the string (just like other types of arrays in C). So what? Consider the --

*following code:*

```
char st1[] = "abc";
char st2[] = "abc";
if ( st1 == st2 )
    printf("Yes");
else
    printf("No");
```

This code prints out *No*. Why? Because the == operator is comparing the *pointer values* of st1 and st2, not the data pointed to by them. The correct way to compare string values is to use the strcmp() library function. (Be sure to include string.h) If the if statement above is replaced with the following:

```
if ( strcmp(st1,st2) == 0 )
    printf("Yes");
else
    printf("No");
```

The code will print out *Yes*. For similar reasons, don't use the other relational operators (<,>, *etc.*) with strings either. Use strcmp() here too.

## 3.3 Not null terminating strings -

C assumes that a string is a character array with a terminating null character. This null character has ASCII value 0 and can be represented as just 0 or '\0'.

This value is used to mark the end of meaningful data in the string. If this value is missing, many C string functions will keep processing data past the end of the meaningful data and often past the

-end of the character array itself until it happens to find a zero byte in memory!

Most C library string functions that create strings will always properly null terminate them. Some do not (*e.g.*,strncpy() ). Be sure to read their descriptions carefully.

## 3.4 Not leaving room for the null terminator-

A C string must have a null terminator at the end of the meaningful data in the string. A common mistake is to not allocate room for this extra character. For example, the string defined below-                char str[30];

Only has room for only 29 (not 30) actually data characters, since a null *must* appear after the last data character.

This can also be a problem with dynamic allocation. Below is the correct way to allocate a string to the exact size needed to hold a copy of another.

```
char * copy_str = malloc( strlen(orig_str) + 1);
strcpy(copy_str, orig_str);
```

The common mistake is to forget to add one to the return value of strlen(). The strlen() function returns a count of the data characters which does *not* include the null terminator.

This type of error can be very hard to detect. It might not cause any problems or only problems in extreme cases. In the case of dynamic allocation, it might corrupt the *heap* (the area of the program's memory used for dynamic allocation) and cause the *next* heap operation (malloc(), free(), *etc.*) to fail.

## 4. Input/Output Errors

### 4.1 Using fgetc(), *etc.* incorrectly

The fgetc(), getc() and getchar() functions all return back an *integer* value. For example, the prototype of fgetc()is:

$$int\ fgetc(\ FILE\ *\ );$$

Sometimes this integer value is really a simple character, but there is one very important case where the return value is **not** a character!

What is this value?  **EOF**  A common misconception of students is that files have a special EOF character at the end. There is no special character stored at the end of a file. EOF is an *integer* error code returned by a function. Here is the**wrong** way to use fgetc():

```
int count_line_size( FILE * fp )
{
  char ch;
  int  cnt = 0;

  while( (ch = fgetc(fp)) != EOF && ch != '\n')
    cnt++;
  return cnt;
}
```

What is wrong with this? The problem occurs in the condition of the while loop. To illustrate, here is the loop rewritten to show what C will do behind the scenes.

```
while( (int) ( ch = (char) fgetc(fp) ) != EOF && ch != '\n')
    cnt++;
```

The return value of fgetc(fp) is cast to char to store the result into ch. Then the value of ch must be cast back to an int to compare it with EOF. So what?

Casting an int value to a char and then back to an int may not give back the original int value. This means in the example above that if fgetc() returns back the EOF value, the casting may change the value so that the comparison later with EOF would be false.

What is the solution? Make the ch variable an int as below:

```
int count_line_size( FILE * fp )
{
  int ch;
  int cnt = 0;
  while( (ch = fgetc(fp)) != EOF && ch != '\n')
    cnt++;
  return cnt;
}
```

**Now** the only hidden cast is in the second comparison.

```
while( (ch = fgetc(fp)) != EOF && ch != ((int) '\n') )
    cnt++;
```

This cast has no harmful effects at all! So, the moral of all this is: **always** use an int variable to store the result of the fgetc(), getc() and getchar().

### 4.2 Using feof() incorrectly-

There is a wide spread misunderstanding of how C's feof() function works. Many programmers use it like Pascal'seof() function. However, C's function works differently!

What's the difference? Pascal's function returns true if the *next* read will fail because of end of file. C's function returns true if the *last* function failed. Here's an example of a misuse of feof():

378

```c
#include <stdio.h>
int main()
{
        FILE * fp = fopen("test.txt", "r");
        char line[100];
        while( ! feof(fp) ) {
        fgets(line, sizeof(line), fp);
        fputs(line, stdout);
}
        fclose(fp);
        return 0;
}
```

This program will print out the last line of the input file *twice*. Why? After the last line is read in and printed out,feof() will still return 0 (false) and the loop will continue. The next fgets() fails and so the line variable holding the contents of the last line is not changed and is printed out again. After this, feof() will return true (since fgets()failed) and the loop ends.

How should this fixed? One way is the following:

```c
#include <stdio.h>
int main()
{
        FILE * fp = fopen("test.txt", "r");
        char line[100];
while( 1 )
{
        fgets(line, sizeof(line), fp);
        if ( feof(fp) )   /* check for EOF right after fgets() */
break;
        fputs(line, stdout);
}
        fclose(fp);
        return 0;
}
```

However, this is not the best way. There is really no reason to use feof() at all. C input functions return values that can be used to check for EOF. For example, fgets returns the NULL pointer on EOF.

*Here's a better version of the program:*

```
#include <stdio.h>
int main()
{
  FILE * fp = fopen("test.txt", "r");
  char line[100];

  while( fgets(line, sizeof(line), fp) != NULL )
    fputs(line, stdout);
  fclose(fp);
  return 0;
}
```

The author has yet to see any student use the feof() function correctly! Incidentally, this discussion also applies to C++ and Java. The eof() method of an istream works just like C's feof().

### 4.3 Leaving characters in the input buffer -

C input (and output) functions buffer data. Buffering stores data in memory and only reads (or writes) the data from (or to) I/O devices when needed. Reading and writing data in big chunks is much more efficient than a byte (or character) at a time. Often the buffering has no effect on programming.

One place where buffering is visible is input using scanf(). The keyboard is usually line buffered. This means that each line input is stored in a buffer. Problems can arise when a program does not process all the data in a line, before it wants to process the next line of input. For example, consider the following code:

```
int x;
char st[31];
printf("Enter an integer: ");
scanf("%d", &x);
printf("Enter a line of text: ");
fgets(st, 31, stdin);
```

The fgets() will not read the line of text that is typed in. Instead, it will probably just read an empty line. In fact, the program will not even wait for an input for the fgets() call. Why? The scanf() call reads the characters needed that represent the integer number read in, but it leaves the '\n' in the input buffer. The fgets() then starts reading data from the input buffer. It finds a '\n' and stops without needing any additional keyboard input.

What's the solution? One simple method is to read and dump all the characters from the input buffer until a '\n' after the scanf() call. Since this is something that might be used in lots of places, it makes sense to make this a function. Here is a function that does just this:

```
/* function dump_line
 * This function reads and dumps any remaining characters on the current input
 * line of a file.
 * Parameter:
 *    fp - pointer to a FILE to read characters from
 * Precondition:
 *    fp points to a open file
 * Postcondition:
 *    the file referenced by fp is positioned at the end of the next line
 *    or the end of the file.
 */

void dump_line( FILE * fp )
{
  int ch;

  while( (ch = fgetc(fp)) != EOF && ch != '\n' )
    /* null body */;
}
```

Here is the code above fixed by using the above function:

```
int x;

char st[31];

printf("Enter an integer: ");

scanf("%d", &x);

dump_line(stdin);

printf("Enter a line of text: ");

fgets(st, 31, stdin);
```

One incorrect solution is to use the following:

```
fflush(stdin);
```

This will compile but its behavior is undefined by the ANSI C standard. The fflush() function is only meant to be used on streams open for output, not input. This method does seem to work with some C compilers, but is completely unportable! Thus, it should not be used.

## 4.4 Using the gets() function-

**Do not use this function!** It does not know how many characters can be safely stored in the string passed to it. Thus, if too many are read, memory will be corrupted.

Many security bugs that have been exploited on the Internet use this fact! Use the fgets() function instead (and read from stdin). But remember that unlike gets(), fgets() does *not*discard a terminating \n from the input.

The scanf() functions can also be used dangerously. The %s format can overwrite the destination string. However, it can be used safely by specifying a width. For example, the format %20s will not read more than 20 characters.

382

# CHAPTER
# ∞ 23- Part –II ∞

## (Live Software Development Using C)

**Mind Drill Note-**

> If you find any error in any code, then don't upset try to de-bug (Fix them) Use every pulse of your mind, if I lead you to 99% then atleast you can Try remaining **1%.**

Auhtor Vs. Student

## 160. Wap for print e-mail Addresses found in any text document.

```c
#include <stdio.h>
#include <ctype.h>
#include <string.h>

int main(void) {
char line[1024];
char address[256];
char *ptr1 = NULL;
char *ptr2 = NULL;

while((fgets(line, 1024, stdin)) != NULL) {
if(strchr(line, '@') != NULL && strchr(line, '.') != NULL)
{
  for(ptr1 = line, ptr2 = address; *ptr1; ptr1++) {
  if(isalpha(*ptr1) || isdigit(*ptr1) ||
    strchr(".-_@", *ptr1) != NULL)
    *ptr2++ = *ptr1;
  else
{
  *ptr2 = '\0';

if(strlen(address) >= 6 && strchr(address, '@') != NULL &&
    strchr(address, '.') != NULL)
printf("%s\n", address);

  ptr2 = address;
  } /* else */
  } /* for */
  } /* if */
  } /* while */

return 0;
}
```

## 161. Wap Program to solve a 3 Variable Linear Equation.

```c
#include<stdio.h>
#include<conio.h>
#include<stdlib.h>
main()
{
clrscr();
float a,b,c,d,l,m,n,k,p,D,q,r,s,x,y,z;
printf("PROGRAM TO SOLVE THREE VARIABLE LINEAR SIMULTANEOUSE QUATIONS");
printf("The equations are of theform:
ax+by+cz+d=0
```

384

```
lx+my+nz+k=0
px+qy+rz+s=0");
printf("Enter the coefficients in the order a,b,c,d,l,m,n,k,p,q,r,s");
scanf("%f%f%f%f%f%f%f%f%f%f%f%f",&a,&b,&c,&d,&l,&m,&n,&k,&p,&q,&r,&s);
printf("The equations you have input are:");
printf(" %.2f*x + %.2f*y + %.2f*z + %.2f = 0",a,b,c,d);
printf(" %.2f*x + %.2f*y + %.2f*z + %.2f = 0",l,m,n,k);
printf(" %.2f*x + %.2f*y + %.2f*z + %.2f = 0",p,q,r,s);
D = (a*m*r+b*p*n+c*l*q)-(a*n*q+b*l*r+c*m*p);
x = ((b*r*k+c*m*s+d*n*q)-(b*n*s+c*q*k+d*m*r))/D;
y = ((a*n*s+c*p*k+d*l*r)-(a*r*k+c*l*s+d*n*p))/D;
z = ((a*q*k+b*l*s+d*m*p)-(a*m*s+b*p*k+d*l*q))/D;

printf("The solutions to the above three equations are :");
printf(" x = %5.2f
 y = %5.2f
 z = %5.2f
",x,y,z);
getch();
return 0;
}
```

**162. wap to Develop a Analog or Digital Clock In "C".**

```
#include<graphics.h>
#include<conio.h>
#include<math.h>
#include<dos.h>
void main()
{
int gd=DETECT,gm;
int x=320,y=240,r=200,i,h,m,s,thetamin,thetasec;
struct   time t;
char n[12][3]={"3","2","1","12","11","10","9","8","7","6","5","4"};
initgraph(&gd,&gm,"f:\arun\tc");\put the directory which contains
egavga.bgi
circle(x,y,210);
setcolor(4);
settextstyle(4,0,5);
for(i=0;i<12;i++)
{
if(i!=3)
outtextxy(x+(r-14)*cos(M_PI/6*i)-10,y-(r-14)*sin(M_PI/6*i)-26,n[i]);
else
outtextxy(x+(r-14)*cos(M_PI/6*i)-20,y-(r-14)*sin(M_PI/6*i)-26,n[i]);
```

```
}
gettime(&t);
printf("The current time is: %2d:%02d:%02d.%02d
",t.ti_hour, t.ti_min,
t.ti_sec, t.ti_hund);
while(!kbhit())
{
setcolor(5);
setfillstyle(1,5);
circle(x,y,10);
floodfill(x,y,5);
gettime(&t);
if(t.ti_min!=m)
{
setcolor(0);
line(x,y,x+(r-60)*cos(thetamin*(M_PI/180)),y-(r-60)*sin(thetamin*(M_PI/180)));
circle(x+(r-80)*cos(thetamin*(M_PI/180)),y-(r-80)*sin(thetamin*(M_PI/180)),10);

line(x,y,x+(r-110)*cos(M_PI/6*h-((m/2)*(M_PI/180))),y-(r-110)*sin(M_PI/6*h
-((m/2)*(M_PI/180))));
circle(x+(r-130)*cos(M_PI/6*h-((m/2)*(M_PI/180))),y-(r-130)*sin(M_PI/6*h-
( (m/2)*(M_PI/180))),10);
}
if(t.ti_hour>12)
t.ti_hour=t.ti_hour-12;
if(t.ti_hour<4)
h=abs(t.ti_hour-3);
else
h=15-t.ti_hour;
m=t.ti_min;
if(t.ti_min<=15)
thetamin=(15-t.ti_min)*6;
else
thetamin=450-t.ti_min*6;
if(t.ti_sec<=15)
thetasec=(15-t.ti_sec)*6;
else
thetasec=450-t.ti_sec*6;
setcolor(4);
line(x,y,x+(r-110)*cos(M_PI/6*h-((m/2)*(M_PI/180))),y-(r-110)*sin(M_PI/6*h
```

```
-((m/2)*(M_PI/180))));
circle(x+(r-130)*cos(M_PI/6*h-((m/2)*(M_PI/180))),y-(r-130)*sin(M_PI/6*h-
((m/2)*(M_PI/180))),10);

line(x,y,x+(r-60)*cos(thetamin*(M_PI/180)),y-(r-60)*sin(thetamin*(M_PI/180)));
circle(x+(r-80)*cos(thetamin*(M_PI/180)),y-(r-80)*sin(thetamin*(M_PI/180)) ,10);
setcolor(15);
line(x,y,x+(r-70)*cos(thetasec*(M_PI/180)),y-(r-70)*sin(thetasec*(M_PI/180)));
delay(1000);
setcolor(0);
line(x,y,x+(r-70)*cos(thetasec*(M_PI/180)),y-(r-70)*sin(thetasec*(M_PI/180)));
}
}
```

## 163. Wap to Print ip addresses found in text"C".

```
#include <stdio.h>
#include <regex.h>
#include <locale.h>
#include <string.h>
#include <stdlib.h>
#include <sys/types.h>
#define IPEXPR   "([0-9]{1,3})\\.([0-9]{1,3})\\.([0-9]{1,3})\\.([0-9]{1,3})"
int main(void)
{
char line[1024];
char *address = NULL;
char delim[] = ",.:;`/\"+-_(){}[]<>*&^%$#@!?~/|\\= \t\r\n";
int retval = 0;
regex_t re;
setlocale(LC_ALL, "");

if(regcomp(&re, IPEXPR, REG_EXTENDED) != 0)
 return 1;

while((fgets(line, 1024, stdin)) != NULL)
{

if(strchr(line, '.') == NULL)
  continue;

address = strtok(line, delim);
 while(address != NULL)
{
  if(strlen(address) <= 15)
```

```c
if((retval = regexec(&re, address, 0, NULL, 0)) == 0)
printf("%s\n", address);
address = strtok(NULL, delim);

    } /* while */
    } /* while */
    return 0;
}
```

## 164. Wap to Print Progress bar "C".

```c
#include<graphics.h>
#include<conio.h>
#include<alloc.h>
#include<dos.h>
void main()
{
int gd=DETECT,gm;
initgraph(&gd,&gm,"c:\tc ");
//put your directory where egavga.bgi is
void  *buffer;
unsigned int size;
setbkcolor(BLUE);
line(230,330,370,330);
line(230,350,370,350);
line(226,335,226,345);
line(226,335,230,330);
line(226,345,230,350);
line(374,335,374,345);
line(374,335,370,330);
line(374,345,370,350);
outtextxy(275,365,"Loading");          //put you text here
int x=232,y=336,x1=236,y1=344;
for(int i=1;i<5;i++)
{
setfillstyle(1,RED);
bar(x,y,x1,y1);
x=x1+2;
x1=x1+6;
}
size=imagesize(232,336,256,344);
buffer=malloc(size);
getimage(232,336,256,344,buffer);
x=232;
int m=0;
while(!kbhit())
{
putimage(x,336,buffer,XOR_PUT);
x=x+2;
```

```c
if(x>=350)
{
m++;
x=232;
if(m==5)                                // m is no of times bar moves
return;
}
putimage(x,336,buffer,XOR_PUT);
delay(20);                              // delay(time) is the speed of moving
bar                                     // less delay means fast and vice versa
}
getch();
}
```
## 165. Develop a Database  software for company in C.
```c
#include <stdio.h>
typedef struct Employee
{
        char fname[20];
        char lname[20];
        char sub_taken[20];
        char last_edu[20];
        char join_date[20];
        int id;
        int age;
        float bsal;
}Employee;

int main(void)
{
        int id;
        FILE *fp,*ft;
        char another,choice;
        Employee emp;
        char fname[20];
        char lname[20];
        long int recsize;

        fp=fopen("EMP.DAT","rb+");
        if(fp==NULL)
        {
                fp=fopen( "EMP.DAT","wb+");
                if(fp==NULL)
                {
                        printf("
Can't Open File");
                        exit();
                }
```

```
            }
            recsize=sizeof(emp);
            while(1)
            {
                    printf("
1.Add Records
2.Delete Records
3.Modify Records
4.List Records
5.Exit");
printf("Enter your choice");
                        fflush(stdin);
                        scanf("%c",&choice);
                        switch(choice)
                        {
                                case'1':
                                        fseek(fp,0,SEEK_END);
                                        another='Y';
                                        while(another=='Y'|| another=='y')
                                        {
printf("Enter the first name,last name,age and basic salary : ");
scanf("%s %d %f",emp.fname,&emp.age,&emp.bsal);
printf(" Enter joining date,id,last education,subject taken");
scanf("%s %d %s %s",emp.join_date,&emp.id,emp.last_edu,emp.sub_taken);
        fwrite(&emp,recsize,1,fp);
        printf(" Add another Record (Y/N): ");

                                                fflush(stdin);
                                                another=getchar();
                                        }
                                        break;
                                case '2':
                                        another='Y';
                                        while(another=='Y'|| another=='y')
                                        {
printf("Enter the id of the employee to be deleted : ");
scanf("%d",&id);
                                ft=fopen("TEMP.DAT","wb");
                                rewind(fp);
                                while(fread(&emp,recsize,1,fp)==1)
                                        {
                                                if(strcmp(emp.id,id)!=0)
                                                fwrite(&emp,recsize,1,ft);
                                        }
                                fclose(fp);
                                fclose(ft);
```

```c
                remove("EMP.DAT");
                rename("TEMP.DAT","EMP.DAT");
        fp=fopen("EMP.DAT","rb+");
        printf("Delete another Record(Y/N): ");
                fflush(stdin);
                another=getchar();
                                        }
                break;
                        case '3':
                                another='Y';
                                while(another=='Y'|| another=='y')
                                {
printf("Enter name of employee to modify : ");
scanf("%s",emp.fname);
                                rewind(fp);
                                while(fread(&emp,recsize,1,fp)==1)
                                        {
                                        if(strcmp(emp.id,id)==0)
                                                {
printf("Enter new fname,new lname,age,basic salary,joining_date,subject taken
and last education : ");
scanf("%s%s%d%f%s%s%s",emp.fname,emp.lname,&emp.age,&emp.bsal,emp
.join_date,emp.sub_taken,emp.last_edu);
fseek(fp,-recsize,SEEK_CUR);
fwrite(&emp,recsize,1,fp);
                                                break;
                                                }
                                                }
printf("Want to Modify another record(Y/N): ");
                fflush(stdin);
                                another=getchar();
                                }
                                break;
                        case '4':
                                rewind(fp);
                                while(fread(&emp,recsize,1,fp)==1)
printf("%s %s %d %g",emp.fname,emp.lname,emp.age,emp.bsal,emp.
join_date,emp.last_edu,emp.sub_taken);
                                break;

                        case '5':
                                fclose(fp);
                                exit();

                }       }       }
```

## 166. C Program To Accept Password.

This is a simple login program in C. While accepting password it masks each character using '*' symbol and display the password in the next line after the user hits Enter key. It also accepts backspaces and acts accordingly.

```c
#include<stdio.h>
#include<conio.h>
char pw[25],ch;
int i;
void main()
{
clrscr();
puts("Enter password");
while(1)
{
if(i<0)
i=0;
ch=getch();
if(ch==13)
break; /*13 is ASCII value of ENTER*/
if(ch==8) /*ASCII value of BACKSPACE*/
{
putch('\b');
putch(NULL);
putch('\b');
-i;
continue;
}
pw[i++]=ch;
ch='*';
putch(ch);
}
pw[i]='\0';
printf("\n\n%s",pw);
getch();
}
```

### Mind Drill Note –

For every "C" Graphics Programming, Make sure that you have installed Graphics Driver according to your motherboard. Unless it you can't run any program that cointains Graphics Programming.

### 167. Develop A Program to Block USB.

```c
#include<stdio.h>
#include<conio.h>
#include<windows.h>          optinal ok!
#include<dos.h>              optinal ok !

void main()
{
system("reg add
HKEY_LOCAL_MACHINE\\SYSTEM\\CurrentControlSet\\Services\\USBSTOR
\/v Start \/t REG_DWORD \/d 4 \/f");
getch();
}
```

### 168. Develop A Program to UnBlock USB.

```c
#include<stdio.h>
#include<conio.h>
#include<windows.h>          ▢ optinal
#include<dos.h>              ▢ optinal
void main()
{
system("reg add
HKEY_LOCAL_MACHINE\\SYSTEM\\CurrentControlSet\\Services\\USBSTOR
\/v Start \/t REG_DWORD \/d 3 \/f");
getch();
}
```

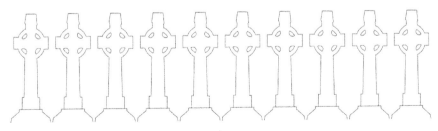

CPSIA information can be obtained at www.ICGtesting.com
Printed in the USA
LVOW04s1721030415

433204LV00015B/627/P

9 781500 533236